designing

Multimedia Web Sites

Stella Gassaway
Gary Davis
Catherine Gregory

Hayden
Books

Hayden Books

Publisher

Lyn Blake

Marketing Manager

Stacy Oldham

Managing Editor

Lisa Wilson

Acquisitions Editor

Laurie Petrycki

Development Editor

Steve Mulder

Copy/Production Editor

Kevin Laseau

Technical Editor

Peter Merholz

Publishing Coordinator

Rachel Byers

Cover Designers

Karen Ruggles

Aren Howell

Book Designer

Anne Jones

Manufacturing Coordinator

Brook Farling

Production Team Supervisor

Laurie Casey

Production Team

Dan Caparo
Cindy Fields
Tricia Flodder
Janelle Herber
Beth Rago

Indexer

Bront Davis

Designing Multimedia Web Sites

Copyright© 1996 by Hayden Books®

Library of Congress Catalog Number: 96-77069

ISBN: 1-56830-308-4

Copyright © 1996 Hayden Books

Printed in the United States of America 1 2 3 4 5 6 7 8 9 0

Warning and Disclaimer

Trademark Acknowledgments

About the Authors

Stella Gassaway Over her 20 years of professional experience as a graphic designer, Stella Gassaway has consistently been at the bleeding edge in the use of digital tools. Her early years were spent primarily in book and publication design, being unconventional with conventional tools.

For the past 10 years Stella has had her own graphic design studio, STELLARViSIONs. The Macintosh computer was introduced at the nascence of the firm with a Mac Plus and a 20MB external drive the size of a breadbox. Far in advance of most studios, STELLARViSIONs was exploring the avenues opened by the use of the Macintosh as a design and production tool.

In 1994, STELLARViSIONs announced the "birth" of its new media division, bYte a tree productions. After years of design with technology, Stella is exploring design experienced through technology—creative intelligence for the digital environment.

Through her role in AIGAlink and as creative director for designOnline's dezine café, Stella works toward her continuing goal to share experiences, knowledge, and the common language of design with designers of all disciplines.

Stella has often been invited to speak about new media and design for the World Wide Web, including the Shocking Your World Macromedia International User Conference.

Member AIGA; Member AIGA Philadelphia Executive Board; Chair, Technology Special Interest Group and AIGAlink Philadelphia (online community and Web site); Member ACD.

stella@vizbyte.com
http://www.vizbyte.com

Gary Davis is the president of Animation House, Inc., a multimedia studio specializing in Web site design and development, 3D animation, and interactive media. With a degree in fine art and graduate studies in art history, Gary gained real experience designing graphics in large advertising agencies. This early work introduced him to the emerging technology of computer-generated imagery. Davis's new interest led to near addiction in digital graphics creation and the possibilities it presents.

Davis states, "I want to spend the rest of my life doing something that satisfies me visually and emotionally, and have found the encompassing nature of the Internet—and particularly the World Wide Web—an important outlet to achieve that goal."

Catherine Gregory is a freelance writer from Evansville, IN. She was a founder of Evansville's monthly *News4U Magazine* and later the editor for the *Evansville Business Journal* and the *Indiana Industrial Journal*. It was during her time at the *Business Journal* that Catherine was introduced to the World Wide Web by the company down the hall at Animation House. She became a freelancer to write the AltaVista Software site's Internet History Section and hasn't been able to go offline since.

Dedications

To Rose Flores Untalan Gassaway, my mother, who has given me strength and vision. *- Stella Gassaway*

I wrote this book with three inspirations always in mind: Seth, Adria, and Elizabeth Gregory. *- Catherine Gregory*

Acknowledgments

My name may be on the cover, but it took a tremendous amount of knowledge and effort to make this book and the multimedia in it. I want to acknowledge all those who made it possible. Steve Mulder for his guidance and encouragement; Gerry Mathews, our digital choreographer, for leading us step by step through the processes in the examples; Stephen Streibig for getting every last byte of material ready for the CD; our staff, especially Gretchen Dykstra and Arthur Knapp, for holding everything together while the book was at a rolling boil and I wasn't getting any sleep; and to my partner in all things, Margaret Anderson, whose chapter outlines, scheduling, organizing, technical writing, interviewing, reviewing, and fresh cups of coffee kept me going until this became a book. *- Stella Gassaway*

This book is the product of a collaborative effort that involved many people. There is NO way it could've been pulled together without the tireless efforts of Tracy Robb, her Photoshop skills, and valuable input.

Many members of the team at Animation House/zoecom, in fact, had a hand in this: Dan Adams, Scott Titzer, Till Krüger, Dino Karl, Phil Bolenbaugh, Tyson Heil, and Stacey Fossmeyer, as well as Jeff King of Object One. A note of special thanks from Catherine Gregory goes to friend and fellow writer Christopher Bruce, for his help in focusing her efforts at a time when she needed some guidance. - *Catherine Gregory*

Hayden Books

The staff of Hayden Books is committed to bringing you the best computer books. What our readers think of Hayden is important to our ability to serve our customers. If you have any comments, no matter how great or how small, we'd appreciate you taking the time to send us a note.

You can reach Hayden Books at the following:

Hayden Books

201 West 103rd Street
Indianapolis, IN 46290
(800) 428-5331 voice
(800) 448-3804 fax

Email addresses:

America Online: Hayden Bks
Internet: **hayden@hayden.com**

Visit the Hayden Books Web site at **http://www.hayden.com**

Contents at a Glance

Table of Contents

ix

Chapter 7: Video: Frame by Frame **275**

introduction

And Now the Second Digital Revolution

Sometimes this profession makes me feel as though I began in the Dark Ages. I

guess I did because Magic Markers were big news then. The greatest technical

difficulty I faced was what layout paper would bleed the least. When I began as

a graphic designer, designers were still speccing hot type. Phototypography was

the new stuff on the block and it would certainly never be as good as metal.

Then came digital type, and designers would never settle for that stuff. No way.

Now we complain about anti-aliased type on the Web. And this is just what's

happened in typography. It's amazing to think I've been through all that; I've

already faced two digital revolutions.

In the first digital revolution, which most designers have barely endured, the desktop computer isolated us from our peers. We became less dependent on expert outside resources for scanning, typesetting, proofing, and image manipulation tasks. In our mad clamor to "have control" over every millimeter of the design and production process, we bought what the software companies sold us: a huge burden of technical responsibility. In the past decade we have taken on more and more responsibility for tasks and expertise that are not our own. We do it all, longing for the past when we worked with a team of knowledgeable professionals to deliver the highest quality projects.

Careful what you wish for; you may find your wish has come true.

The second digital revolution is upon us, turning everything we have grown accustomed to upside down. The Internet removes us from isolation. To design for this new medium takes greater expertise than one person alone can master. Designers must learn again how to cooperate and direct other creative and technical partners. No matter how many books you buy, no matter how many tips and tricks authors such as us can give you, there is no substitute for professional expertise. We tell this to prospective clients every day, so we too should heed this advice. In this digital revolution we must face the truth; we must join together with engineers, audio technicians, video editors, musicians, animators, and many others to produce work for this new medium.

With all of this revolutionary stuff going on, we mustn't forget that some things don't change. The same creative intelligence applies to the new media. Without the skills to organize information, convey concepts, and implement strategies, design is replaced by decoration. We must apply thinking as we always have. We must blend old systems to create the hybrids of the future.

Gary Davis, Catherine Gregory, and I have written this book to give you a basic understanding of what it takes to create multimedia elements for the Web and how to integrate them into a site. No doubt you picked it up and checked it out because you want to be able to add the bells and whistles necessary to capture the attention of those who visit the sites you design. You want to animate a logo, incorporate music, make video accessible, and generally do some cool stuff.

Within this book you will find suggestions, tips, and URLs to sites that help you keep in touch with the pulse of technology and that feature techniques and design solutions we hope will inspire you. You will learn what tools you need to take advantage of the evolving Web landscape. These examples are just plain good design, the result of both intellectual and creative skill.

"Confusion and clutter are the failures of design, not the attributes of information."

—Edward R. Tufte

When you begin to look at these examples in the text, on CD-ROM, or on the Web, I'm sure you'll find these aren't merely bells and whistles, but well-integrated elements expanding the quality and content of the sites within which they reside. It is essential to eliminate confusion and clutter at a site and to create interactive elements enhancing the information and contributing to the content. This doesn't mean be boring; this means be creative.

Ask yourself:

- Am I designing for the future?

- Am I looking at things from a new perspective?

If you are still thinking of creating Web "pages," think again. The Web is a flatland no more. The page is dead. The Web has evolved into a multi-dimensional space, informative, provocative, and extremely chaotic. With the introduction of tables in browsers, designers were finally able to have the grid control on a page to which we were accustomed. Now with the addition of frames, the real challenge is upon us. How do we design true multilevel access to information in designated regions called frames that can individually display an HTML document residing anywhere on the Internet? Now we can be in two places at once. So are we anywhere at all?

As designers, it is our responsibility to aid the viewer's navigation through cyberspace. We cannot organize the Internet; its chaos is its power. But we can give viewers we guide through it a sense of order, place, understanding, and access. This new medium gives us the opportunity to design an environment that is vibrant, exciting, informative, and entertaining.

3

At first it looked as though the Web would be a simple, logical step for print designers to take: a step from the printed page to the illuminated page. But technology has already changed that. The technology that drives the Web is evolving at speeds singeing everything in site. The incredible speed of technological change demands tenacity and team work.

We hope this book will help you to be part of this second revolution.

Stella Gassaway
bYte a tree multimedia productions
`http://www.vizbyte.com`

chapter

1

 Gary Davis & Catherine Gregory

Initial Considerations of Web Multimedia

Since its introduction to the public in 1992, the World Wide Web, with all of

its futuristic capabilities, has attracted the attention of the multimedia

industry across the globe. Excited by the sky's-the-limit possibilities the Web

places at their feet, engineers and artists are scrambling to lead the way in

development and design that the incredible medium offers. As hardware,

software, and browser companies present designers with more wonderful

tools of creation, the risks of using them poorly become greater.

Since excellent Web design will become more prevalent, it's vital that the multimedia designer quickly find the way to the front of the pack of this highly transitional medium in order to stay there. By first comprehending the basic structure supporting good design technique, we as designers may continue on the path to mastering the task.

There are three elements in multimedia Web site development that transport multimedia designers into the highest category of excellence.

> *The Three Considerations of the Multimedia Web Site Designer*
>
> ① *Determine the message and its intended audience.*
>
> ② *Design how the message is best presented.*
>
> ③ *Create the design in an efficient and creative manner.*

- Determining the message and its intended audience

- Designing how the message is best presented

- Creating the design in an efficient and creative manner

This chapter focuses on the first set of considerations. Chapter 2 focuses on the designer's considerations for *design*, followed by Chapter 3's list of considerations for efficient *implementation* of the design. In order to prepare for these three steps, we need to recognize a brief description of the medium at its broadest level, the Internet.

The Nature of the Internet

The Internet is a medium of metaphors. In the first years of the Web, it will be understood through comparisons to other media. It's important that as Web designers we understand the points of reference used by the constant stream of wide-eyed new users. The Internet's identity is slowly coming into focus as multimedia shapes it (see Figure 1.1).

In 1950 people thought of television as half radio, half movie theater. The children that grew up with it certainly never divided it into such a description. TV was TV. It consistently improved, but the idea of sitting around the RCA on Monday nights to listen to Jack Benny or going to the all-day matinee for a nickel on Saturdays was a very foreign concept to children in 1960. What today's adults do to steer and mold the Internet over the next few months, years, and decades has an unlimited scope at this point (see Figure 1.2).

figure 1.1

The Internet remains in its infancy. It will be fascinating to watch how multimedia will influence its growth.

figure 1.2

Home theater had humble beginnings.

Multimedia is poised to take the Internet to even higher levels of home theater and telephony than the majority of the modern world uses already. The capabilities of live or captured video and audio, virtual reality, and interactivity are fast turning the Net into a vital tool for not only the obvious areas of communication and entertainment, but the fields of medicine, education, business, and finance. The faces of all these dimensions will change and therefore change the world as we know it now because of the Web's use of multimedia.

The Internet today is an incubator of thought—a spawning ground for a paradigm of thinking and communication. Communication between person and person, person and machine, and machine and machine means the limitations of electronic communication are now thrown away even though our dependencies are increased. Interactive television, the automated home, and video phones are all becoming realities.

What the future holds is limited only by the imagination. These ebbs and flows of thought will take us into directions we haven't even dreamt of. Yet, one thing will remain constant: we will always need an interface connecting us to one another. By using the Internet as our point of contact, the need for good, intuitive design on the Web becomes more than desirable—it is essential if we are to understand each other. It is essential for us as Web designers to comprehend the magnitude of the task at hand in order to be successful. The ultimate goal is to communicate a message in the most appropriate and appealing way to best reach the desired audience (see Figure 1.3).

figure 1.3

The Internet can be used to deliver messages like no other and all other media before.

The Metaphors

Since we did not grow up with the Internet, we will begin to explain its nature through those very universal frames of reference, that of common media. It's essential to understand those commonalities to best utilize them for good design.

The Internet can function as a billboard, a magazine page, a TV, and even a telephone (see Figure 1.4). The most exciting sites on the Web implement multimedia well, whether it's a brief splash or multiple implementations. It would be a very rare Web page, though, that would want to enlist all those concepts at once. Sensory overload is a sure way to disturb and annoy the Net user enough to never want to visit a site again. Then again, depending on the site's intent, it's important to make a page fun by making use of the Web's most appealing feature, interactivity.

figure 1.4

Read urban diary at The Place to experience a great example of metaphor use and interactive Web site design (http://www.art.uiuc.edu/ludgate/the/place.html).

In the broadest sense of the word, interactivity is a method of allowing the user control over what is presented onscreen through programmed choices. This can be as simple as menu options or as complex as a virtual reality environment or digital game. It's important for effect, as well as bandwidth considerations, to use interactivity in order to enhance the site's purpose or message, not to overburden or confuse the intent.

To use a Web page as a TV, therefore, we may include the choice of a short video to clarify a point or present an example. A Shock Bauble placed strategically acts as a billboard for quick emphasis of a concept. Used by Web designers, a CU-SeeMe event presents the user with a choice to participate in communication much like the telephone does. RealAudio, which enables for streaming audio, may be used for a promoted live broadcast.

NOTE

Shock Baubles are tiny Shockwave files that weigh in under 12K. The Shock Bauble Showcase is found at `http://207.69.132.225/abtboble.htm`. Shock Baubles are aptly described as attractive and without deep meaning. They run the gamut of combinations of visual, audible, and interactive files. They're also free and claim the capability to be easily placed on a page (see Figure 1.5).

figure 1.5

The caption under this Shock Bauble at `http://207.69.132.225/ourbobl/hum1.htm` reads, "The dimensions of this piece are 592 pixels wide by 132 pixels tall and it is a smidgeon over 6K in total file size. Shockwave files don't have to be big to be neat."

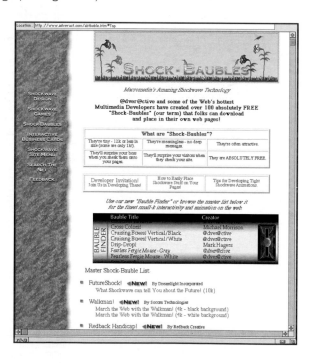

The key is in keeping the site's intent clearly in mind. By giving the user choices in how the site's message is presented or emphasized, we raise the chances that the site's intent is satisfied. If we give the user too many choices, chances are the user will be distracted from the intended message.

While a Web page is no substitution for TV, printed pages, or billboards, it still integrates all those technologies and uses elements of each medium's methods for distribution of information. In group forums, for instance, the Web combines nearly every different type of communication and yet goes beyond them. It uses a big graphic like a billboard to draw in the audience, text like a magazine page, and still allows for one-on-one interaction (see Figure 1.4). After product information is presented, the Web forum enables the user to interact with all levels of users in the quest to better understand the technology spotlighted.

Print, TV, telephone, interactivity, video, audio, billboards, and magazine ads all can be replicated in the Web environment. In each case it boils down to attention to detail, what constitutes good design, how the clients' needs are met, and how the task is executed. We may use each of these elements to get the intended message across (see Figure 1.8). Good designers use them well by carefully weighing the advantages and disadvantages of each against the purpose of the site.

About CU-SeeMe

CU-SeeMe by White Pine is desktop video conferencing software for real time person-to-person or group conferencing. CU-SeeMe offers full-color video, audio, chat window, and white board communications. It enables participation in live conferences, broadcasts, or chats. CU-SeeMe requires at least a 28.8Kbps modem to be launched from Web pages for video, a 14.4Kbps modem for audio-only.

The Group Forum

A true Web hybrid, the concept behind group forum software applications can be described as a cross between a newsgroup and video conferencing. Like a newsgroup, group forum software has predetermined, dedicated subject matter that is discussed through text and may be enhanced with digital images. Like video conferencing, the discussion is live, although it may be open participation. Video conferences are traditionally exclusive between selected parties.

Large corporations are becoming more attuned to the advantages of group forums. This software enables a widely scattered staff to hold a meeting including graphical material, no matter what time zone a member of the group happens to be in. As long as they have access to the Net, they can be there.

Open forums are used to present product information and allow discussion among experts, new users, and potential purchasers. The group forum concept applies to multimedia design because its various uses, whether Internet or intranet, open or closed, will require informative, attention-grabbing content surrounding them (see Figure 1.6 and 1.7).

11

figure 1.6

The AltaVista Software site hosts ForumForum, a virtual space created specifically for live discussion and document sharing for both public and private, corporate and personal use.

figure 1.7

The AltaVista Software site's Roundtable section offers the user the opportunity to interact with other users, even experts in group discussions.

figure 1.8

In order to get the message across clearly, a good designer will consider many techniques. The Harley-Davidson site's Shockwave introduction immediately puts the user in the rider's seat with sound and movement (http://www.harley-davidson.com/homcb).

Its Dynamic Nature

In its beginning, the Internet was informational only. Its sole purpose was to enable the exchange of ideas through onscreen text. With the introduction of the World Wide Web and its possibilities for multimedia, the Internet is now about the design and presentation of information and how it is exchanged.

As designers we have to consider not only the continuously changing nature of the Internet but how that promotes change within the sites. In order to draw people back, a site must be designed to be modified easily, whether to add new information or new technology. Main menus particularly need to be continuously updated to attract viewers' attention.

In the original zoecom intro page, for instance, a virtual zoetrope is centered above the company logo at the top of the page (see Figure 1.9). The page is balanced by the tiered clickable sections' titles with a revolving globe graphic and light text messages at the bottom. About a year later, the next incarnation of the same page adds appeal without compromising the original effect or tone of its predecessor (see Figure 1.10). The various changes made on this version—the reverse in background color, elimination of the hyphen in the logo, text additions, shifts in element locations—all work together to capture the user's attention. The new information presented in text and graphic form invites the viewer to see what lies beyond this first page.

figure 1.9

The initial zoecom introductory page.

figure 1.10

The next version adds information through text and graphics (`http://www.zoecom.com`).

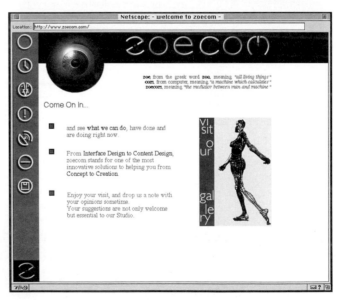

Also, how will the Web site change the face of the business it represents? Some sites will need changes made on a daily, weekly, or monthly basis. Who will be doing it? The design house or an employee of the client? It must be designed in such a way as to efficiently implement any modifications.

A sense of satisfaction can push the budding Web multimedia designer into stagnation. It's extremely tempting to become complacent after mastering a method or tool of design because it is such an exotic new art. But as the evolving medium continues its transformation, the best designers will not allow themselves to become caught in a shortsighted paradigm. Constantly looking at the tools and technologies with fresh eyes in order to implement them in innovative ways is part of the responsibility of designers reaching for high status as Web designers.

Its Economic Nature

The unique economic opportunities that exist through the use of the Net is one way Web sites differ from the media to which they compare. Designers and publishers are given the opportunity to create "works of art" that implement animation, video, audio, and interactivity without a multi-million-dollar investment.

figure 1.11

The Web offers an expansive medium for some of the most creative techniques ever developed at what can be little expense to the creator. This QT movie that may have been made from some-one's camcorder video adds dramatic power to the intended message to entice visitors to Lake Tahoe (http://www.gotahoe.com/tahoe/pages/scrapbook/hmp/qtmovies/ski2.mov).

There are several factors that make the Web the most economical use of multimedia known.

- Combines the basic elements of print advertising, radio and television, and CD-ROM publishing into one package,

- Easily implements previously produced content

- Has a universal market reach every moment of every day.

The Web therefore creates opportunities for an unprecedented ratio of cost per individual involved in receiving the messages through multimedia.

Since most Internet service providers enable 5-10MB of hard disk space for a Web page housed at their site, most of us are given an ample amount of "clean canvas" to work with. With proper file optimizations, the total size for even an extremely large site is almost never as high as 5MB, unless large files for download are included.

Given a site's boundaries, it makes sense to use all the other media's best features. The economics of the Web are such that it doesn't necessarily need to cost any more to do an eye-popping, audio-enhanced design than a stagnant, unbalanced, graphics-only design. When pre-existing elements such as audio or video tapes are provided by the client the designer is allowed economical ways to implement multimedia in a site. This makes multimedia especially desirable when working with a page that needs to be refined and/or enhanced.

Only in instances that require all new elements to be produced is high cost a factor. By using good design principles and existing multimedia a project has the capability to take on grandiose proportions and become an award-winning site for relatively little financial investment. Once again, it's all about paying close attention to detail.

The First Considerations

A site's message or purposes are determined by any number of variables: a mega-corporation wanting to use the Web for a leg in a marketing campaign; a home user wanting a personal site; or a free-thinker wanting to create a stir through the ease and low cost of Web publishing. The reasons are as varied as are human needs. After you have determined what the site will communicate, the next step is to determine who you want to visit the site and who will be most likely to see it. The multimedia Web site designer then looks at the different elements of multimedia available in order to match these "tools" to the message and the audience.

Determining the Audience

For companies preparing their first Web site or updating their current one, the tried and true methods of audience identification are the place to begin. This includes all the internal data of previous surveys, sales history lists, and marketing department statistics, as well as any research from outside agencies. After this audience has been identified, it is narrowed to current Web users and those who will be Web users soon.

TIP

Resources for Web Trends

- Harrison Digital Internet/World-Wide-Web Demographics site (`http://www.harrisondigital.com/hd_dem.html`) contains a long listing of comprehensible, serious statistics, projections, and survey results.

- The INTERNET SOCIETY site at `http://www.isoc.org/` has information harder to assimilate but easily credible.

- The Wahlstrom Report site, published by Wahlstrom & Company, the directory marketing specialists, gauges and reports market trends including Internet growth (`http://www.wahlstrom.com/wahlrprt.html`).

- Yahoo's list of resources are at `http://www.yahoo.com/Computers and Internet/Internet/Statistics and Demographics`.

- Nielsen, the famous information-gatherers, are at `http://www.nielsenmedia.com/commercenet/`.

"What Message Will My Audience Expect on the Web?"

While the Web audience is growing exponentially and will continue to broaden as the Web transforms, it is still limited to a small percentage of the world's population. Language barriers narrow it down even further. Therefore, your initial audience is relatively select and easy to identify.

The follow-up questions include: Should the site include enough information to draw a larger audience? Should it be designed in such a way to address a narrow audience now and bring in a broader one later? Should it be limited only to focus on attracting and maintaining the original audience? What are the ways to accomplish the answers to these questions?

Matching the Presentation to the Audience's Needs

By answering the previous questions you determine what the site's audience will look for. A highly technical audience may want loads of text with a smattering of graphics. Therefore, would a four-frame 3-D model get an idea across faster than, or in addition to, a three-paragraph explanation? How much file space will it require? Is its effectiveness worth its efficiency? Users' computers should enable them to quickly view a short Director video. Is this something they'll find helpful (see Figure 1.12)?

figure 1.12

No one wants to bother with so many plug-ins that they don't have time to soak in the site's hard information.

A youthful audience is drawn to information with bold design, movement, and short amounts of text. Will these users have the patience to download a plug-in? What will their general equipment be like? A daily online newspaper's readers probably won't want to be distracted by a looping GIF animation on the stock market page. A soft drink site's viewers would probably enjoy seeing one on any page.

The wonder of multimedia is that it enables hard information to be presented in a relatively light manner. By using an animation that illustrates the foundation of a highly technical explanation first, for instance, the written details are much easier to comprehend (see Figures 1.13 and 1.14).

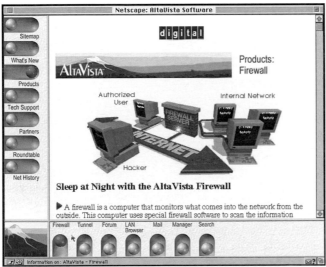

figure 1.13

AltaVista's page illustrating how a firewall works (http://altavista.software.digital.com/products/firewall/howork/nfintro.htm) contains a perfect example of looking at cool stuff for basic information that smoothly prepares the user for hard information.

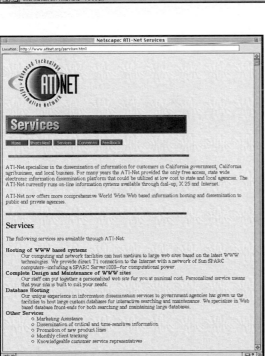

figure 1.14

A dry presentation of information is not likely to broaden an audience. http://www.netxpress.co.uk/product_overview.html

19

The Pointcast news site at `http://www.pointcast.com` takes its screensaver's multimedia elements and enables the audience to personalize the presentation to match the individual's preferences. Animated headlines for the type of news the user deems interesting move across the screen when it's not in use (see Figure 1.15). The Pointcast screensaver is not only fun and informative, it offers an excellent implementation of user interface.

figure 1.15

The Pointcast
screensaver
(`http://www.`
`pointcast.com`)
enables you to fine
tune built-in
multimedia to fit
your desires.

Multimedia presentation can be valuable and appropriate in nearly any instance. As shown in the preceding examples, it enables the designer to reach many audiences without being patronizing or distracting.

What's Available in Multimedia

After the site's audience has been determined, many multimedia designers look to see if their previous knowledge can be used to meet the site's needs. A quick overview of the technology available will help you decide if there is any multimedia worth investigation to implement on your next site. Later chapters of this book contain detailed discussions of many of the multimedia elements we have used and come to prefer.

Graphics

Virtually every Web designer is familiar with the elements of graphics. While graphics aren't considered "multimedia" per se, they are an important cornerstone in the foundation of most Web sites and must be carefully considered along with any multimedia.

Graphics make it possible to include high-impact illustrations and still maintain a small file size. Most software programs are cross-platform-compatible as well as recognized by most browsers. When combined with multimedia tools such as JavaScript or RealAudio, graphics offer alternatives to byte-heavy animation or video programs. A thorough understanding of how to use graphics on the Web enables more creativity and more advanced implementation of multimedia elements without compromising bandwidth limitations.

There are many design books available for designing graphics on the Web. Chapter 4, "Graphics: The Foundation for All Multimedia Design," covers some of the finer points of graphics implementation every multimedia designer needs to consider. One of our favorite books, David Siegel's *Creating Killer Web Sites*, provides an excellent in-depth look at Web graphics.

Animation

Computer animation has made huge strides in the last decade. Now the Web offers another place for these moving pictures. Animation is extremely effective for educating and illustrating. Inline plug-ins enable animations to be as much a part of a site's look as the background color or logo, which has made them even more popular. No one will dispute how much animation can draw attention (see Figure 1.16).

There are some drawbacks to the use of animation on the Web. For one thing, the best software for its creation is pricey. Like all computer technology, though, we have recently witnessed its availability increase dramatically as its consumer cost continues to take a downward turn. Another obstacle is animation's weight. Animation file size has to be carefully monitored. The clever designer can use several methods, though, to overcome this, as we show in Chapter 5, "Animation: Dancing, Spinning, and Jiggling in Cyberspace." Finally, not every audience member has the equipment to view and therefore be affected by a site's animation. What else can we offer as substitution?

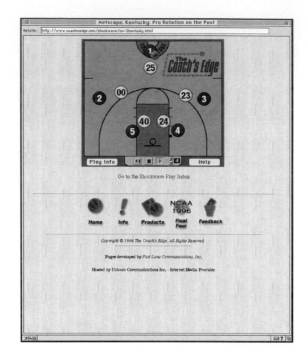

figure 1.16

The diagram pages at The Coach's Edge site let you get in on the action with Shockwave play-by-play animations (http://www. coachesedge. com).

Sound

Perhaps the most often overlooked multimedia element for Web design, digital audio has the effectiveness of communication through yet another sense: hearing. Still in the less-than-perfected stages of development, Web sound requires an indulgent listener in order to meet bandwidth requirements. The use of audio, therefore, is usually but not always limited to specific messaging needs (see Figure 1.17). It won't be long, however, before Web users are used to browsing to background music straight from a site.

Different types of audio technologies fill different needs for sound. Streaming Shockwave Audio and RealAudio, for instance, transmit live or recorded sound, and their capability for streaming eliminates the traditional, lengthy download time. Streaming audio clips play live and on-demand sound from the Web browser over connections of 14.4Kbps and faster. There are several other formats that fill different needs, as discussed in Chapter 6, "Audio: An Earful of Atmosphere." The chapter offers considerations for you to weigh against your skills and resources to best fit the site's purpose.

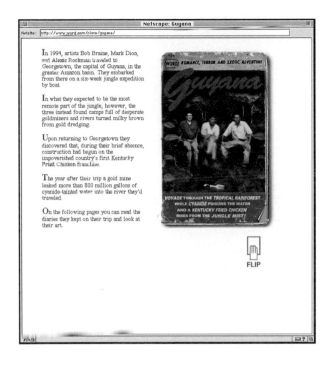

In 1994, artists Bob Braine, Mark Dion, and Alexis Rockman traveled to Georgetown, the capital of Guyana, in the greater Amazon basin. They embarked from there on a six-week jungle expedition by boat.

In what they expected to be the most remote part of the jungle, however, the three instead found camps full of desperate goldminers and rivers turned milky brown from gold dredging.

Upon returning to Georgetown they discovered that, during their brief absence, construction had begun on the impoverished country's first Kentucky Fried Chicken franchise.

The year after their trip a gold mine leaked more than 800 million gallons of cyanide-tainted water into the river they'd traveled.

On the following pages you can read the diaries they kept on their trip and look at their art.

figure 1.17

Listen to the drums beating a message from deep within the rainforest in this story at The Word site (http://www.word.com/place/guyana). RealAudio makes you feel as if you are virtually exploring Guyana.

Video

There's no argument that video clips are some of the most entertaining and effective ways to communicate (see Figure 1.18). Refinement of the multimedia software for the Web and the addition of inline plug-ins for its use make video easier than ever to incorporate into a site. Chapter 7, "Video: Frame by Frame," goes through examples of well-designed uses of video on the Web.

Because video has the capability to add sound synchronized within the file, it can bring a user even closer to a complete experience than previously mentioned multimedia (see Figure 1.19). More than listening to a recording and/or looking at a still image, a video with sound draws its audience into the event and perhaps suspends disbelief of the experience for a moment. Download time can be a burden for users whose browsers don't enable instant streaming, in which case the video must be brief for the sake of size. Because video has become such a desirable multimedia element for the Web, software companies are racing to make compression algorithms that enable more effective delivery of video at a higher quality.

figure 1.18

Animation House's embedded Quicktime ant informs the user of step-by-step animation technique (http://animationhouse.com).

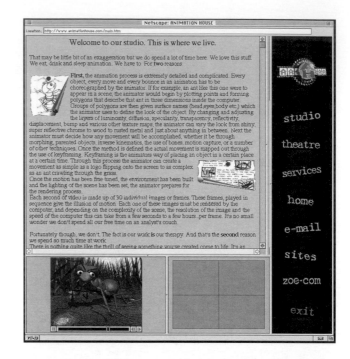

figure 1.19

This site for a Japanese television program devoted to underwater life enables the Web user to really experience a fish's point of view through a QT movie (http://seatv.nttlabs.com/seatv/aquarium).

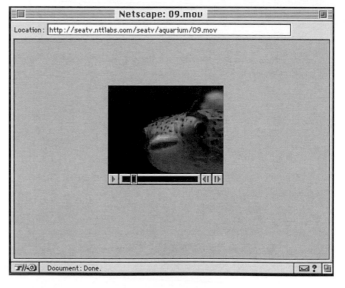

Virtual Reality

When the Virtual Reality Modeling Language (VRML) was first introduced in 1994, its mind-exploding potential was recognized by the leaders in Web technology. VRML offers Web designers an unprecedented ability to communicate and educate. Virtual reality gives the designer a truer feeling for a third dimension to offer viewers, with the added capability of user movement and control (see Figure 1.20).

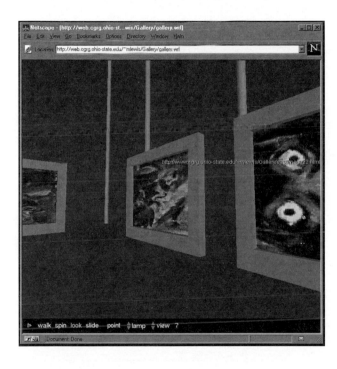

figure 1.20

At the Dream Abalufia Gallery you "virtually" walk down corridors to view art (http://www. cgrg.ohio-state.edu/ ~mlewis/Gallery).

Most Web site designers are familiar with virtual reality environments. Its use as an animation tool is also discussed in Chapter 5 and as an interactive tool in Chapter 8, "Interactivity: A Richer Experience." As the number of browsers adding inline plug-ins to allow the technology to be accessed grows, the number of Web viewers who find it useful and/or entertaining will grow as well. And as this number increases, new versions of VRML will contain new features and be easier to learn. As new versions of the VRML language continue to improve, not only will features be added, but VRML will become easier to learn, too.

Interactivity

Multimedia applications have transformed the Web from a publishing medium to an interactive medium. New technology such as Java, JavaScript, VRML, and Shockwave are used to enable the user to have expanded control over the choices the designer includes on a site. The word "interactive" has come to represent the most dramatic demonstrations of user control, particularly in panoramic environments, games, and virtual reality worlds (see Figures 1.21).

figure 1.21

At the CNN site visitors may participate in a poll at Take A Stand then immediately view the latest results by clicking The Tally (http:// allpolitics. com/).

Including a complex interaction such as a game into any site is a large project in itself and usually the main focus of the site. In Chapter 8, various aspects of sites built around interactive elements are discussed.

Determining Which Multimedia Elements to Use

One of the trickiest steps when making decisions for a Web site design is how to match multimedia options to the determined messages and their audience. Usually lack of access is the first factor in throwing out a choice. If you don't have the software or knowledge, you can quickly eliminate a killer idea.

The following questions don't take that factor into account; you'll have to make that call. But they will help you quickly make several important decisions on the road to a well-thought-out multimedia Web site.

Matching to the Message

● What is the most important message that needs to be conveyed on this Web site?

● Which multimedia elements will say or help say it the most effectively (see Figure 2.22)?

figure 1.22

One the Wildernet site includes audio samples of The Throne of Drones album (*http://www.wilder.net/stc/sombient/throne/*).

27

● Of a prioritized list of other information, which need special attention drawn to them?

● What information needs to be offered over and over (imprinted)?

● What are the best ways to do this?

● How can messages be leveraged to other parts of the site? (see Figure 1.23)

figure 1.23

This splashscreen Glf animation provides the segue from the Women's Wire site opening page to its section on developing careers (`http://www.women.com/work/go`).

Matching to the Audience

- What type of access to the Web will the greatest number of my audience have?

- What kind of computer equipment will they use?

- Will they be home users or office users?

- What kind of browsers will they be using (see Figure 1.24)?

- What is the lowest common denominator for choosing file formats, software, plug-ins, and browser support?

- Does my audience require the lowest common denominator or can I specialize?

- Is my audience mixed enough that I should offer both (see Figure 1.25)?

- Does my audience expect to be impressed by this particular site?

- Will multimedia elements reinforce audience perception of my company/organization/client in a positive way?

figure 1.24

This FAO Schwartz Toys site's pages are attention-grabbing, contain brief information, download quickly, and can be viewed by most browsers (`http://www.faoschwarz.com/faohome.html`).

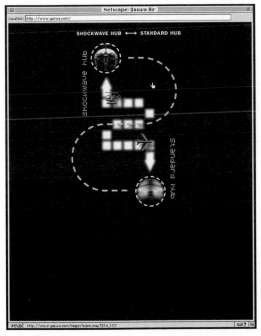

figure 1.25

The opening page of the QASWA site offers the user the choice of viewing Shocked or unShocked (`http://www.qaswa.com`).

Determining Technical Compatibilities

If the multimedia material is through plug-in only, then what browsers support it? Who will be able to download it, and importantly, will everyone else see a blank page or broken icons? If the multimedia element is relegated to one page or section, the alternative browser user will be able to see the rest of the site without having pages broken up by blank areas of missing segments. Such a situation certainly hinders reading text left on the page.

You can divide plug-ins into three categories: Those embedded in Netscape Navigator and/or Microsoft Internet Explorer (called controls in Explorer), mainstream plug-ins that are *recommended* by Netscape, and the rest. Of course, if you use a Navigator plug-in, you are nearly guaranteed that those browser users will be able to benefit from them and have access to your multimedia. In the next category, mainstream plug-ins often serve multiple purposes so many users will either have them or be willing to download them. It's risky to use a plug-in from the third category because the chances of a wide number of users having it are slim. You can narrow that risk by alerting users to the fact that the plug-in is needed for the site and offer a link to download it.

TIP

Narrow the risk of losing viewers from using an unknown plug-in by alerting them to the fact that it's needed for the site and offering a link to download it.

It is recommended you first try to make use of browser-embedded plug-ins in order to hit the broadest audience. Also, Internet Explorer has the capabilities to use Netscape plug-ins and provides an ActiveX plug-in for Netscape users to view its ActiveX-enabled Web sites. These are often cross-platform-compatible, especially for the major plug-ins. Cross platform development for ActiveX will be made available soon.

Second, should you use a mainstream plug-in, always check its platform compatibility against its intended audience, as listed in the tables in the next section. This can be accomplished quickly by checking through Browserwatch (`http://www.browserwatch.com/`). Browserwatch will also alert you to the most recent advances and additions made in plug-in technology.

Navigator Built-In/Explorer Compatible Plug-Ins

Manufacturer	Product	Function	OS Compatibility
Netscape	Live3D	3D VRML plug-in enables the user to access VRML worlds; runs interactive, multiuser Java applications	Windows 95, NT, and 3.1 Macintosh
Netscape	LiveAudio	An asynchronous sound-playing plug-in	Windows 95, NT, and 3.1 Macintosh
Netscape	LiveVideo	Plays AVI movie files	Windows 95, NT, and 3.1
Macromedia	Shockwave for Authorware	Enables user interaction with Authorware pieces to deliver a detailed, interactive multimedia experience	Windows 95, NT, and 3.1 Macintosh and Power Mac
Macromedia	Shockwave for Director	Interaction with Director movies, sound and more within the browser window.	Windows 95, NT, and 3.1 Macintosh and Power Mac
Apple	QuickTime	Automatically plays QuickTime movies	Windows 95, NT, and 3.1 Macintosh and Power Mac
Microsoft	Video for Windows	Plays Video for Windows movies	Windows 95, NT, and 3.1
VREAM	WIRL Virtual World	Proprietary VRML plug-in enabling 3D environment viewing and object manipulation using sophisticated controls such as collision detection and gravity.	

Mainstream Plug-Ins for Images

MANUFACTURER	PRODUCT	FUNCTION	OS COMPATIBILITY
Ncompass	ActiveX	Enables Navigator users to run applets created through Microsoft's ActiveX Controls.	Windows 95 and NT
Omniview	Bubbleviewer	Enables users to experience location in a 360-degree environment	Windows 95 and NT Power Mac
Corel	CMX Viewer	Views vector graphics	Windows 95 and NT
Iterated Systems	Fractal Viewer	Enables the use of fractal images in a highly compressed, resolution-independent form.	Windows 95 and NT Macintosh
Infinop	Lightning Strike	Optimized wavelet image codec provides high compression ratios	Windows 95, NT, and 3.1 Macintosh UNIX
Macromedia	Shockwave for FreeHand	Allows users to interact with FreeHand art and graphics	Windows 95, NT, and 3.1 Macintosh
Summus	Wavelet Image	Wavelet-based image-compression and transmission	Windows 95, NT, and 3.1 Macintosh and Power Mac
Autodesk	WHIP	Views, sends and shares 2D vector data and design content	Windows 95 and NT

Mainstream Plug-Ins for Presentation

MANUFACTURER	PRODUCT	FUNCTION	OS COMPATIBILITY
Adobe	Acrobat 3.0	Views, prints, and maintains integrity of page layout through its Portable Document Format page layout	Windows 95, NT, and 3.1 Macintosh and Power Mac

MANUFACTURER	PRODUCT	FUNCTION	OS COMPATIBILITY
Net-Scene	PointPlus	Views PowerPoint and other presentations	Windows 95, NT, and 3.1
Microsoft	PowerPoint Animation Player & Publisher	Views and publishes PowerPoint animations and presentations	Windows 95 and NT

Mainstream Plug-Ins for 3D and Animation

MANUFACTURER	PRODUCT	FUNCTION	OS COMPATIBILITY
Ncompass	ActiveX	Enables Navigator users to run applets created through Microsoft's ActiveX Controls.	Windows 95 and NT
Silicon Graphics	Cosmo Player	VRML 2.0 browser	Windows 95 and NT Irix
FutureWave	FutureSplash	Vector-based animated graphics and drawings in files that are remarkably small and play in real time	Windows 95, NT, and 3.1 Macintosh and Power Mac
Aimtech	IconAuthor	Multimedia applications authoring tool	Windows 95, NT, and 3.1
mBed Software	mBed	Enables multimedia animations to be embedded directly into HTML.	Windows 95 and 3.1 Macintosh and Power Mac
Kinetix	Topper	Embeds 3D scenes created from 3D Studio and 3D Studio Max; supports Virtual Reality Behavior Language that adds animation to VRML worlds	Windows 95 and NT
Integrated Data Systems	VRealm	VRML support that adds several object features and multimedia	Windows 95 and NT
Plastic Thought	Web-Active	Displays movable 3D images	Macintosh and Power Mac

continues

33

MANUFACTURER	PRODUCT	FUNCTION	OS COMPATIBILITY
Data Views	WebXpresso	Display 2D and 3D Drawings, graphs and controls; supports real-time interaction	Windows 95 and NT Unix
Apple	Whurlplug	3D viewer for QuickDraw 3D	Macintosh

Mainstream Plug-Ins for Audio and Video

MANUFACTURER	PRODUCT	FUNCTION	OS COMPATIBILITY
Open 2 U	ACTION	Used to embed MPEG movies with synch-ronized sound into HTML pages	Windows 95 and NT
Ncompass	ActiveX	Enables Navigator users to run applets created through Microsoft's ActiveX Controls.	Windows 95 and NT
Diagigami	Cine Web	Brings real-time, streaming audio/video to the Web using standard movie and audio files	Windows 95, NT, and 3.1
Iterated Systems	CoolFusion	Streaming Video for Windows AVI plug-in	Windows 95
LiveUpdate	Crescendo	Version 2 delivers higher-quality stereo MIDI music to the Web; Crescendo Plus adds streaming	Windows 95, NT, and 3.1 Macintosh
SSEYO	Koan	High-quality generative organic MIDI music for the Web; small files, long play	Windows 95, NT, and 3.1
Knowledge Engineering	MacZilla	A Navigator 2.0 Mac plug-in that does practically everything	Macintosh
Yamaha Corp	MIDPLUG	For Netscape, offers the impact of sound and music accom-paniment	Windows 95 and 3.1 Power Mac

MANUFACTURER	PRODUCT	FUNCTION	OS COMPATIBILITY
Intelligence at Large	MovieStar	Allows Netscape to view QuickTime movies from a Web site.	Windows 95 Macintosh
FastMan	RapidTransit	Decompresses and plays music that has been compressed up to 40:1	Windows 95 and NT Macintosh
Progressive Networks	RealAudio	Provides live and on-demand real-time audio over 14.4Kbps or faster	Windows 95, NT, and 3.1 Macintosh and Power Mac
Totally Hip	Sizzler	Simultaneous viewing and interaction through streaming video	Windows 95, NT, and 3.1, Macintosh and Power Mac
MVP Solutions	Talker	Enables your Web site to talk to Mac users; uses a simple text file	Macintosh
Voxware	ToolVox	High-quality speech audio in Web pages	Windows 95 and 3.1 Macintosh
VDOnet	VDOLive	Compresses video images without compromising quality on the receiving end	Windows 95, NT, and 3.1
Vivo Software	VivoActive Player	Streaming video plug-in for Netscape	Windows 95, NT, and 3.1

To keep on top of new multimedia plug-in developments, we suggest that you bookmark these three sites:

● Browserwatch at `http://browserwatch.iworld.com/plug-in.html`

● Netscape's list at `http://home.netscape.com/comprod/products/navigator/version_2.0/plugins/index.html`

● Yahoo's list at `http://www.yahoo.com/Computers_and_Internet/Internet/World_Wide_Web/Browsers/Netscape_Navigator/Plug_Ins/`

Limiting Plug-Ins

After a specific plug-in has been chosen, the thoughtful designer will continue to use it throughout the site for different multimedia (see Figure 1.26). One plug-in may allow for several different combinations of GIF animation. If someone needs to download 17 different plug-ins, you've got to have one exceedingly special site.

figure 1.26

This site's use of one plug-in is effective and efficient (http://www.zoecom.com).

Further information on the way plug-ins are configured to go from server to client can be found in Appendix B, "What Every Multimedia Designer Should Know About MIME Types." This offers a simplified explanation and rather detailed reference for ways you can double-check or troubleshoot the method of transmission for your plug-in files.

chapter

2

 Gary Davis & Catherine Gregory

The Art of Multimedia Web Site Design

All designers have habits that serve them well. We can only advise from our

own experiences. The following guidelines are the ones we fall back on time

and time again. Some are used naturally, with no effort. Others come to

mind only when we've hit a block and have to be reminded of the tried and

true methods that work every time to move that block.

For the multimedia designer who wants to use the Web, or the Web designer who wants to implement multimedia, this chapter offers all the basic knowledge and much more to ensure that your site's design is planned well.

Quite often when we become stuck on an idea or method we need to remind ourselves how to create a different way of doing things. At the beginning of this chapter are methods that help us challenge the thought process to keep us on top of the game.

The upcoming section, "What Makes Good Design," covers design fundamentals as they apply to multimedia for the Web. This serves to remind seasoned designers of certain guides and offers insight for those new to the scene. The section "Navigation Considerations and Design" goes over important elements for what makes up a Web site's feel and ease of use.

The last section of this chapter, "The First Steps of Design," offers a checklist of steps to consider and take before you begin the actual construction of your site. The general steps for building and implementing are offered in Chapter 3, "Building, Implementing, Testing."

Challenge the Thought Process

Once we designers understand the mechanics of using multimedia thoughtfully, there is yet another consideration: using multimedia *creatively*.

Creativity is generally thought of as part of a person's nature, a predisposition one comes into the world with. The ability to quickly grasp technology is thought of in the same way, although as the polar opposite to being creative. Now the two are linked arm-in-arm within this brand new medium called the World Wide Web (see figure 2.1).

Since most of us fall somewhere in between the two talents, implementing them both takes some special and, hopefully, pleasurable effort. This book does not focus on multimedia technology. Rather the focus is on how to approach the technology in ways that will set off creative sparks for Web site designers. At the least, it will serve as a guide to distinguish between valid and poor design.

Instructing a person on how to think in a creative manner is material that could fill volumes. If a few fundamental guidelines, however, are kept in mind, then the functional multimedia Web site designer will reach levels seen or imagined but never before grasped.

figure 2.1

Is creative thought a natural or learned characteristic? What's your idea?

- **Fresh vision.** Use your most comfortable frame of reference for problem solving, then immediately try to think of something else. Whether dealing with an initial concept or using a multimedia tool, ask, "Can this be done another way? What are the ways? Are any of them better?" Would a logo, for instance, be more effective on a different side of the page? Would an animation be just as effective if it were reduced to fewer frames?

- **Discrimination.** What is truly pleasing? If you feel excited from an interactive experience you designed, and you continue to enjoy it after the initial thrill, then other people probably will, too. Trust your gut but remember that shock for its own sake won't be universally appreciated.

- **Experimentation.** Deadlines aren't friendly to this guideline, but they are the one element of cutting-edge design that can't be avoided. Deadlines are the reason behind curtailed social lives as well as the reason behind industry and peer recognition. This is where the commitment to achievement is most evident. In order to be good at creating content, the designer must know how to weigh the different options in order to choose. There are two subcategories in the experimentation guideline:

① **Show No Fear.** Sure, it's a bit dramatic, but sometimes we designers need to be reminded that a little courage can go a long way. It's okay if a new route doesn't take you where you had hoped. You probably learned a lot on the way, including some other paths to try.

② **Break Rules.** This applies to design as well as technology and is essential to the experimentation process. If the broken rule messes everything up, then don't do it again. It may, however, open new avenues (see Figure 2.2).

figure 2.2

The zoecom VRML section (http://www.zoecom.com) takes multimedia Web technology to places never before imagined.

What Makes Good Design

Whether you're dealing with a fine art painting, a Post Neo-Modern sculpture, or a superhero comic book cover, there are elemental requirements that separate the good from the otherwise. The same holds true for Web pages, and it certainly goes deeper than visual presentation. That, however, is where it begins.

The question always comes back to how to design a site for the Web and make it exciting, exhilarating, fun, and interactive. How do we make a Web site so wonderful people want to come back for more?

There's much to consider. It's important to keep in mind not to be too one-dimensional. How can the site be informative or educational, and yet leave room for product promotion? Just as in traditional modern advertising, from billboards on expressways to 60-second TV spots, we designers always have to consider the short attention span of the late 20th-century citizen.

By offering choices of brief interactions like options for sound or video clips or links to pop-up windows that add detail to statements in the main text, the site won't be overwhelming, yet it is enabled for product promotion in enticing ways that give the user control, a very important element for appeal. In other words, the method of the offering (see Figure 2.3) is equally important as the interactivity, and all must work cohesively toward the ultimate goal of delivering the intended message.

> ### The Keen Eye and Clever Mind
>
> *A woman sits in a bare room, the afternoon light streams through the window to her left, a floor lamp is in the corner, and a camera on a tripod is pointed toward her. Two photographers have been instructed to go in the room and snap her picture. The first person enters the room quietly, looks through the viewer, and pushes the button. The second person enters the room whistling, which causes the woman's eyes to widen and relax her expression. The photographer adjusts the lamp shade to cast more artificial light on the wall behind her, which creates a barely noticeable halo-like effect behind the woman's head. He then looks through the viewer and pushes the button. When the two photographs are compared, although they have both captured the woman's image within a balanced frame, which one is more pleasing? Innovation (whistling) and attention to detail (adjusting the shade) are keys to creating better design.*

41

Graphic Design

Pages written about graphic design fill volumes. The Web designer that keeps in mind the following graphic design basics will find they soon become a natural part of the design process. Use these basics as a checklist, and when every element is implemented, you, the designer, are halfway through the design process. The graphic design considerations are followed by a checklist for multimedia design and then navigational design considerations.

figure 2.3

7Up's index page
(`http://`
`www.7up.com`) uses
clever graphics to
guide and link to the
site's different
sections.

Balance

Composition is everything. A balanced page is absolutely essential to drawing and maintaining the user's attention in a pleasing manner. Master the following approach and as confidence builds, creative thought expands.

If you begin with a minimalist view of the way a page should look, then carefully add elements, chances are that a page won't become over-burdened or unbalanced. Begin with the three most important elements to the message, for example, the logo, a photograph, and some text. Depending on the placement of the page—as an introductory page, the first page of a section, or a page with one specific purpose—decide which of the three elements is the most important, and place the other elements around it in such a way to draw the user's attention to it first or longest (see Figure 2.4).

figure 2.4

Elle Magazine's first
page (`http://`
`www.ellemag.com`)
contains three main
elements: the
header, the column
of images along
the left, and the
text body.

43

A commercial site's introductory page, for instance, has the purpose of familiarizing the user with the logo, whether it's brand new, a variation of an old one, or as a way of stating "You are here." The logo may be reduced even to the point of only appearing at the bottom of the page thereafter. If it remains at the top of the pages, no matter how small, it will draw the user's attention first, even if it's only for a split second (see Figure 2.5).

Because the dimensions of a standard screen page are 640×480 pixels, the designer is initially obliged to work within those horizontal layout param-eters. In fact, after the toolbar and other browser-displayed elements are taken into account, a screen page is reduced even more. The traditions of page design allow for certain guidelines for the placement of text and images. This is ideal for opening nonscrolling pages. Once a page includes information that requires scrolling, either vertically or horizontally, the initial layout grid is obsolete and the dimensions must be readjusted to fit the length of page. Two rules of thumb:

- Never allow a page to be scrolled through vertically more than three screen lengths or 1,440 pixels;

- Never allow a page to be scrolled through more than two screen widths or 1,280 pixels.

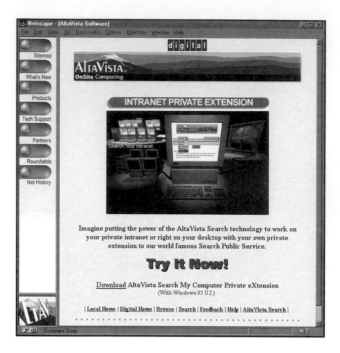

figure 2.5

The first page of the Alta Vista Software's (`http://altavista.software.digital.com`) Internet Private Extensions not only describes how the product works, but reminds you of the site's identity in the lower- right corner, all within 640×480 pixels.

Another way to change the pixel dimensions of a page is through the addition of frames. In order to be acceptable to the viewer, frames must have an identifiable purpose beyond creating a vertical layout, and they must be designed to quietly enhance the function of the content frame. Allow the design to determine whether a page is horizontal or vertical. Unless a pattern is required by your client, allow yourself only to be guided, but never limited, by layout grids. Over-structured principles and layout grids only serve to limit one's imagination, which in turn limits the potential of the design.

The old rule was "No matter what the layout is, always place text on the left and images on the right or it looks awkward." We see examples of the opposite of that standard all the time. Instead use guidelines dealing with weight and space to balance a page and please the eye. Since images are weightier than text, heavier fonts for the text block can add balance against a large image. White space is an important element that allows the eye to rest and enhances the power of the message (see Figure 2.6).

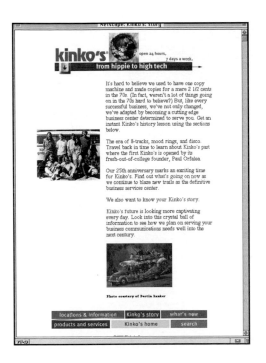

figure 2.6

The kinko's site at `http://` *`www.kinkos.com` uses clean and simple, yet effective, layout on every page.*

45

After you determine the placement of the page's most important element, you must balance the other two against it as well as against each other. (Think of arranging a group of pictures on a wall.) If the text looks too lightweight, make it heavier with color or a larger font. If the image is too overpowering, lighten it by reducing or cropping it. If a page, whether predesigned or in its genesis, looks stale, try centering a side-justified element, or the opposite, moving a centered element over (see Figure 2.7). It's amazing what a small detail can do to improve the page's overall composition (see Figures 2.8 and 2.9).

figure 2.7

The CNN site at
http://cnn.com
exemplifies a well-
balanced page using
images and the
navigation bar
against the text.

figure 2.8

The subtle elements
of a poorly balanced
page...

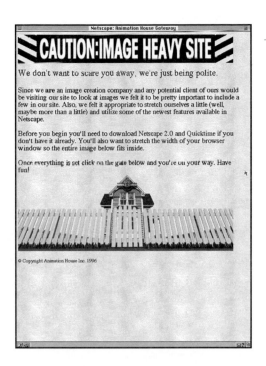

figure 2.9

...compared with a well-balanced page make a dramatic difference, as seen at http://www.animationhouse.com.

Be willing to walk away from a page for a few hours if it doesn't seem quite right. It's amazing what a night's rest or evening at the movies can do for a fresh perspective. Another trick is to print the page out and hang it on a wall. Seeing it in black-and-white can make a huge difference. If that doesn't offer a revelation, hang it upside down and study it again.

Visual Uniformity

A consistent layout is pleasing to the eye. It's disturbing for a user to move through a site that has graphically complex pages contrasting very plain pages. A fairly even balance is pleasing and helps set the stage for fun multimedia surprises (see Figure 2.10).

TIP

Use a lengthy page only if it's likely be printed to be read. Try to never have a page that takes more than three complete screen scrolls to get through. Even if the site is on a level that has pages purely text-based, give users the opportunity to "turn the page," so to speak. At the least, it allows them the opportunity to take a split second to further absorb what they've read. If you're using images, though and, especially if you're using multimedia, never allow the page to go on at great length. It could take a very long time to download if there are elements used throughout its length.

figure 2.10

This innocent-seeming page at http://www.zoecom.com hides an inviting surprise: The hand motions the viewer to come closer.

Color Palette

Coloration is one of the easiest ways to implement continuity in a site. A company's signature colors can be used as a constant reminder to viewers of what site they are at or what the level of that site is. Palette on the Web is limited by the lowest common denominator of screen capabilities at 256 colors. It's easier to choose colors from a client's brochure or logo and let Photoshop or DeBabelizer work its magic on them to prepare them for the Web. Because this doesn't always work for all platforms, you may have to consult the Macintosh palette or the Netscape color cube to tweak them to an acceptable hue.

Tip

Color Psychology

It's been found that...

● Warm colors (yellows) appear closer; cool colors (blues) recede.

- Bright colors project excitement.

- Pastels seem delicate.

- Grayed colors impact the viewer as reserved and sophisticated.

- Muddy brown colors produce a feeling of warmth and more casualness.

- People over 30 are affected much more strongly by color than those younger.

- Women are more responsive to and opinionated about colors and graphics than males.

- Women, in general, demonstrate a significantly greater preference for the color violet than their male counterparts. They register an aversion for the color brown.

- More people prefer reds and blues with highly saturated red being the favorite. There is no significant discrepancy for the different levels of saturation of blue.

- Different parts of the retina focus on blue and red, however, a combination of blue and red can make text and graphics appear to jump.

- Red and green combinations don't contrast well next to one another.

- Yellow on black is the most effective for gaining attention.

Typography

HTML limits typographic maneuverability, and bandwidth limits any text style created as a graphic file. The Web designer's choices, therefore, are narrow from the start. Typography, the arrangement and appearance of text, is still an important consideration for uniformity of a site. Before creating a page, decide how to use paragraph indents, blank line separations, drop caps, bold, italics, and type size to create a look for the text. Don't forget that text that is created within a graphics software program such as Photoshop can be just as useful, as well as beautiful and effective for short messages (see Figure 2.11).

Templates

Page templates may also be used to provide visual uniformity and are another way to tip users off as to where they are. Page templates are created using a grid built within specific margins like those that desktop publishers use. Text blocks and image elements are placed using rectangles as guides. Don't forget the importance of white space as a design element. Depending on the site's purpose, keep the number of templates limited or they lose their effectiveness to create continuity.

figure 2.11

The elaborate typography for this personal site at http:// www.mcp.com/ people/mulder *is a example of classic design techniques meeting with modern technology.*

The template is one way to create a foundation for the site's continuity (see Figures 2.12, 2.13, and 2.14). Keep in mind that the site's identity determines whether templates are to be limited. A site that uses colors, fonts, images, or multimedia elements for continuity may chuck a template-limited design out the virtual window.

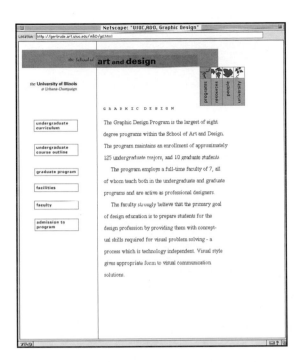

figure 2.12

The University of
Illinois School of Art
and Design at
`http://`
`gertrude.art.`
`uiuc.edu/A&D/`
`gd.html`.

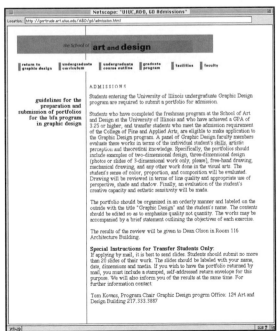

figure 2.13

Example 2 from the
University of Illinois
School of Art and
Design at `http://`
`gertrude.art.`
`uiuc.edu/A&D/gd/`
`admission.`
`html`.

51

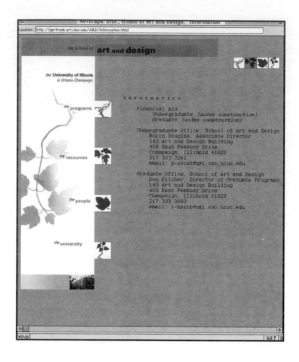

figure 2.14

Example 3 from the
University of Illinois
School of Art and
Design at `http://`
`gertrude.art.`
`uiuc.edu/A&D/`
`information.html`.

Images

The Internet magazine @tlas is an excellent example of how to maintain
consistency throughout a very deep site (see Figure 2.15) (`http://`
`atlas.organic.com/atlas/summer_ddx.html`). The summer issue's
photography section uses a back and forth icon that is a design element
pulled from the home page's directory icon. It's also an excellent example
of innovative design, with its combination of the influence of Victorian
advertising graphics with common Indo/Asian graphics (see Figure 2.16).
Through the inclusion of the icons, the user is able to maintain a sense of
bearings and will instantly recognize a page from the issue, even if it is
happened upon through a search engine.

Navigational Menu

Even without using browser-limited frames, a Web site may maintain
consistency by including the page's menu on the first page of every new
section (see Figure 2.17). This is accomplished by copying and pasting on
the determined pages. Including the page's menu not only creates a visual
consistency, but aids viewer navigation.

figure 2.15

The @tlas (`http://atlas.organic.com/atlas/summer_ddx.html`) directional buttons' icon is pulled directly out of...

figure 2.16

...the photography section first page header.

figure 2.17

The CNN site
(`http://cnn.com`)
includes its menu on
the first page of
every section.

Timing

Consistent load time adds continuity. While deeper pages may take a bit longer to load, don't feel you can take advantage of users' attention spans simply because they are interested. The Internet user, especially the surfer, is not known for great patience. If you're anxious to add new applications to a site, there are tricks to using them well so that none of these basic elements of timing are sacrificed.

While the ways to manipulate multimedia within the bandwidth boundaries are discussed at length in the following chapters, always keep in mind that small files mean short download time. Sometimes choices have to be made of one element over another, and quite often experimentation is the only way to make the decision. A well-designed interactive experience is generally a powerful medium (see Figure 2.18).

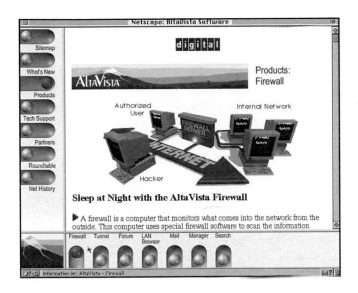

figure 2.18

Multimedia can make a fact-grinding experience pleasant, even thrilling (`http://altavista.software.digital.com`).

TIP

Always remember two things:

① Good Web page design is like a good piece of art: It is balanced and well composed.

② A great-looking image or multimedia design doesn't need to take up any more space or bandwidth than a bad design.

Multimedia Design

The successful multimedia Web designer always keeps in mind to tell a story or paint a picture whenever practical. That's because multimedia's effects will enhance even the driest information. A wordy, technical explanation that uses animation, video, or audio to give a more immediate comprehension is a wordy, technical explanation that is fun to read. But because the Web has bandwidth limitations and select users that are further limited by their computers' capabilities, the Web designer has more considerations to weigh than other multimedia designers.

Purpose

The purpose of the multimedia element must be carefully considered, especially in light of the different baud rates of dial-up users. Does the element really serve a good purpose for its message and the audience? That is, does it truly enhance the communication or illustrate the point? If a dial-up user has to wait an hour to download a page, it better be poignant. For the designer who is on the fence about whether to include a multimedia element, a quick perusal of the following should help you make the decision.

Bad Reasons for Using Multimedia on a Web Site

- **To look cool.** Looking cool is not cool if it's at the expense of file size or has no meaning. We stress the point once again: a big file size means slow downloading, especially for users with less-than-powerful equipment. The cool look won't be seen by anyone who has to wait long to see it, and that amounts to a significant number of people. It won't be appreciated by anyone at all if it has absolutely no meaning or aesthetic value (see Figure 2.19).

figure 2.19

Just because it's
Shockwave doesn't
mean it's cool.

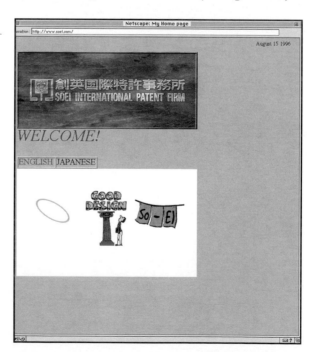

- **Because you have the tools to do it.** Sorry. Just because a designer has a powerful computer and some good software isn't reason enough to include multimedia in a site. It will only draw attention to the fact that the designer doesn't know the best ways to use the tools for the Web.

- **Because you know how to create it.** This is a terrible reason to add multimedia to a site. It doesn't matter, for example, if the designer is the most gifted animator to walk the earth because no one will see an overburdened Web page. Remember this basic rule of thumb: limit GIF animations to one per page (see Figure 2.20). They are very effective sprinkled throughout a site and still get the point across that the designer is talented if there is only one on the page.

figure 2.20

There are over 10 animations going on in this page at once!

- **Because there's a new plug-in available.** There's a myth floating about that jumping on a plug-in bandwagon assures multiple hits. While this may be true for a few days, it's not reason enough to include a multimedia element in a Web site (see Figure 2.21).

figure 2.21

Too many plug-ins can mean a page full of broken icons.

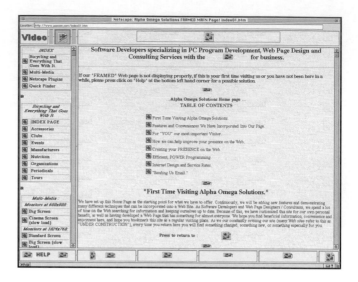

- **Because you see an opportunity.** There are a million opportunities available. Every one cannot be implemented because there's not enough bandwidth. This is not interactive television…yet.

Good Reasons for Using Multimedia on a Web Site

- **To be cool.** The designer who knows that being cool means having multimedia quickly available to most viewers in a balanced and constructive way is the designer who uses the element successfully (see Figure 2.22).

- **To draw attention.** A good example of this is a simple animation with a small file size on a home page. It's appealing without being distracting from the main message. It brings a viewer in (see Figure 2.23).

- **To maintain attention and enhance information.** When a site's message gets too text-heavy, it's a nice touch to break up the visual elements of the page, as well as offer a break from reading, with a multimedia element that conveys part of the overall message in its own unique way (see Figure 2.24 and 2.25).

figure 2.22

The Mediaband site at `http://www.mediaband.com/mediaband/mb.html`, featuring the Marc Canter Show, is full of well-designed Shockwave elements that attract, entertain, and add to messages and interactions.

figure 2.23

The small animations at `http://blindspot.com` can draw big attention.

figure 2.24

An animation can be a powerful information tool (`http://www.prophet.com`).

figure 2.25

The news ticker in the upper-left corner of c/net's index page (`http://cnet.com`) is an eye-catching information medium.

● **To inform and educate.** There are limits to text, and as VRML is improved and more widely used, Internet users will see more and more of it used to offer quick comprehension of complex subjects. The same goes for interactivity (see Figures 2.26 and 2.27).

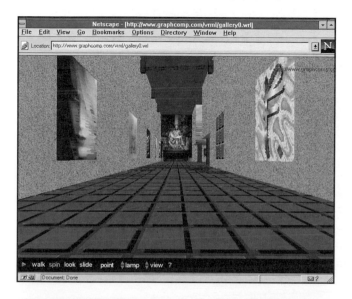

figure 2.26

The GraphComp site offers viewers a real interactive and cultural treat through VRML at `http:// www.graphcomp. com/vrml/ gallery0.wrl`.

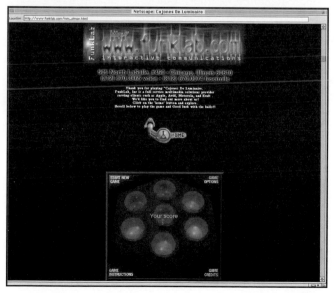

figure 2.27

Keep your brain plastic by playing virtual Simon, a sequencing skills game using different colors and music tones, on the FunkLab site (`http:// www.funklab.com/ mm_simon`).

- **Because it can be kept to a small file size.** This is a poor reason alone, but it certainly must be connected with every other good reason.

TIP

The Optimal File Size

The following information came from `http://www.wsdot.wa.gov./webmaster/webdesign/guide/transfer.htm` and lists optimal speeds.

Size 14.4 Modem (the lowest common denominator)

10 K File	5.7 seconds
25 K File	14.2 seconds
50 K File	28.4 seconds

This information leads us to believe that any page under 50K will be viewable by most Web users.

- **In other words, because all the advantages far outweigh any disadvantages.** Just remember to keep in mind that if the element's purpose is to draw attention, enhance, thrill, or entertain, keep the file size to an absolute minimum, or the viewer will be annoyed by its presence. If the multimedia element is there to serve a larger purpose, then a larger file size will be tolerated.

Balance

The multimedia element must also make visual sense within the page. This means the animation, applet, or audio screen needs to be in graphical balance with the rest of the page (see Figures 2.28 and 2.29). Regardless of the screen's illusion and the fact that Web designers are really dealing with a black cathode ray tube, balance goes back to the process learned in Design 101. Weigh the page design against these basic elements, the viewer's interest, readability and recognition, and its intended purpose.

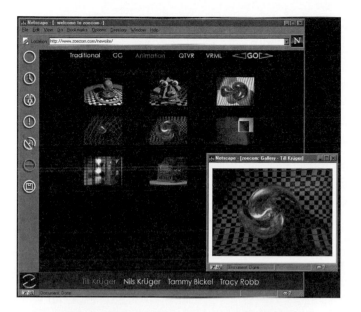

figure 2.28

This pop-up window at `http://www.zoecom.com` figures into the rest of the page without upsetting the graphical balance.

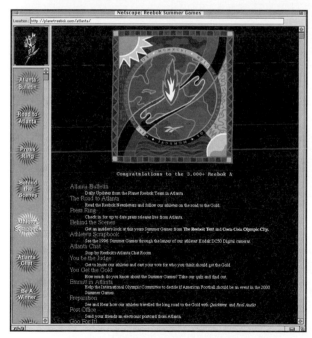

figure 2.29

At Planet Reebok (`http://planetreebok.com/atlanta`) see a great example of balance. The small GIF animation in the upper-left corner along with the framed menu bar and inner frame layout set the tempo for this site's success.

Consistency

Innovation is good, but it's *consistency* that gives instant recognition. Innovation causes the viewer to pause; consistency causes the viewer to identify. One of the most successful and obvious uses of this philosophy is the Absolut Vodka print campaign. What magazine reader doesn't instantly recognize the shape of the bottle, no matter what variations of materials, medium, or background are used in the advertisement?

Besides using a product's silhouette over and over, there are other ways to develop consistency. The Web designer has a unique set of tools to create consistency as well as unique opportunities to implement it. After logo design, color palette and font limitations are the next most widely used elements for creating recognition. The Web designer also has all the multimedia tools to choose from in order to go to unprecedented limits.

Imagine an Absolut bottle that rotates using four-frame GIF animation, stands in front of a Shockwave lightning storm, (see Figure 2.30) and enables the user to watch and hear a short Director video on how to make the perfect vodka martini, shaken not stirred?

figure 2.30

This lightning storm, with all its sound effects, can be found on the Mediaband Web site at http://www.mediaband.com/dp/banner.html.

On a Web site the designer has a choice of several elements to maintain uniformity. The use of frames offers the easiest way of maintaining a consistent theme (see Figure 2.31). That way navigation buttons, corner icons, and logos are never removed from the viewer's field of vision no matter how deep into a site the Web traveler proceeds.

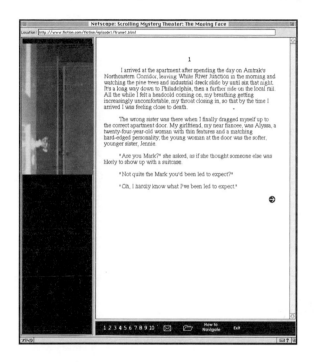

figure 2.31

The Fiction Workshop at http://fiction.com/fiction/episode1.htm uses frames to present aspects of a modern mystery for its audience to uncover clues.

There are several ways unique to the Web to maintain uniformity within a site through standard design elements as well as the new technology in the following information.

Frames

Unique to the Web, HTML frames are one of the easiest ways to create a consistent multimedia element. Implementing frames correctly is one of the biggest challenges.

Interactive Interface

This is the type of design element that makes a site fun. Realize that fun can be understated and elegant. There are several ways you can incorporate multimedia in an interactive interface. Some examples include menu buttons that change color when the mouse rests on them (see Figure 2.32) or move when they're clicked. There's also the use of audio with the sound of a bell, a snap, a whoosh, a beep on or chimes each time a link is clicked.

figure 2.32

At *http://
www.hayden.com*
the menu buttons
fade when your
mouse rests on
them.

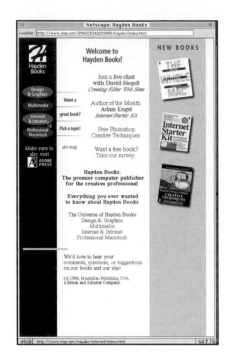

Use and Style of Animation

Using animation throughout a site at determined places is a wonderfully effective way to thread uniformity. One of the best examples we found is on the Neville Brothers' site found at `http://www.comm.net/nevilles/moveit.html` (see Figure 2.33). Simple animations of brightly colored, primitive drawings are the focal point in each of the headers on the first page of each section. These include stars that turn into candles, flapping birds, snapping gators, and a laughing moon that leaps over the horizon, all created in the same highly stylized form.

A similar effect using a much different style is achieved on The Word site at `http://www.word.com`. Tiny graphic elements within the headers of each of the sections have simple animated effects, such as a pipe that puffs smoke, a garbage can that oozes slime, a blinking scull, and a winking George Washington (see Figures 2.34 and 2.35).

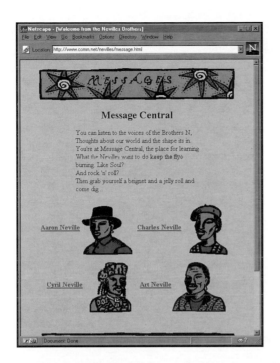

figure 2.33

The Neville Brothers' site at http://www.comm.net/nevilles uses animation as an element of consistency in the headers of each section.

figure 2.34

At the Word site (http://www.word.com/desire/) these lips that represent the Desire section are saying ... something (???)

figure 2.35

In the Habit section
of Word (*http://*
www.word.com/
habit) the tiny
puffs of smoke tie in
with all the other
little section header
animations.

Background Audio

There's a definite chasm between soothing and annoying when it comes
to background sound on the Web. It certainly can be one of the most
pleasant ways to link a continuous element throughout the various pages.
Because a RealAudio file plays on even after the user has left the page
where it was triggered, it is a simple method to implement sounds for
surfing. One example of this method is The Lil Sound Web Page at `http://`
`/www.monmouth.com/~lwallenstein/`
`music1.html` which uses MIDI files to offer
computer generated versions of contemporary
music on every page of the site (see Figure 2.36).

The Multimedia Web Designer's
Elements for Consistency

- *Color Palette*
- *Typography*
- *Navigational Menu*
- *Frames*
- *Interactive Interface*
- *Use of Animation*
- *Style of Animation*
- *Background Audio*

Bandwidth

Balance of the bandwidth is another important
consideration. If you feel strongly about implementing a large multimedia piece, the rest of the
page should be simplified so download time isn't
out of synch with the other pages on the site.

Eliminating large graphics on the page is quite often enough to achieve this bandwidth balance (see Figure 2.37).

figure 2.36

The Lil Sound Web Site offers a large number of choices for background music on its site at `http://www.monmouth.com/~lwallenstein/music1.html`.

figure 2.37

On the Mission: Impossible site graphics are kept to a minimum throughout in order to allow the game to download easily (`http://mission.com`).

Bandwidth considerations are also dependent on your audience. A corporate intranet, whose users have an ISDN-speed connection, can certainly bear the burden of large files with ease. Perhaps your message is targeted at high-end Web users, including 14.4 modem owners isn't a priority. A far-reaching site will definitely want to think in terms of the lowest common denominator.

Navigation Considerations and Design

With Web design still in its infancy, many designers don't take some of the technological aspects of it into consideration, focusing on its design elements. Navigation is two-fold, and in order to create it successfully, you must consider what moves it, HTML and JavaScript, as well as its visual intuitiveness. Navigability is as important to site design as the graphical look. The following navigational considerations will help you from overlooking some of the most important details in site development.

Weighing the Various Limitations

The first step in determining a navigational design is to define the site's intention. After a site's purpose or purposes have been determined, and therefore its audience, it's up to the designer to develop a plan that best allows the viewer to see the messages. At this point your previous browser considerations need to be looked at again.

Netscape Navigator may be king of the browsers, but it's not the only one out there, and Internet Explorer is no lightweight contender. How much you or your client may want the attention of the less-enhanced browser users is a very legitimate consideration. If you want to exploit the capabilities of the Big Guy browsers and also need to include the other users, you must offer two sites that closely reflect one another.

Frames are a design element that give the user a sense of control and greater focus. Fear of being distracted away from the original purpose is greatly lessened when navigational icons or buttons are included in a framed site (see Figure 2.38). Some refer to the area of the window that stays constant as the "cyberspace sextant."

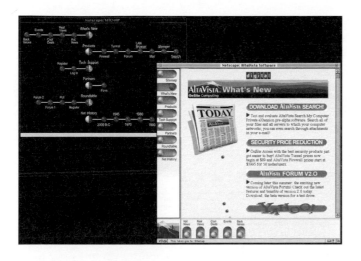

figure 2.38

The ability to get around easily within a site is as important as its content (http:// altavista.software. digital.com).

By creating a menu frame, the content frame is created—the frame that displays different areas of the site or other sites. Each frame has a different URL. The menu frame contains all the navigation tools and can point to and bring up the information in the kinetic window frame. The menu frame aids in several ways. It enables the user to rejoin the site or its home page with ease; the menu frame maintains a visual and functional point of reference.

Be warned though; improper use of frames can cause confusion and actually destroy the navigational benefits it was intended for. A site that is tightly structured around more than two frames may limit its flexibility.

The way a visitor moves through a site not only reflects the intuition of the designer, it also mirrors the intuition for the user. This is a crucial point, therefore, for a well-designed site. If the navigation is not intuitive, the chances of keeping the attention of the casual or impatient user are greatly minimized.

An intuitive site offers the user as much ease of navigation as a walk around a town square. The site's order and direction have logical place-ment because the designer has anticipated the user's navigational needs and addressed each one (see Figure 2.39).

figure 2.39

Levi's site (`http://levi.com/inner-seam/us/vol2/iss2/`) has excellent navigation and an interesting menu bar along the bottom of each page.

Linear vs Nonlinear

NOTE

Linear—A continuous, chronological movement or experience.

Nonlinear—As applied to Web navigation, it's the work or an event in which the designer's initial parameters and the user's intuition meet. In a multimedia experience it is the user who ultimately determines the outcome or the actual form of the work.

To be linear…or not to be linear. This critical navigation issue is addressed for many sites. The technology is the same, but the design is different (see Figures 2.40 and 2.41). The navigational tools that are an intrinsic part of a nonlinear site enable the user to move intuitively through it because everything the user needs is onscreen. With the World Wide Web and the wonderful technologies that have sprung up because of it, designers can create ways for Net travelers to jump from page to page, section to section, or site to site, and never lose track of their origin or ultimate destination.

figure 2.40

Linear navigation is appropriate for specific needs.

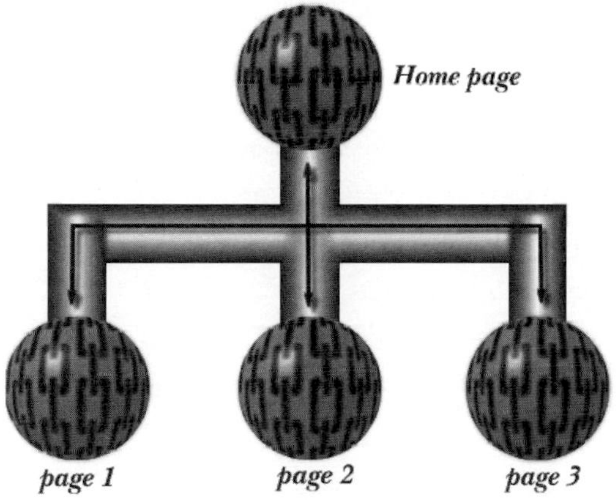

figure 2.41

Nonlinear navigation is preferred for specific sections of large, multilevel sites.

Linear navigation is appropriate for specific situations such as lengthy manuscripts that the user may want to print out, in a gallery or product display setting, or for a timeline. Government sites use linear navigation to move through legislative documentation. The Indiana University Law School Web site found at `http://www.law.indiana.edu/codes/in/incode.help.html` even includes instructions on linear navigation on the first page of the section called Using the Indiana Code.

When designing for lengthy text, it's sometimes best to break a document into sections and provide directional icons at the end of the page to enable a user to go on to the following section or review the previous section. The icons can also serve as a method to take the visitor back to the table of contents (see Figure 2.42).

figure 2.42

Use buttons such as these for linear navigation.

Nonlinear navigation has quickly become the preferred choice for any sophisticated site, whether personal or commercial. Framed menus are an immediate indicator to Internet users that browsing the site is efficient and focused.

The odds of users forgetting their original purpose are greatly diminished when given the option to go immediately to any section on the site without having to use a Back or Forward button or having to return to a home page to be reminded of choices. This is especially important on sites that use the Web to present information that might be lost through a deep and convoluted path (see Figure 2.43).

figure 2.43

The static menu at `http://projectcool.com/coolest` *ensures that the Web traveler won't become lost or confused.*

Navigation Features

The benefits of a nonlinear site far outweigh the added time needed for its development and creation. An ever-present menu, for instance, encourages the user to hide the browser's toolbar, which creates a cleaner presentation. By displaying links to every other section, a nonlinear site gives the user a constant sense of direction and control of that direction.

Three features are often found on nonlinear sites; frames, pop-up windows, and site maps. As a designer it's important to familiarize yourself with these navigational elements as they relate to multimedia.

Frames

Because more browsers are able to display frames, frames are popping up on Web sites everywhere. The opportunities that frames enable for multimedia are as exciting as the ease of navigation they present. Like all well-intended innovations, frames are misused as often as not.

Placing the site's menu within the static surroundings of a window screen is the simplest way to provide nonlinear operability. GIF animations or Java applets can be included within the frames to add excitement and, as long as they're well designed, won't compromise speed or distract from the main message of the site.

TIP

To only allow certain browser users the benefits of nonlinear navigation with frames is to ignore several million other Internet users, until all other browsers add the function. The most thoroughly designed sites have two versions if frames are used in one (see Figure 2.44). Multimedia enhancements are much more limited in the nonframed variation, but the graphical look can be identical to the framed one. This requires including the menu on the first page of each section; a matter of copying and pasting HTML code.

The AltaVista Software site (`http://altavista.software. digital.com`) is a stellar example of excellent use of the combination of multimedia elements and imaginative design for navigation. The site's navigational layout was developed by first addressing the feeling of frustration that comes from losing track of one's position in relation to the rest of a Web site. Since this was planned as an enormous site, it was imperative to give the user directional bearings (see Figure 2.45).

figure 2.44

*The first page of the
AltaVista site
(`http://
altavista.software.
digital.com`) gives
the user a choice of
frames
or not.*

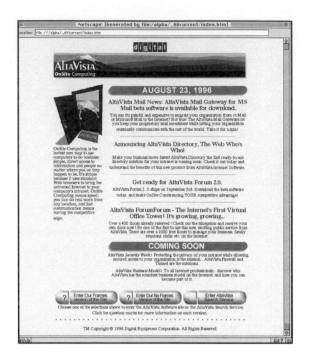

figure 2.45

*The AltaVista
Software site offers
cutting-edge
navigability. It has a
visually appealing
menu; its frames
offer the designer
an in-place palette
for multimedia
effects as well as
ever-present
directions for
the user.*

Shortly before the project began, Netscape released frames capabilities. Even though it was possible to maintain a menu on every page of a site before frames, the designers objected to the fact that the menu needed to be reloaded every time a window changed. Even if a menu is cached, it has to be redrawn, and if it's in a table, the page is recalculated each time the window changes. They felt that the time involved in that process conflicted with the patience level of the average Web traveler and therefore made it impractical. A site menu within a static frame section, however, eliminated the reload dilemma.

Just as frames can be a wonderful addition to a site, their misuse is also seen throughout the Web (see Figure 2.46).

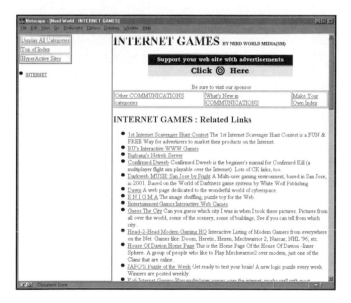

figure 2.46

These frames use up way too much real estate!

Limit the use of framed menus for sites that:

- Invite the user to link to other sites
- Are divided into several sections
- Want to implement multimedia effects within the menu
- By virtue of their large size require sophisticated navigation tools

Don't use frames if they're unnecessary; there's no need for two separate URLs when a click map and a back button or Home link are sufficient.

JavaScript for Pop-Up Windows

This fun and cool design method of using JavaScript to trigger pop-up windows is mentioned in navigation development because it eliminates going from one spot to another and yet brings forth as much information as a window offers. Pop-up windows enable the world to be brought to your feet, so to speak, without you leaving your page. They can be very effective when used properly (see Figure 2.47).

figure 2.47

A pop-up can be like traveling in a bumper car. They don't always go far, but they're lots of fun (http:// projectcool.com/ coolest).

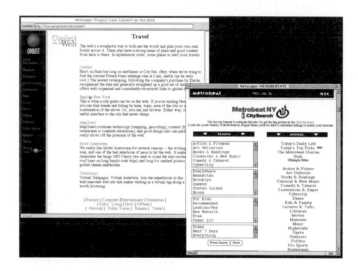

Because JavaScript capabilities aren't available on many browsers besides Netscape and Internet Explorer, many visitors will see absolutely nothing happen when a JavaScript hot spot is clicked (see Figure 2.48). If you must have all users able to see your site, you probably won't want to use any multimedia, or else create a second, text-only version. To find the JavaScript code for pop-ups click View Document Frame Source. This is how the JavaScript appears within the HTML code:

```
<script language="JavaScript">
<!--
  function popup (url){
        popwindow=window.open(url,'popwindow',
'scrollbars=yes,resizable=yes,status=no,width=400,height=350')

  }
// -->
</script>
```

It is becoming increasingly popular for many designers to use pop-ups as a means to go to another Web browser window without leaving the original site. It helps ensure that users will return to the original page they linked from (see Figure 2.49).

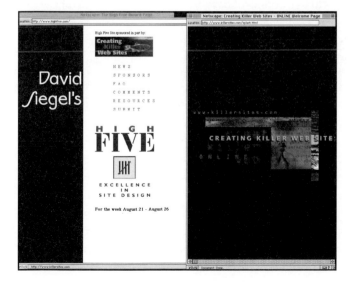

figure 2.49

Pop-up windows at David Siegel's High Five site (`http:// highfive.com`) enable you to view the page you just left.

The design for the AltaVista Software site's History Section unfolded nearly as rapidly as the new technology became available. Originally it was proposed to be a text-heavy, book-like section with several graphic illustrations to balance and ease the visual aspect. At one point, however, this was dismissed in favor of a more pleasurable, Web-friendly design that offered the information through an interactive timeline (see Figure 2.50).

figure 2.50

AltaVista's History Section presented a unique challenge (`http://altavista.software.digital.com/inethistory/nfintro.htm`).

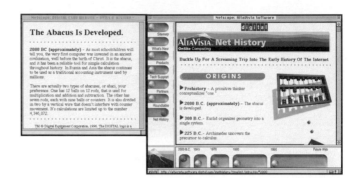

Once the graphical concept for the different timeline sections evolved, the question was how to offer more detailed information than just dates and events. Simultaneously, while the designers researched the newest beta version of Netscape, pop-up windows were presented. This brand new capability, accomplished with JavaScript, was the obvious answer to the question posed. Within a couple of days, the design team learned how to implement these new developments specifically for the History Section. Pop-up windows enhance the navigation of this timeline by presenting bits of information that the user toggles on or off with a single click of the mouse.

JavaScript, in fact, enhanced the navigation interaction in more than one way. It was used to write the coding that triggered the GIF-animated spheres in the menu to roll across the bar and change colors for the submenu in the frames (see Figure 2.51). JavaScript was chosen over HTML because its command set had the capability to extend a smooth interface for the various functions within each frame. HTML was not capable at the time of supporting more than one function. By using JavaScript to trigger the GIF animations, the HTML-coded frame stayed cached, otherwise, the whole frame would have been required to refresh, delaying the animation and the function.

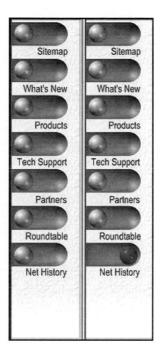

figure 2.51

GIF spheres move
with the help of
JavaScript.

JavaScript triggered GIFs are just one way to implement a multimedia-enhanced navigation tool. Any multimedia application can be used to create a special effect for a tool that's clicked or rolled over. Just remember the user ends up downloading the application and requiring its plug-in in order to experience the effect.

The Site Map

Site maps can be the most wonderful navigational tools when created correctly. The clickable site map is about the friendliest way a site can enable its visitors to move around and explore. Make it visually striking and a site map is a total pleasure to use (see Figure 2.52).

The decision was made, for example, to include the site map in the AltaVista site for several reasons. Not only do its 3D spheres lend cohesiveness to the site's design, but they also help to familiarize the user with the three-dimensional effect. This is important for future revision options of the site, since virtual reality technology will undoubtedly have a large impact on Web site design.

figure 2.52

Site maps are fast becoming essential tools for navigation design. The site map for the AltaVista software site (http://altavista.digital.software.com) was created not only for the present but to be enhanced for the future.

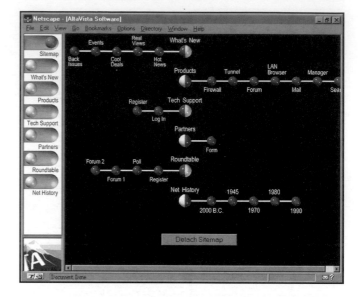

In its beginnings, as illustrated previously in Figure 2.52, the map is truly two-dimensional despite its 3D graphics. The plan for the site, however, indicates that its levels will grow into several layers, so that a two-dimensional map will be too complex for a user to want to read. A three-dimensional virtual model that could be seen on all sides would enable fast and easy comprehension of the map's deeper levels. It would also include a large thrill factor for many users (see Figure 2.53).

The site map as it stands holds large appeal for users who prefer an interactive experience. It offers an alternative method of navigation, and enables more direct access for the user by eliminating a mouse click. While the information is the point of the site, making it fun or an interesting challenge to get to the information is one of the greatest assets of this medium. The thought behind this site map exemplifies the use of good planning on many levels, including preparing for the future (see Figure 2.54).

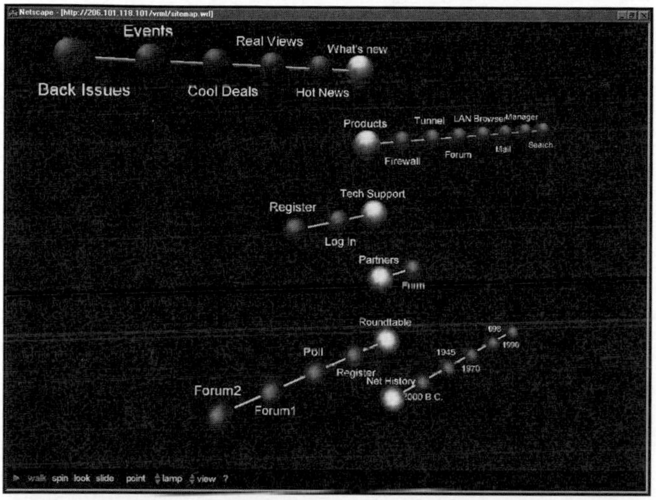

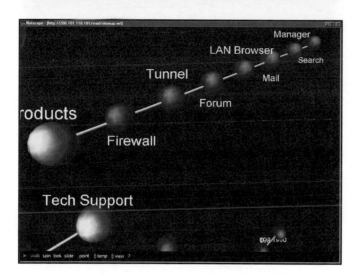

figure 2.53

The site map
evolved, shown in
a beta version.

figure 2.54

The viewer will be
allowed to walk into
and move through
the site map's virtual
world.

The First Steps in Design

We've discussed the most basic elements of good site design, including
navigation considerations. This section includes the beginning steps to
take, whether you're working with a client or developing a personal
project. Details for implementing multimedia in a Web site are included in
the later chapters. These steps enable the designer to make an initial plan.

Proposal

Determining the client's needs affects the flow, look, page layout, and depth of the site.

By writing down everything that needs to be included in a Web site, you firm up the site's purposes and goals. The proposal needs to include a detailed breakdown of every section, its message, and the elements, whether multimedia or not, that will be used to communicate those messages. Don't be intimidated at the thought of putting the plan into writing. Remember, it's a proposal, not a contract.

If it's a lengthy project, you can almost be guaranteed it will be much different at its birth than at its conception. A written proposal merely acts as a starting point and a guide. The designer who stays on top of Web news will hear about several ideas that can totally change a site's look or method. Be prepared to be flexible.

Navigation

In order to best identify the movement of the site, a flow chart enables the concepts to gel (see Figure 2.55). After the client's needs have been determined, the well-organized designer creates a flow chart to illustrate his or her thoughts and allow for client feedback. It's easier to change a Web site's direction at this stage than after it's online. It's the flow chart that combines linear thought with nonlinear navigation.

figure 2.55

Flow charts can be as simple or complex as the client's needs.

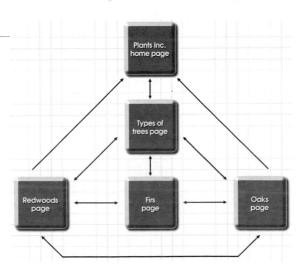

A Web site's flow chart begins with the home page, or page that contains the menu. From there it branches into each section, which branches into their various sub-sections. Each section appropriately links to the sections and/or subsections they need to. It's up to you and your client to decide the most logical flow of the site.

The Look

Deciding the look of the site involves several aspects. If the templates are the foundation, as discussed, then you decide the colors. Because of bandwidth and color limitations, it is important to make choices for the site early on. Due to the potential vastness of a Web site, some companies or corporations develop a metaphor for their sites in order to create a well-defined Internet identification.

In order to develop a site metaphor, the creative process must be implemented. Try to remember to implement colors and imagery that reflect the company's character. Although contemporary design enables a no-holds-barred approach, use common sense, create original graphics, and attend to details to the point of going an extra 10 percent in the content development (see Figure 2.56).

figure 2.56

The Marc Canter Show is an easy metaphor to spot. Haven't we all wanted our own talk/variety television show? (http:// www.mediaband. com/index.html)

The Menu

A result of defining the site's sections, navigational path, and look, the menu is the most important visual and mechanical element of the Web site and needs to be treated with thoughtful consideration (see Figure 2.57). Not only must it be clear to the user what section each button clicks to, the buttons themselves must be visually appealing and should show either through movement or a color change which one has been activated. At the same time, the menu can't be distracting from the rest of the window.

figure 2.57

The little fishie at the bottom of the Killersites site (`http://killersites.com`) aids in navigating through the sections. You always know where you are because the menu stays on the left.

The Structure

File directory design cannot be emphasized enough as a determining factor for proper Web site design (see Figure 2.58). The way the file directory is set up separates the wise from the naive. The time put into the flow chart allows you to accurately determine the kind of directory that will be needed.

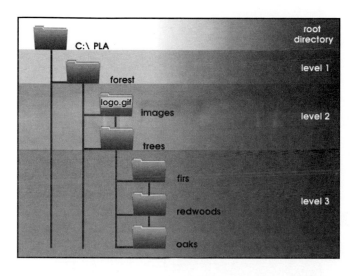

figure 2.58

The file directory is often overlooked by Web site designers, even though it's essential to the practicality of the site.

Some structure that may be included in your file directory includes an images folder, a movies (AVI, QuickTime) folder, or a cgi-bin folder. It is entirely dependent on what the job entails in order to create a modular foundation. These modules create great efficiency and also set up a structure that prepares it for ease of modification in the future or as the site is being developed.

Unfortunately, many Web designers give little or no consideration to a meticulous file directory. The result is much like taking everything in your filing cabinet and throwing it into a single manila folder. If such a site needs a modification or updating, the entire system must be torn down and rebuilt. It's a very poor use of time. The well-designed file directory, on the other hand, is a thing of beauty. The designer and the client can be reassured that modifications can be made with ease and logic.

The Hierarchical File Directory Structure

The following are guidelines you can use to achieve a well-organized structure:

① Create a main directory (see Figure 2.59). Under this heading exists everything in the site. This is like the file cabinet, only it's not as difficult to move when it's time to dust behind the furniture and magnets don't stick to it.

87

figure 2.59

The main directory is the easy part. Don't give in to the temptation to throw all the files into it in an unorganized state.

② Create different levels of directories. The designer will first designate directories for widely used images or text, such as headers, logos, or directions that are used on various pages throughout the site. These documents are placed in one directory appropriately named, such as images or guides. This facilitates changes that must be made, since the change(s) will affect all the pages that share that directory (see Figure 2.60).

NOTE

As the levels of directories become deeper, many people begin to refer to them as subdirectories or folders. Quite often these terms stem from a background in Unix, DOS, or Macintosh computers. In this book, for the sake of uniformity, they will continue to be referred to as directories.

③ Organize the files. These are the visual and directional components of the site. They always end with an extension, such as .htm or .gif. Be sure to name them logically so that they're easy to identify. It's important to limit the number of files within a directory to a maximum of 15. Otherwise it becomes too time-consuming to find a file and the point of this method is lost. It is best to use more directories; they're free and don't take up any space in the office.

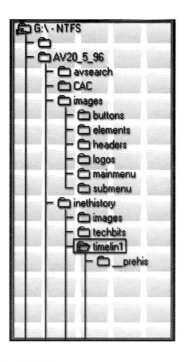

figure 2.60

This well-organized file directory saves untold man-hours during the site development.

How to Make It Relative

The following is a step-by-step example of how to maintain relative reference within the file directory structure. Many designers are familiar with directories designed with HTML links in a linear flow, starting with the root directory. Computer programmers refer to this method as using an "absolute pathname." This is quickly becoming obsolete in Web site design. Even the most uninitiated designer working on a simple home page should always use relative pathnames for the file directories. Using relative pathnames instills good habits and broad comprehension as well as provides the mobility required for server transition.

The relatively referenced file directory enables the designer to take complete advantage of its modularity as well as the site's mobility. This is absolutely imperative due to the swiftly changing nature of the Web, its technologies, and the effects of those changes on the growing trend of server specialization. It also meets the needs that enables a site to be moved from a local drive to a server drive simply and efficiently and still allow for easy changes and revisions. The example of a relatively referenced, hierarchical structure illustrates the method enabling the ease of movement and change for any site and all of its components.

The First Page

While the first page of any site may not be the first page created, it is usually the first impression, and almost always exemplifies the site's total identifying visual factors. It, therefore, must be the first page designed. Its visual appeal must get the viewer to pause first, then stay long enough to read a brief but arresting message. This also means not allowing the user a choice to scroll on the first page or pages. If scrolling can't be helped, keep it to an absolute minimum; try hard to keep these first messages on a single screen.

After the site has the viewer's attention, it takes a few pages to pull out the big guns. The home or introductory page is the gateway to the bigger messages, so it must draw the user in with exciting graphics that don't take long to load. If they do, the whole purpose is defeated because the average user won't wait long to see them no matter how interesting you say the site is.

That's why it's so important to use graphical elements on the first page that have been carefully considered from all angles. Sometimes something as simple as a bold background color can add incredible draw behind a quiet image and text, or you can use the opposite case of a softly colored background to contrast a bold image and strong text. The designer that becomes comfortable with creating a first page using simple elements then is placed in the position to implement some multimedia. A GIF animation or VRML model of a 3D object that is smaller than the size of a single GIF image can be quite exciting and still quick to load (see Figure 2.61).

figure 2.61

This corner of the AltaVista site illustrates how the small file size of a GIF animation makes it a perfect multimedia element on a home page.

chapter

3

Gary Davis & Catherine Gregory

Building, Implementing, Testing

As stated at the beginning of Chapter 1, the last set of considerations in

multimedia Web site development is for "Creating the design in an efficient

and creative manner." To help clarify what may seem like an overwhelming

task after reviewing the many determining factors discussed in the first two

chapters, this chapter offers the third and final group of considerations you

make when beginning a multimedia Web site.

The following chapters focus on solutions to applying multimedia creations to Web pages. This chapter offers an overall view of general building considerations. Such considerations range from the most efficient way to scan images to methods for testing your work.

Multimedia for the Web is a work-in-process. The considerations we include for the methods used in general building, implementing, and testing will help get you started before you read more detailed methods for specific multimedia use in the later chapters.

The Building Process

Start broad, then move in. This method enables the designer to "sketch" a basic architecture for the site and then methodically fill in all the wonderful details. This ensures your site has a beginning, an end, and supporting parameters.

Quite often we begin with a list of every issue that must be addressed within the site. This enables us to identify a rough order of content. Quickly sketched flow charts are helpful at this stage. Begin your hierarchical file structure now, and as files are created it will be obvious how to place them.

The steps that follow also enable a team of designers to see what tasks or areas can be taken over by each member. If a site is designed by one person, the list enables him or her to see beyond what may seem to be an overwhelmingly complex project.

Design Templates

The template, in its broadest sense, may be defined as the guiding look of the site. It will include all or some of the following elements beginning with a layout, header and footer designs, colors, graphical fonts, the navigation menu, and any multimedia elements chosen to serve a role. Such multimedia could be looping audio playing throughout the site, a sound or animation occurring when a button or icon is clicked or rolled over, or a framed header that includes a GIF animation.

The template, quite logically, is the first step in the building process. It is up to the designer to determine whether it may be inappropriate for every page to use the master template defined by the first page. This depends on the depth, style, content, message, and variety of the site. Some sites will use a different template for nearly every section. The more a template's elements are adhered to—whether it's a header font, frame size, or basic colors—the more uniform a site will be (see Figures 3.1 and 3.2). The more often the template is used, the easier it is for the designer to place content. Different templates may be designed for deeper levels of the site.

It is ultimately up to you to decide how uniform a site needs to be. This is based on the site's purpose as well as time and profitability constraints.

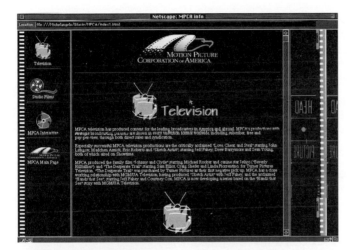

figure 3.1

A site's template is the first structure built; it establishes the look and therefore the identity of the site.

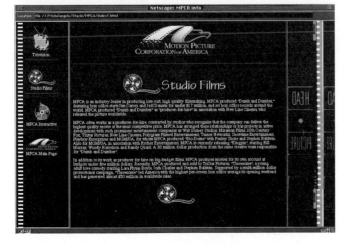

figure 3.2

To a user one page may seem entirely different from another even though they use the same template.

Large corporate sites with multilevels may like to use a different template for each level. Be aware, however, that because sites of this type are constantly revising and adding new content, the templates are not strictly adhered to. Presentation of content is more important than sticking within the boundaries of a previously used template. Continuity is maintained by choosing from the several elements of the original, or master, template.

TIP

Make sure you're happy with the entire look of the home page, including colors, fonts, and layout before you carry any of it over to the other pages.

Place Frames

Frames are often established as an element of the template's layout. If a site is going to use frames, this is the first layout element built. The most common use of frames is to keep the navigation menu constant while allowing the content window to bring up any page of the site or other sites.

Frames may also be used to lead to a more narrow navigation path or create multimedia effects within the different sections of a site. In order to change two frames with one click a Java applet or JavaScript is required.

Determine Window Size and Tables

Frames establish the size of the content window, which in turn determines how HTML tables fit within that window. Tables are used at this time to establish your margins, columns, and rows.

If you don't use frames, tables are used to establish much of the layout of a template. In a non-framed site a table is used to determine the menu's location and dimensions, as well as other elements such as blocks of text.

Comments

Place your HTML comments next to organize the header, text, background images, graphics, footer, and anything else you will want to find quickly within all that code. This is particularly helpful when doing a highly structured site, whether you're working with a team or alone. The need for comments increases with the complexity of the site.

Font Types and Graphic Images

Now that the canvas is prepared it's time to think about what to put on it. This is a good point to begin considering font types and what graphics you want to see as part of the template design. This step quite often is developed simultaneously as the following one.

Menu Images

If a framed menu is part of the design, it is often the first framed area filled in with content. Because a framed menu is so visible in a site, its menu's buttons, fonts, and background are usually created before the main background and headers. The images used for the menu help determine the color and size of images used throughout the site. This is also the time you jump to JavaScript, Java, or your application of choice to implement any movement within the frames.

We found the examples for the moving buttons in Figures 3.3 and 3.4 through the Java Boutique site at `http://weber.u.washington.edu/~jgurney/java/`. The Java applet code that moves them is also offered on the site and follows here. This code, as contained within the <APPLET </APPLET> tags, describes the various button image frames and defines when they appear onscreen. Anything in a <PARAM> tag is recognized by Java browsers and ignored by non-Java browsers. The site encourages you to use the code for your own purposes.

```
<APPLET
codebase="classes"
CODE="ANButton.class" WIDTH=130 HEIGHT=98>
SIZE of button images
<PARAM NAME="image1" VALUE="images/tvbg.jpg">
BACKGROUND image
<PARAM NAME="image2" VALUE="images/tvdn.jpg">
DOWN image
<PARAM NAME="image3" VALUE="images/tvup1.jpg">             UP
image(s)
...
<PARAM NAME="image9" VALUE="images/tvup9.jpg">
<PARAM NAME="pause" VALUE="200">
Pause between images in ms (optinal, defaults to 200)
<PARAM NAME="x" VALUE="19">
LEFT pos. to draw sub-images
<PARAM NAME="y" VALUE="19">
TOP pos. to draw sub-images
<PARAM NAME="dest" VALUE="http://www.math.uni-hamburg.de/
~fm5a014/">URL to navigate to
</APPLET>
```

figure 3.3

This is an example
of animated buttons
from The Java
Boutique site
(weber.
u.washington.
edu/~jgurney/
java/).

figure 3.4

To give an idea of
the movement, we
show three frames
used from each
animation.

Organize and Prepare Images

The methods of image preparation are well known to the experienced
Web designer. It's an early step in the process of building so that images
are ready to be used. Many designers are furnished with images by their
clients, although few are digitized and Web-ready. General steps for
making images useable in HTML are included in the following sidebar.
Chapter 4 discusses the steps for creating images for the Web in detail.

The other images needing preparation (even creation) are those that give the site its personality. They include the background, the menu buttons or icons, the logo, a repeated image if one will be used, and any other illustrations so that the total number of graphics remains under 50K. Graphics creation is discussed in Chapter 4, "Graphics: The Foundation for All Multimedia Design," and is written about in detail in the book *Creating Killer Web Sites* by David Siegel.

An oversized image reduced in HTML with HEIGHT and WIDTH tags runs the risk of an unnecessarily large file. Make the image the correct size in Photoshop or DeBabelizer for the Web page, even if you have an image used in more than one place on the site at different sizes.

After the GIF or JPEG file is placed in HTML, it needs to be checked on the browser immediately so that size adjustments can be made. Despite the use of a template, you may determine that an image's dimensions may need to be fine-tuned once it's seen on the page. This prevents a need to completely redo the page after other content has been placed.

> ### *General Steps for Image Preparation*
>
> ① Determine the approximate final dimensions of the image in pixels.
>
> ② Scan the image at twice the size decided in Step 1 or at twice the resolution.
>
> ③ Place, manipulate, and save in software program of choice. (We use Photoshop or DeBabelizer.)
>
> ④ Scale image to determined size.
>
> ⑤ Place in file format of choice, adjust colors, compress, and save this image.
>
> ⑥ Place image in HTML.
>
> ⑦ View image. If the size needs to be adjusted, go back to the file saved in Step 3, resize, and repeat next two steps.

97

Create the Pages

The home page is generally the first page designed because it is the source for the movement through the rest of the site. Whether a site is linear or nonlinear, the index page contains the links to the first pages of every section. Create this page before you move on to anything else (see Figure 3.5).

figure 3.5

Design the home page first (`http://www.entropy8.com`*).*

Usually next in the creation process is the top page of the site, if one has been included. Some Web users find them annoying because when they click a link they want to go directly to a home page. If built properly to load *very* quickly, and if there is an added purpose beyond branding or establishing the site's tone, top pages can be a real boon to a site (see Figure 3.8). Top pages are in fact very useful to alerting a user of needed plug-ins and are the place to provide links to them.

While there are always exceptions to the most common uses of the Web, nearly every site, whether it's commercial or personal, is divided into sections as evidenced by the menu buttons. The next step in the building process is making the first pages of each section. In a highly uniform site the different sections' first pages use the initial template with variations determined by the content and the amount of creativity allowed the designer. A less structured site may use entirely different layouts for the first pages of its sections. After these pages have been completed, the sections' pages are filled with content (see Figure 3.6).

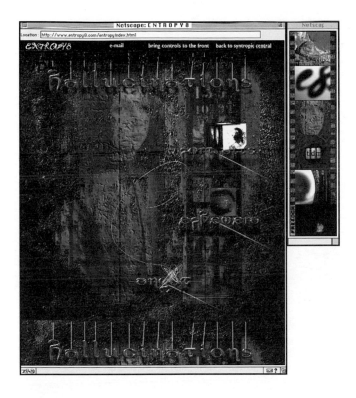

figure 3.6

*Build a page once
you know the
section it falls in and
that section's first
page is built
(http:/
www.entropy8.
com/).*

The main rule to remember when building is: "Simpler is better." This applies to any method the designer uses to achieve the look of a page or a function of a multimedia technology. If a page's tables have several cells, see if they can be reduced effectively. If an animation has 16 frames, see if there's any way to cut it down without harming its integrity.

Page Names

- **Splash Page**—Sometimes called a splash screen, this is a fairly recent innovation in site design (see figure 3.7). The splash page loads quickly (not more than 15 seconds) and never carries more than a brief message. It is often times a way to distract and entertain the viewer while plug-ins are loading. The splash page may be static or it may use layers that load in a determined sequence. It may disappear to bring up an intro or home page or it may require a click to go to the following page. This is one of the last pages built.

figure 3.7

Entropy 8 site's
splash page loads in
about five seconds
and stays onscreen.

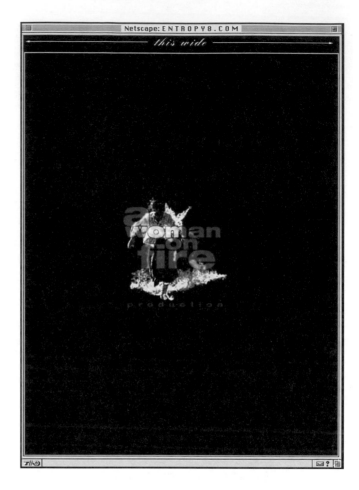

- **Introductory, Intro, or Top Page**—This page is weightier in content than a splash screen (see figure 3.8). The top page usually announces what is needed to view the site; it may include the option to go to a framed or non-framed version of the site. If a top page is used on a particularly large site, this is quite often where the site's search option is presented. Build this near the end of construction of the site, after all the content has been worked in. It may make a difference for what you include on the page.

figure 3.8

The intro page at
Entropy 8 not only
repeats the splash
page's advice for
screen width but also
offers instructions
about browser needs
and Options
adjustments for the
user's optimal
viewing.

- **Home Page**—This page is the main identifier for the site and is the
  first page to introduce the navigation menu. Because the home page
  always features the menu, it is generally the first page built (see
  figure 3.6).

Implementing the Multimedia Elements

The complex high-tech design elements are best saved for last, as they
require serious focus and need the established structure of the site to
guide their file size and direction (see Figure 3.9). This does not apply all
the time, but it can be an effective rule-of-thumb. Elements such as
moving menu buttons or a continuously-looping, framed animation are

part of the first page design. It should be reiterated that these multimedia files built in the early stages of the site's construction need to be kept minuscule and simple in order not to interfere with quick loading and to enable other, larger files to be built into the site.

figure 3.9

Save the razzmatazz for last when you know the rest of the site is orderly (`http://www.entropy8.com`).

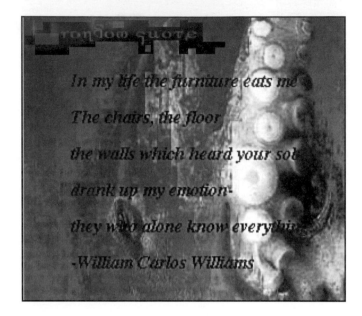

Simple Animations, Audio, and Video

Animations that are elements of the site's look, such as flipping menu buttons or a looping logo icon, are generally created early in site construction. Other simple animations illustrating content or drawing attention to a section header are left to the later stages of the building process. Depending on time constraints, they are often added after the site has been up for some time. It's not unusual to go to a favorite site and discover that a formerly static graphic has come alive.

TIP

There's a surefire trick to draw attention to the most important element on a page: animate it.

The same advice applies to audio and simple, or soundless, video uses. Pop them in toward the end of building the site. Tweaking these files can be time-consuming, so it's best to be nearly finished with the rest of the site (see Figure 3.10).

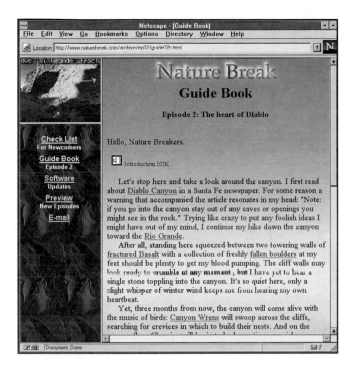

figure 3.10

This page on the Nature Break site (`http://www. naturebreak. com`) includes two multimedia technologies: an interactive pan- orama and an audio clip.

Complex Interactions and Video with Audio

When complex interactive experiences, such as games, virtual reality worlds, or video movies are used on a site they are usually huge drawing cards the site is built around. Often one designer works on such a technol- ogy while another builds the site to house it. If you plan to do both simultaneously, don't. Treat the site as one project and the complex multimedia experience as another. When one is completed, the other's direction will be clearer than if you attempt to do both at once (see Figure 3.11).

103

The zoloft site is an elaborate game of intrigue built around the premise of a highly controlled society that engages the user as a spy. Shockwave is used to simulate the view from hidden surveillance cameras and simulate conversations overheard through secret microphones and phone taps. This site is an excellent example of how to interweave multimedia so completely into a site that it's nearly impossible to tell where the message leaves off and the effects begin. Because an unShocked version of the site is available, this tells us that the storyline can metaphorically be consid- ered the egg, we mean chicken...

figure 3.11

*Which came first:
the site or the
multimedia
experience?
(http://
spectacle.com/
zoloft/initia-
tion/
interface.html).*

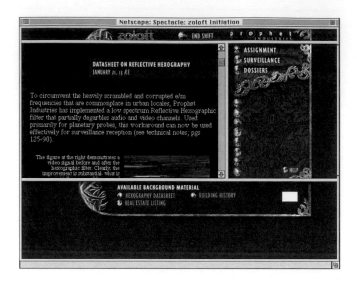

Testing

Checking and testing is an ongoing step in the production process. As each new link is added to a site and each image is placed, the designer must make sure that everything works the way it was intended to, if not better. The easiest way to check the look and function of your Web page as you develop it is to split your screen into two windows with the HTML on one side and a view of the page on the other (see Figure 3.12). If this bothers you because it reduces the size of the HTML document, then keep your browser accessible so that you can refer to it easily.

figure 3.12

*Keep your HTML
document next to
its result to ensure
that the page looks
and acts as it's
intended.*

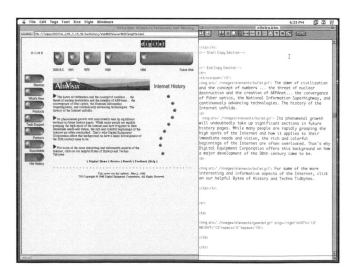

TIP

After making a change in your HTML document you must go up to Options, choose the Network Preferences file, and clear the cache or set your cache to 0 during testing (see figure 3.13). Otherwise your revision will not be evident on the page you view, even if you reload it.

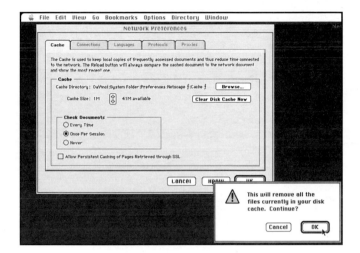

figure 3.13

Clear the cache in Network Preferences in order to see your HTML changes.

Interactive sites particularly must be tested for intuitiveness and effectiveness before they go online. Whenever possible, test how intuitive the different aspects of a site are on a human guinea pig. Quiet observation of a user's behavior can tell you a lot about whether interactive elements, colors, page design, or navigation layout needs to be tweaked or revamped. Any willing volunteer will do, whether it's the neighbor kid, your father-in-law, the insurance guy down the hall, or the package delivery lady. This is also the best way to be sure that your design and any written instructions for experiencing it are clearly understandable, which leads to positive email, as opposed to complaints, whines, and generally snide remarks.

It can be surprising the way colors look or the way multimedia behave on other operating systems, so don't wait until your page is online to find out (see Figures 3.14 and 3.15). All the most common platforms need to checked including Mac, PC, and any others you deem appropriate. The platform test can be the least convenient, depending on the equipment in the studio, office, or home where the site is created. Testing each page on different platforms and browsers is integral for fine-tuning.

figure 3.14

*What looks perfect
on a PC…*

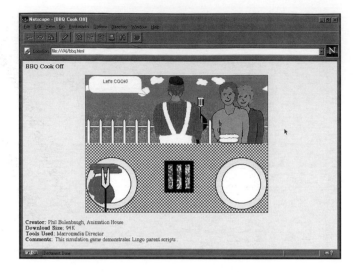

figure 3.15

*…may be different
on a Mac.*

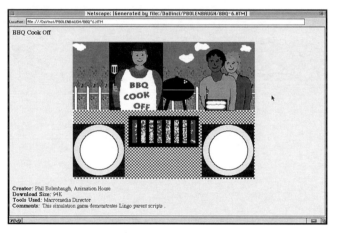

The easiest way to do this is to have more than one operating system
networked within your working space. If you don't have the luxury of a
multiplatform set-up, there are a couple of different ways to view how the
site looks on a platform other than the one it was built on.

The next best method of doing this is to load a beta site onto the server you use. This way you can call your friend who has a different operating system and ask how it looks or go over there and do it yourself. This does require having a friend with a different OS than you. Be sure to look at your site using other browsers, too.

The other way to test your site is to save to a portable storage system such as a disk, SyQuest, Jaz, Zip, or optical drive disc or cartridge, depending on the size of the site and portable media equipment preferred. This method requires software that formats the disk for the other operating system (see Figure 3.16) and software that translates the disk's files to be viewed by the other system. If, for example, a site is created on a Mac, then software such as MacLinkPlus converts the files from HTML to ASCII and image graphics to raw data and saves them to a PC-formatted disk in order to be viewed by the PC. Don't forget to name the file using the 8.3 rule when creating the site if you will be testing it this way.

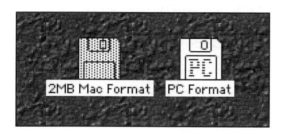

figure 3.16

Look on your Mac's desktop to see which operating system the disk is formatted for.

Always test on a Mac and PC using Netscape Navigator and Internet Explorer. To learn more about what technologies work best with what operating systems and browsers, refer to chapters 4 through 8.

When the site is finished, it needs to have a thorough final check. Use the following guidelines to place your site on the Web with confidence.

- Each graphic element is placed correctly.

- All text is proofed.

- Text flows correctly.

- All links work and indicate when they've been used through HTML LINK and VLINK code.

- All multimedia elements work correctly.

- The entire site looks and functions properly on all operating systems.

- "Footers" for email, trademarks, and other information are included at the bottom of every page.

chapter

4

 by Gary Davis and Catherine Gregory

Graphics: The Foundation for All Multimedia Design

One of the key supports of a well-designed Web site is a strong proficiency in

the development of Web graphics. This chapter leads you through the unfolding

process that takes place to create a cutting-edge, graphics-appropriate site

design. The file formats, software programs, techniques, and choices featured

offer you unique uses for graphics within new sites as well as enhancements

for current sites. The knowledge acquired will aid in efficient site development

planning that will be continued throughout the remainder of the book.

The focus of this book is multimedia. This chapter doesn't pretend to cover graphics in great depth, but it underscores some of the graphical elements of a site's design that set the stage for multimedia. GIF and JPEG file formats, the most widely used graphic file formats for the Web, are touched on, as well as two of the most often used programs, Adobe Photoshop and Equilibrium's DeBabelizer. We take a walk through the art gallery section of the zoecom site and focus on the choices for different graphic elements and how they were implemented.

> **NOTE**
>
> For an excellent resource that covers Web graphics issues in depth, check out David Siegel's *Creating Killer Web Sites* (Hayden Books).

Nuts and Bolts

There are several things the multimedia Web site designer must have from the outset, including skills in graphic design and the technology needed for using it on the Web. This section reviews how to scan images and the file formats and tools necessary for graphics creation on the Web.

About Digital Images for the Web

In the digital world there are two types of graphic images: vector-based and raster-based. The site designer must have a clear understanding of the two types, and their strengths and limitations, in order to effectively build graphics for the Web.

Vector Images

Vector images are created on your computer screen through mathematical formulas. Because their descriptions depend on the geometric locations of points, lines, and curves they can be scaled to any size without loss of resolution (see Figure 4.1).

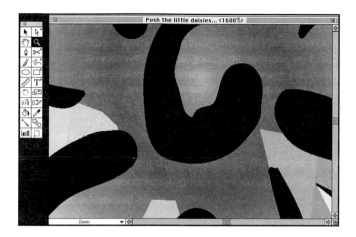

figure 4.1

Close-up of a vector image.

The advantages of vector-described images is that their file sizes are generally significantly smaller than raster images. This is because the information used to create them is described in concise mathematical formulas. This enables greater transfer and display efficiency due to the smaller storage space that raster images require.

Magnification or diminishment of a vector image will not affect its quality. A vector file can also be layered, which means the user can turn off or on the screen-display of different portions of the graphic information, which may be desired for printing purposes.

Most graphic designers are familiar with vector graphics through the use of image creation software programs such as Macromedia FreeHand and Adobe Illustrator. These graphics are not used regularly on the Web because the plug-ins required to view them are not yet embedded within most browsers. There is a FutureSplash plug-in for Netscape that implements vector graphics in its animation. A discussion of the increasing interest in vector design is included in this chapter's section "Image Editor Options."

EPS

Vector images for the Web are commonly described through PostScript, the image description language developed by Adobe. The Encapsulated Postscript (EPS) file format allows the graphic material to be transferred from one program to be documented in another. EPS translates graphics and text into descriptions to a printer that then draws them based on the encapsulated code. These images are often created in Illustrator or FreeHand, and may be then edited in raster-based applications such as Photoshop or xRes if desired. You should note that the image file will be permanently changed to a raster image if this is done, however.

111

Some of the best uses for vector images are for illustrative purposes or logos consisting of flat or shaded areas of hue. Color may be assigned to a vector formula in one of two basic ways: for a broad or narrow outline or to fill in an area with solid or gradated color.

Raster Images

Raster images are pixel-based graphics where each and every pixel contains its own color and bit depth information. Bit depth is determined by the number of colors, or palette, for the image to choose from. File sizes can increase exponentially when size and bit depth are increased. File sizes can be determined by multiplying an image's width and height by its bit depth, also expressed as "bytes." A 24-bit RGB image, for example, contains three bytes of data per pixel. An 8-bit RGB image contains one byte and a black and white image only one eighth of a bit per pixel. A 640×480, 24-bit RGB image would use 640×480×3 or 921,600 bytes. A kilobyte consists of 1,024 bytes, so this image would be exactly 900K—obviously much too large for a standard Web site. The benefit of these greater bit depths is that the greater the amount of available colors, the more accurately photographic and finely detailed images are reproduced. (see Figure 4.2).

figure 4.2

Close-up of a raster image.

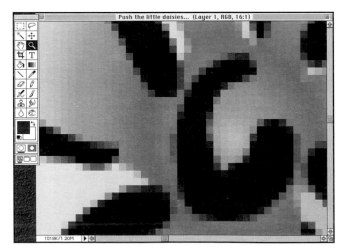

NOTE

The word "pixel" is the shortened term for "picture element," defined as one of the many tiny dots that make up a screen image.

TABLE 4.1

Bit Depth and Colors

BIT DEPTH	NUMBER OF COLORS
1	2
2	4
3	8
4	16
5	32
6	64
7	128
8	256
24	16 million plus

Raster images will never be replaced by vector for graphic display of photography or other detailed images. The quality of appearance of raster images is dependent on the vast color palette that is used.

While there is an infinite number of digital colors available, in order to have their work seen, Web designers must limit themselves to the number that most computers can view. The majority of computers connected to the Internet are capable of displaying 256 colors at once, or 8-bit color.

Because Netscape Navigator is the preferred Web browser, and because its major contender Internet Explorer is compatible to so many of its features, it's wise (not to mention easier) for you to design your Web graphics using the 216 colors that make up the Netscape color palette (see Figure 4.3). The Netscape 216 Color Palette with hex numbers and values can be found at `http://www59.metronet.com/colors/`. What this ultimately means is that the images you create for the Web are color-limited, another one of the challenging conditions of the medium.

figure 4.3

The Netscape Color
Cube colors
(http://
mvassist.pair.com/
Articles/
NS2colors.html).

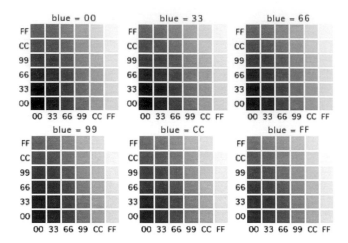

You may use your editing software for the process of dithering to expand your color options. Dithering uses colors from the available palette to create the illusion of colors that are not included. The method is visually effective but expensive from the standpoint of file size because dithered images are harder to compress than non-dithered. Proceed cautiously.

Anti-aliasing is another consideration that involves color during the creation process. When an image is aliased, its edges are visibly jagged against the background color. In order to smooth the edge's appearance the designer implements the image creation software's anti-alias setting to choose the mediating colors. Anti-aliasing will add a significant number of colors to an image that make it less compressible. It's up to you to decide whether or not these smoothed edges are worth the added file size weight.

Scanning Images

There are a few rules about scanning to go over before we begin a deeper look at graphics for the Web. First, for the sake of time, it's important to determine what size an image needs to be before it's scanned. As we mentioned in Chapter 3, we always scan an image at its original dimensions and about twice the resolution *or* twice the dimensions at its original resolution.

It would be overkill to ever scan an original-sized image at over 150 dpi for the Web, but you do want to *begin* with 24-bit color. Photoshop and DeBabelizer are much better at converting the images to a smaller color palette than most scanner software.

During the scanning process is also the time to crop an image to the size needed. There's no reason to place an over-sized file in the image editing program. Cropping is also vital in keeping file size minimal.

Never allow a Web image to reduce its resolution lower than 72 dpi, which is the ratio that most monitor screens display. Any image that has a lower resolution than that will appear pixelated. An image with a higher resolution will appear at the screen's maximum dpi.

An image no wider than 487 pixels works well on all platforms, should be quick to download, prevents horizontal scrolling, and prints on one page.

After the image is scanned and you are ready to manipulate it in preparation for the Web, be sure to save the original in a separate file. That way if the image you're working with becomes degraded as you experiment with its optimization, you don't have to re-scan in order to start fresh.

Choosing the Formats

While most Web site designers are familiar with the differences between JPEG and GIF file formats, a quick overview of their characteristics offers some insight into clever use of both. A well-designed combination of the two file formats can make a Web page snap visually, and a thorough understanding of their differences is the way you make these formats work effectively.

GIF87a and 89a

The GIF (Graphical Interchange Format) file format was originally intended to serve as a medium for exchanging images over CompuServe, which introduced the GIF in 1987. With the introduction of the World Wide Web in 1992, new interest developed in this paragon of a file format. GIF is the most prevalent graphic file format on the Web because all computer browsers were built to read it through any platform. With a maximum of 256 distinct colors, it meets the capabilities of most of today's computer monitors.

GIF files are created through raster images. The 216 colors Netscape enables you to work with should be reduced to as few as possible to be effective as a GIF file, which averages a compression ratio of 4:1. A GIF image loses no visual information during compression, so it always looks like the original one you've created.

Because GIF compression is light, the file to be compressed must be kept small through various techniques. File size can be optimized by making certain that the image is closely cropped, the number of colors are reduced to the minimum acceptable, and color contrast has been minimized.

Creating GIF Files

GIF in Photoshop:

① Open the original RGB image.

② Pull down the Mode menu and select Indexed Color.

③ Select the number of bits/pixel (see Figure 4.4).

figure 4.4

In Photoshop's Indexed Color window.

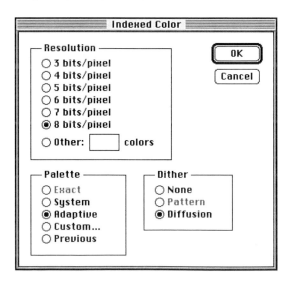

Select Adaptive if you want the software to choose the colors or Custom if you want to choose from the Netscape Color Cube.

Select Diffusion if dithering.

④ Save the file with the GIF extension (see Figure 4.5).

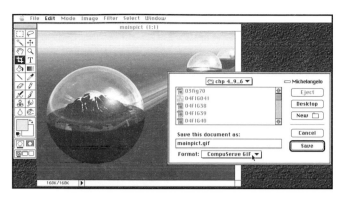

figure 4.5

*Saving as
CompuServe GIF.*

GIF file in DeBabelizer:

① Open the image.

② Pull down the Palette menu and select Options (see Figure 4.6).
Decide whether to dither the background color. If you do want to you
must:

    a.   Pick the dithering percentage.

    b.   Pick the background color.

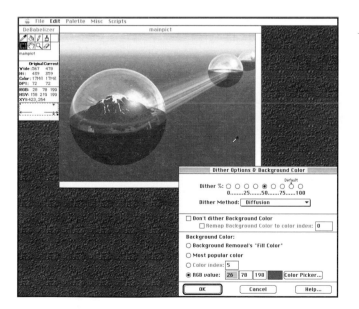

figure 4.6

*Choosing dithering
and background
options.*

③ Go back to Options and choose pixel depth by making comparisons.
Press Control-Z to undo and redo the image.

a. Select Translate.

b. Select Clear All to wipe out previous settings.

c. Reduce colors to your satisfaction.

④ Save the file with the GIF extension.

figure 4.7

Saving the GIF in DeBabelizer.

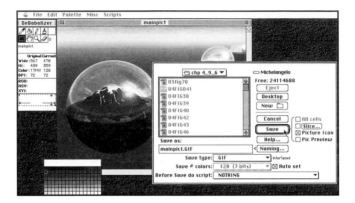

Text images take longer to load than HTML text, so they're definitely not best for lengthy descriptions.

NOTE

Text images disallow words to be grabbed by search engines. Designers that use text images should also use an ALT text tag that repeats the text so that the search engines will recognize it.

GIF89a is basically the same as its predecessor GIF87a with a few added features, including capabilities for transparency, interlacing, and animation. Transparency and interlacing are a couple of the outstanding features that makes GIF89 so popular from the graphic designer's point of view. GIF89 interlacing capabilities were developed to put the user at ease while the page downloads. Interlacing enables the graphic file to load in what appears to be layers, so that the user has an idea of what will appear on-screen. Because it increases file size, interlacing should be used only for images that you wish to be seen quickly or as a preview.

Transparency is the capability to enable a background to show through one or more colors that is chosen by the designer. Photoshop has an excellent plug-in called GIF89 export, which has a real-time preview and the capability to select any number of colors from the images actual color palette. There can be problems when interlacing and transparency are used on the same page, so it's best to choose one over the other. Otherwise an interlaced transparent image may appear without the transparency, or the image may not be completed.

JPEG

JPEG stands for the Joint Photographic Experts Group, the committee that standardized this image compression medium. With a capacity for 16.7 million colors (24-bit), JPEG was designed to compress photographic images. JPEG's development takes advantage of limitations of the human eye in order to radically compress an image file without detectable loss of detail.

As with GIF, JPEG is raster-based. JPEG's compression formula is based on separating the image into zones and removing brightness information from color hues. A certain amount of image information is lost through JPEG—a little with low compression, a lot with high. JPEG's compression ratio can run as high as 100:1 but usually begins at about 10:1, depending on how high the designer sets the quality. JPEG can decode in phases, the same effect as GIF's interlacing. This is referred to as a "progressive JPEG." All the major browsers support JPEG and the rest are not far behind.

Highly flexible and embraced by all major browsers, JPEG offers the designer a choice between file size and image quality of varying degrees. With some experimentation the designer can often select a very small file size with no detectable image distortion. With JPEG, file size is reduced through the quality settings of the software used, such as Photoshop or DeBabelizer. Reducing JPEG file size is simple, therefore, because the programs analyze and choose the method automatically. It's simply up to you to accept or adjust the level.

JPEG has limitations. Images that use few colors don't translate as well as in GIF and don't save at a smaller file size. At the time of this writing, most computers don't meet JPEG's capacity for 24-bit color—over 16 million colors—but with technology advancing at its current rate, computers'

119

color capacities will increase affordably, and the demand for JPEG will undoubtedly soar. Until then, 8-bit monitors will continue to display JPEG images at their capacity.

Creating JPEG Files

JPEG in Photoshop:

① Open the image.

② Select Quality from the Mode menu. Select Medium or High.

③ Save the file with a JPEG extension.

JPEG in DeBabelizer:

① Open the image.

② Set Quality to the compression rate you choose.

③ Save the file with the JPEG extension.

When a Web page contains several graphic elements in its design, separate those elements into a few reasonably-sized files. The designer must carefully weigh, however, how much to ask the server to send in comparison to the size of the files. It's usually better to send five reasonably sized files than 30 tiny ones or one huge file.

The Comparison Rule

The best rule to use when deciding which file format to use is this: Always compare the image qualities and compressed file sizes of JPEG and GIF. So much hinges on who your audience is and what your messages are. Sometimes a JPEG file is bigger than the GIF file of the same image, but the JPEG's look makes it worth the extra few seconds of download time (see Figures 4.8 and 4.9). If a page has a lot going on, you may decide to settle on a poorer quality image because it's worth the 1KB you save.

There are as many variables as there are reasons for Web pages. Comparing GIF and JPEG is always worth an extra few minutes and leaves you feeling confident that you made the wisest choice. There is often no better guidance than experience, and your own will enable you to quickly assess when it's not necessary to make a GIF/JPEG comparison. Refer to the sidebar on "Exceptions to the Comparison Rule" in the meantime.

figure 4.8

JPEG image, file size 52K.

figure 4.9

GIF image, file size 52K.

121

On a visual level, GIF and JPEG present comparable grayscale images. JPEG, however, wins the compression competition but takes longer to decode and view. This is an example of the trade-offs that a designer must weigh against the intent of the site's message.

The Up-And-Coming Technology

It seems as if new technology for Web site creation becomes available nearly every day. PNG and Lightning Strike are just two increasingly popular examples of new formats to find cool images on the Web. We briefly explain both of them in the following sections. Use the URL addresses to explore them further and decide if you may like to use them.

Exceptions to the Comparison Rule

Go exclusively to GIF if:

- You have a simple line drawing with relatively large areas of eight or less colors

- You need to use transparency

- You want to animate the image

Go exclusively to JPEG if:

- You have a large photo

- You have a big image with a lot of color

PNG

`http://www.boutell.com/boutell/png/`

Pronounced "ping," this format's name is the acronym for Portable Network Graphics. It was developed specifically to be a substitute for GIF, which is entangled in a legal debate over royalties. Like GIF, PNG offers lossless compression. Among other things, it features support for 1-, 2-, 4- and 8-bit color palettes and 1-, 2-, 4-, 8- and 16-bit grayscale. PNG has multiple CRCs, the error-checking technique that enables file integrity to be checked without viewing. The non-patented format uses common file corruption detection and has a two-dimensional interlacing scheme. For even more information, check out the site at `http://quest.jpl.nasa.gov/PNG/`.

Lightning Strike

`http://www.infinop.com`

This system is causing quite a stir with its capabilities for very high image compression ratios for large images that have download speeds comparable to JPEGs. Its formula is based on wavelets, mathematical functions that divide data into different frequency components and then study each component with a resolution matched to its scale. There is a Lightning Strike plug-in available, as well as an ActiveX component and Java applet to support Lightning Strike compressed images.

Choosing the Tools

Image manipulating software is as important to the Web designer as the proper set of tools is to any artisan. We turn our focus to Photoshop and DeBabelizer, two raster-based programs preferred by graphic designers for manipulating graphic images for the Web. However, new software programs, each with its own unique set of features, are gaining the interest of designers as the potential of the Web becomes more widely recognized.

This section briefly touches on some of the major players, including those specializing in vector-based graphics. As mentioned earlier in this chapter, these graphics, which have their roots in Adobe's PostScript language (PS), have become increasingly popular for Web-based graphics for a number of reasons. One is that file sizes, as opposed to raster-based imagery, can be exponentially smaller in size (kilobytes). The encapsulated postscript file format (EPS) exists only as fields or areas defined mathematically, these areas are then filled with a specific color or graduation of color between two hues.

Even though programs such as Photoshop and xRes provide multiple layers and undo features, vector-based illustration software such as Adobe Illustrator and Macromedia FreeHand offers unparalleled control and editing capabilities for the imagery they create. Text graphics are a perfect example because raster-based images, once sized, cannot be enlarged or reshaped without some degradation of the original image. Vector-based graphics are mathematically calculated and may be resized at will with no degradation at all. Even though the number of vector-based images used on the Internet will not reach the level of raster-based or photographic imagery, its uses can be shown as effective solutions for many designers.

DeBabelizer

http://www.equilibrium.com/

Equilibrium Software's DeBabelizer is Macintosh- and SGI-based (though its forthcoming version will support Windows, too). It provides you with the ability to freely manipulate the Netscape 216 color palette as well as much larger palettes. DeBabelizer enables Web designers to create GIF images with 8 to 16 colors. Reducing colors to such few choices enables solid, well-defined color through the elimination of the risk of pixelation from dithering. Dithering control and batch processing are features DeBabelizer offers, taking the tediousness out of manually processing a GIF animation or collection of images. DeBabelizer has a broad range for accepting and outputting file formats, which adds to its versatility. It automatically reads over 60 different formats and writes over 45.

When DeBabelizing a color palette to reduce colors, DeBabelizer dithers an image down to the prominent colors and usually does a truly excellent job. Occasionally there is an instance when a file must be reduced to so few colors that the designer needs to select the colors that will best represent its original look instead of allowing DeBabelizer to choose. This may be the case when creating a GIF animation, or for an image that needs to be used on an already heavy page. Selecting the Translation option enables you to hand pick the colors (see Figure 4.10). Do be warned, this method can take quite a bit of experimentation until you get the hang of it. It offers, however, an excellent way to keep file size down and keep all those great elements you had originally envisioned on the page.

figure 4.10

Translation in DeBabelizer.

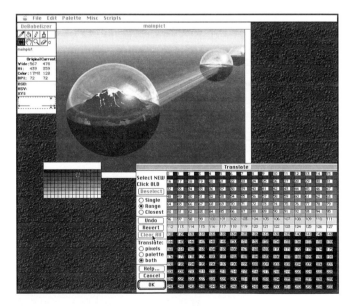

Photoshop

`http://www.adobe.com/prodindex/photoshop/`

Like DeBabelizer, Adobe Photoshop enables you to prepare raster images for the Web. Unlike DeBabelizer, Photoshop doesn't offer detailed control for color selection often used when reducing palettes or batch processing. Photoshop was created for image creation and manipulation on Macs and PCs. It provides the ability to create a seemingly unlimited number of effects that can be used with photographic, graphic, and video image files.

Photoshop's long list of features includes:

- Numerous choices for selecting ways to enhance or distort photo images.

- The ability to adjust image size, mode, resolution, bit depth, brightness, contrast, color, and levels.

- A broad range of creative possibilities available through specialized filters, layers, channels, and editing tools.

Image Editor Options

Listed here are a few increasingly popular image manipulators and some of their features. To learn more about them check out the URLs provided.

FreeHand

`http://www.macromedia.com/software/freehand/`

Macromedia's cross-platform image creator enables you to make vector- or raster-based art for the Web. By moving your native vector files onto the Web you can take advantage of Shockwave. FreeHand also attaches links and embeds fonts within Shockwave graphics. FreeHand integrates with all major graphics applications and for many of them, FreeHand opens their file formats and lets you move the graphics using a simple interface. It offers a detailed collection of creation and modification tools and multiple page design and layout capabilities.

GIF Construction Set

`http://www.mindworkshop.com/alchemy/gifcon.html`

GIF Construction Set for Windows is a shareware collection of tools for working with multiple-block GIF files. Not only does it creates transparent GIF files and looping animations, it will serve as a fully-compliant Windows GIF viewer application and is capable of being a GIF viewer "helper" application for Web browsers. The GIF Construction Set also adds, edits, and deletes comment blocks and will add non-destructive text to images as plain text blocks. Among other things, GIF Construction Set converts AVI video clips to animated GIF, creates animated text banners, and adds special effect transitions to still graphics.

Graphics Converter Gold

http://www.imsisoft.com/products/grphcgld.html

This shareware is a comprehensive image file conversion and management utility for Windows. Graphics Converter Gold has many features including support for over 70 vector, raster, and fax file formats. It enables you to browse through large graphics files to find the images needed and offers support for OLE (object linking and embedding) technology that will update edited graphics images in any documents containing them. Graphics Converter Gold also enables you to organize graphics files into custom directories and provides powerful image manipulation tools.

Graphic Workshop

http://www.mindworkshop.com/alchemy/gww.html

This increasingly popular program is for working with bitmapped graphic files. Graphic Workshop handles and converts most of the popular file formats, including FLI and QuickTime animations. It offers many image manipulation tools, thumbnails, and slide shows. Graphic Workshop maintains an image database with keyword searching, runs any function in batch mode, and uses virtual memory to work with large images.

NIH Image

http://rsb.info.nih.gov/nih-image/

This public domain image processing and analysis program was created for the Macintosh. NIH Image not only acquires, displays, edits, enhances, and analyzes images, but it animates them as well. It reads and writes TIFF, PICT, PICS, and MacPaint files, provides compatibility with many other applications, and supports many standard image processing functions. NIH Image also measures defined regions and flips, rotates, inverts, and scales selections.

Paint Shop Pro

`http://www.jasc.com/product.html`

Paint Shop Pro is an image viewing, editing, and converting shareware program for Windows. It supports over 30 image formats and several drawing and painting tools. Paint Shop Pro provides dockable toolbars, enhanced selection options, and built-in special effects filters. Paint Shop Pro features support for Progressive JPEG, Mac PICT, and PNG with transparency.

ThumbsPlus

`http://www.cerious.com`

This graphics image and clip-art browsing and catalog program features the ability to select thumbnail size and color depth and offers several unique features that enhance file organization. ThumbsPlus enables extensive viewing and supports the most common file formats. ThumbsPlus also offers OLE client support.

xRes

`http://www.macromedia.com/software/xres/`

This speedy, high resolution bitmap editor for Macs and PCs creates multilayer collages from high resolution raster images. xRes is integrated for graphics QuarkXPress and Adobe Illustrator EPS files. Its well-planned tool set includes artistic brushes, textures, floating text objects, a gradient designer, and color-based masking. xRes makes rasterizing and composing vector artwork created in Import Photoshop files simple with its multiple levels of undo. xRes is capable of batch processing large, high resolution files.

127

Case Study: The zoecom Art Gallery

An art gallery on the zoecom Web site (`http://www.zoecom.com`) illustrates the creative thought process behind Web graphics (see Figure 4.12). With many artists struggling to find a gallery to represent them, this graphically intensive site provides an alternative way for artists to market their works through an online gallery. As such, the zoecom site is a perfect example of graphics choices Web designers can use to set their sites apart, whether they use multimedia or not.

figure 4.11

Excellent graphics are evident in the zoecom logo.

figure 4.12

The zoecom art gallery's page is an example of a clean, stark look balanced on a white background.

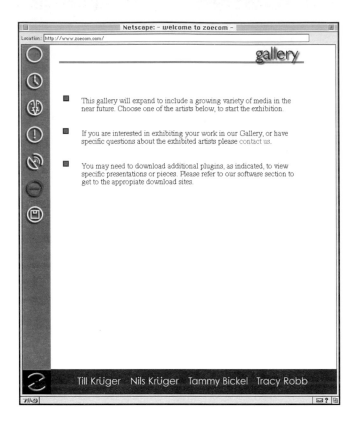

The Concept

The design process begins with a concept, and there are usually several avenues to explore. In this circumstance, the first thought was to recreate the artists' catalogs using the slide show technique. This method is easily implemented in a linear Web site requiring only a navigational path that moves forward and back. The first page of the gallery can have one button that leads to all the collections that follow in a particular pattern (see Figure 4.13).

Netscape: - welcome to zoecom -
Back
Forward
Home
Reload
Images
Open
Print
Find
Stop
Location: http://www.zoecom.com/
Tracy Robb
Photography
Till Krüger Nils Krüger Tammy Bickel Tracy Robb

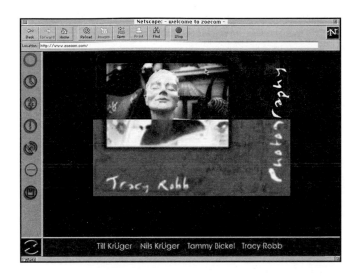

figure 4.13

This site's page is an example of a simple way to begin a slide show (`http://www.zoecom.com`).

A contemporary art gallery, however, doesn't make a mark for itself with traditional simplicity, online or not. The obvious alternative was to provide four buttons, one for each artist and set the stage for adding new artists. When the initial design thought was formulated, it was then time to think of an approach to distinguish each.

To show each exhibitor's collection to its best advantage, we thought that creating an atmosphere around each show would further separate and identify it from the others. We achieved this by creating a "site within a site" for each of the four artists (see Figure 4.14). These unique-to-each graphical elements can then be implemented on the pages of the subsites to create individual online atmospheres that help shape the reactions of the Internet visitors.

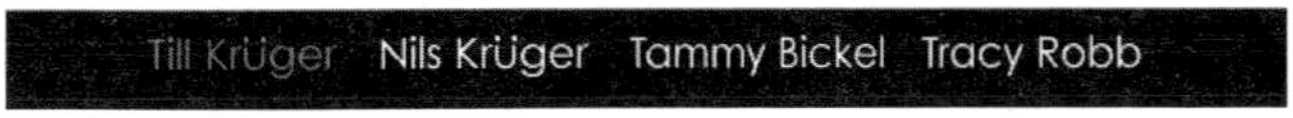

Till Krüger Nils Krüger Tammy Bickel Tracy Robb

figure 4.14

The four artists' names act as gates to their exhibits.

One of the best characteristics of this gallery site is its commitment to offer each artist a totally unique environment. New artists will be encouraged to create an atmosphere reflecting his or her work. The zoecom site was conceived with the future in mind, and part of each new artist's responsibility will be to develop a presentation concept and to work with the designer to integrate that concept into the whole site. Automated slide shows and RealAudio enhancements are just a couple of the multi-media elements that this site's design may easily add to the graphically intense art presentations.

The Look and The Process

The highly stylized icons in the menu frame set the tone for the site's clean, contemporary feeling. The Photoshop-created icons reflect international symbols made interesting with bright colors. The icons were made using the GIF file format because of its capability for transparency, using 4-bit color depth. A rollover script written in JavaScript was used to activate the colored variations.

When the arrow pointer touches one of the icons, a message appears at the bottom of the page explaining where the icon leads (see Figure 4.15). When the arrow pointer touches the green encircled bar the message "Our gallery presents various artists" shows up on the narrow status bar. The JavaScript technique for creating this effect, called an "onMouseOver event," can be found at `http://home.netscape.com/eng/mozilla/3.0/handbook/javascript/`. This URL, in fact, includes many wonderful JavaScript techniques.

Click the gallery icon and the content frame changes to another page that announces the Gallery, with four names listed in the newly formed bottom frame.

These names, created in Photoshop, are links to each artist's section. JavaScript along with Photoshop layers were used to create the illusion of the icons' color change when the mouse rests on them and the color change when they are "pushed in." This simple technique assures that the different layers, each containing a separate version of the icon, do not shift but line up perfectly when placed over the top of each other.

As the user goes further into the site, a cohesive feeling for the whole gallery section is contained even as each subsite reveals its own individual atmosphere. Before developing each artist's subsite, we created the one element of continuity, the direction arrows, using a GIF image with 4-bit color (see Figure 4.16).

figure 4.15

As the mouse passes over a menu icon, an explanation of the section it opens is shown on the bottom frame.

figure 4.16

The arrows' bright color was created with 4-bit color.

Till Krüger

As president of zoecom, Till Krüger is also head designer. Till chose to display his art pieces in a way that reflects the diversity of his collection and the basis of his business. The surreal drawings and gesturing hand fade into the black background to create a startling introduction to his section of the gallery. The animated hand was created by flat scanning one of the design team's actual hands into different frames and then placing each frame in Photoshop. The background was then painted in and made transparent and saved in GIF. The hand image was then placed in an HTML table in order to place it precisely over the image behind it. The black background was saved in JPEG because its continuous tone would not have compressed as well had it been saved as a GIF.

Till's five media categories are listed across the top of the page. The right-to-left placement of the types of art allows the viewer to infer the chronology of the artist's development (see Figure 4.17). By beginning with his freehand drawings and etchings and ending with his VRML environments, the site visitor senses the natural transitions involved in his choices of media.

figure 4.17

The first page of Till Krüger's section invites the viewer to explore four categories that demonstrate his art.

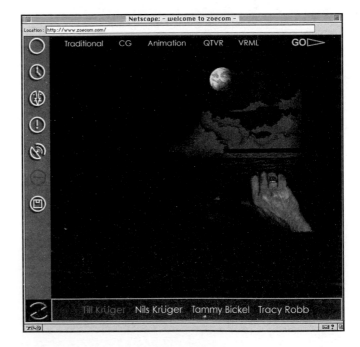

By using HTML and JavaScript coding, thumbnails of Krüger's art increase to a viewable size in a new window when they're clicked (see Figure 4.18). Pop-up windows are used in the interactive media of animation, QuickTime VR, and VRML (see Figure 4.19).

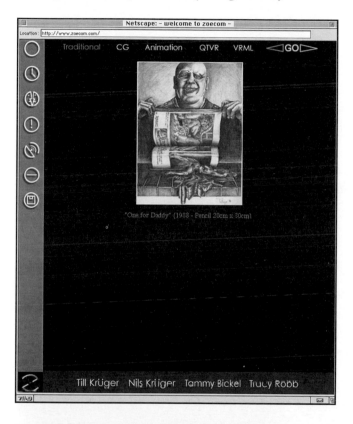

figure 4.18

An enlargement from a thumbnail on the traditional page.

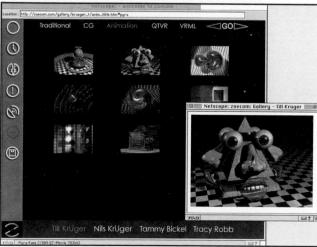

figure 4.19

Pop-up windows are used with the interactive art.

Nils Krüger

In order to create an individual look for Nils Krüger's site we used stark black or white backgrounds with small, contrasting blocks of italicized HTML text to set a light balance for his powerful, industrial sculptures (see Figure 4.20).

figure 4.20

Nils Krüger's site has a simple elements balanced against his forceful sculpture.

The younger Krüger brother, Nils, is a metal sculptor. His work has an immediate effect on the viewer. Charming and disturbing at the same time, Nils' dramatic pieces require museum-like surroundings in this virtual gallery. The artist's comments are also offered to the viewer as a way of understanding the creator's intent. The two-element layout combines the brief statements with the look of the page and adds to the similarity of a book color-plate (see Figure 4.21).

NOTE

In the print publishing world a color-plate is a full color illustration that is often printed on glossier, heavier paper than the text pages.

Because each piece serves as an illustration of his whole statement, Nils' display furthers the idea of the symbiotic relationship between the words and the images. Considering that Nils' pieces are so powerful it was decided that there was no need to cram the page with a lot of design.

figure 4.21

We thought of Nils Krüger's Photoshop images as color-plates in order to get the digital effects he was looking for.

Interest is added by mixing the right and left balance of the text and image along with the black-and-white elements of the text and background. This also enables continuity to be created without effort and enables the viewer to concentrate on the artwork.

Nils' pages came from a Photoshop file created for his catalog. GIF was used for the majority of the page because of its lossless compression and is perfectly suited for black on white or white on black. Nils' blocks of text are italicized HTML font. JPEG was chosen for the photographic images, using high-quality and medium compression settings in Photoshop.

Tammy Bickel

Tammy Bickel's ethereal 3D metal work display takes an entirely different approach from anyone else's. Tammy's gallery section was created from her brochure designed in Photoshop. Because she had chosen the deep plum color for her brochure, we used it for her Web display. Not only are her pieces photographed with color-intensive backgrounds, but there is more color on her color-plates' backgrounds. Photoshop-created text fonts continue the thread of whimsy inspired by her sculpture (see Figure 4.22). JPEG was used for her section because it had worked effectively for Nils' section, which was similarly designed.

135

figure 4.22

Feminine elements found in the mixture of font types draw attention to the airiness of Tammy Bickel's metal works.

Tammy's section concentrates on balancing the playfulness and whimsy reflected in her functional metal forms with a little text and the deep plum background that adds interest through its color. Because most of her pieces are photographed against natural backgrounds, the strong color complements, contrasts, and adds continuity to her virtual exhibition. The use of a mixture of stylized, different-colored fonts for the text aids in balancing the image elements (see Figure 4.23).

figure 4.23

Fancy fonts were worth the extra effort to create a unique atmosphere for Tammy's exhibition.

The elements for Tammy's site were sent to us as a Photoshop file. This enabled us to separate the elements, rearrange them as needed, and save them as JPEGs. In the original design, for instance, "Garden Sculpture" had been underneath the photograph. The text didn't line up correctly and it interfered with the balance because the Go arrows (see Figure 4.24) had to be included.

figure 4.24

The directional arrows required the design elements in the Photoshop file to be rearranged to achieve this look.

Because different operating systems don't readily support unusual HTML fonts and not all browsers support HTML 3.2 standards yet, text for these pages was typed and arranged in Photoshop (see Figure 4.25) and turned into a JPEG file. This outcome is visually superior to GIF and the file is about the same size. A nest of tables in HTML was built to contain the different elements involved in the pages (see Figure 4.26). Height and width were specified within the table cells through HTML. Each cell held one image. On the front page of Tammy's site, for instance, the photo image was one element, "Metalwork by" was one element, and "Tammy Bickel" another. The blocks of text were saved as cropped JPEG images.

figure 4.25

*Separate JPEG files
created the text on
this Web page.*

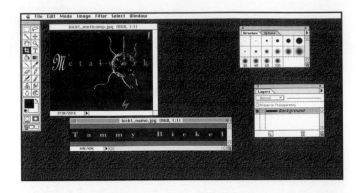

figure 4.26

*The different graphic
elements were
nested in HTML
tables.*

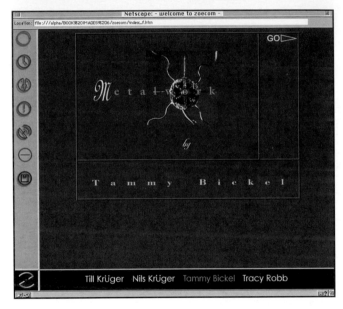

Tracy Robb

When you click to Tracy Robb's section you see a photographic negative
that is quickly layered over by a positive image. The use of layering is a
good introduction to a photographer's Web site (see Figure 4.27). The
startling use of negatives from photographs that are not from of the same
image as the positives encourages viewers to reload the page and double-
check what they just saw.

This layering effect is accomplished through the LOWSRC HTML tag
extension:

```
<img src="images/robbt_xman.jpg" lowsrc="images/
robbt_xman_lo.jpg" >
```

The browser loads the LOWSRC first, followed by the SRC. Only Netscape
supports this effect.

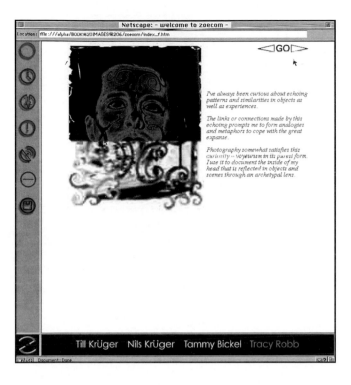

figure 4.27

The positive layers cover the negative slowly enough to add effect.

The use of stark backgrounds behind the images shines a virtual spotlight on the artwork balanced by the artist's descriptions (see Figure 4.28). Tracy's work was prepared in Photoshop using the most basic methods and saved in JPEG because there is no other file format specific for photography.

figure 4.28

This Chicago cityscape layers over a negative of gravestones.

chapter

5

By Stella Gassaway

Animation: Dancing, Spinning, and Jiggling in Cyberspace

The opportunities for animation within a Web site are rapidly increasing as

Web browsers continue to expand their capabilities. These advances have

eliminated choppy sequencing and the annoying, many-stepped procedures a

visitor previously had to endure to view the briefest animation. As the brows-

ing environment has improved, the tools for authoring animation for the Web

have become more numerous, more sophisticated, and yet simpler to use.

This chapter discusses both the design issues and technical challenges involved in animating for the Web. Animated elements should be integral to the design, enhancing and furthering the goal of the Web site. Our emphasis will be on animation that is simple, clever, and quick to load, and that can be created by a design studio without extensive technical expertise or heavy investment in new software.

We have divided the chapter into three sections. In the first section we will look at choosing when and where to add animation to such elements as logos or icons, characters, text, navigational elements, or informational graphics at a site. In the second section we will review basic concepts and techniques of animation and discuss some useful software tools. In the final section we will cover the software options for building and delivering animation on the Web and the pros and cons of various approaches or file formats. Here we will take you through step-by-step examples from our experience. Separating the design process and the technical process in this way is artificial and for the purposes of chapter organization only—in a working studio technical constraints should spur creative solutions.

Once we understand the best ways to use animation in Web site design, the exciting possibilities are endless. Thoughtful use of animation is one of the best ways to enhance a site's effectiveness and popularity.

Animating a Web Site: Design Issues

We're all tempted to add movement to show off what we can do or to lure a visitor into our Web site. The challenge is to create an animation that has meaning and a reason for being. The site you are designing may already have static elements that long to be animated. Often an element will call out to you, "Please...I can move, really I can."

Technically, animation is not movement at all, but the illusion of movement created by a series of still images. Objects appear to move across the screen, rotate, grow larger or smaller, distort, or transform themselves. Even if the object itself does not move, there might be a change in its color, transparency, or light source.

Often the sites we design are based on graphic elements and content that has been created for print projects. It takes careful thought and quite a bit of testing to find out what kind of dimension and movement you want to add to flat objects to bring them to life. An obvious example is an illustration of an object that has motion associated with it in everyday life, such as the steam out of a hot cup of coffee or a camera flashing (see Figure 5.1). These objects are typically considered "inanimate." Characters, illustrated figures, or cartoons are natural candidates for motion.

figure 5.1

A flashing camera on the viewing instructions page of `http://www.vizbYte.com`. *Check it out on the CD-ROM.*

In other cases the material for a site may be based on a moving medium, such as television, and the animation can mimic the motion viewers are accustomed to seeing. Animation can help explain a concept or give life to text that might otherwise have little impact on the viewer.

What message does the animation deliver? What story does it tell? What atmosphere does it create? The answers to these questions will tell you whether there is integrity of purpose to your animation. As with all work designed for new media, test the reaction to the animation on a few of the folks in the studio to get some immediate reactions. Make adjustments and test it some more.

143

NOTE

In the discussions that follow, wherever file formats or software is mentioned in passing, refer to the extensive discussion of technical issues in the second part of the chapter.

Animated Logos and Icons

Spinning logos are a bore; if you've seen one you've seen them all. Most visitors to a site, even those new to the Web, will have had their fill of this syndrome from television. The rampant overuse of the 3D logo rotating and glinting in space has soured most designers (but, alas, not all clients) on this unimaginative use of animation.

A logo or icon can be, however, an element you wish to introduce with emphasis or keep in the forefront of the viewer's attention. Instead of implementing meaningless motion, look for an animated growth or sequence that builds the logo, or a repeating element that is not too intrusive.

Just as designers often make scathing remarks about the use of too many typefaces on a single page, the same remarks will be made about a Web site that looks like a drive down a Las Vegas street at night. The animated elements you add to a site should always enhance the experience. Consider whether to loop the animated sequence. Does the animation looping make sense? Will the viewer grow weary of the animation? Does looping the animation distract the viewer?

We've seen a few sites where so many things are spinning, blinking, or running around that you don't remember why you even came to the site. If you decide to put more than one animated element on the page, think about the speed and frequency of repetition in the animations. Don't worry; if someone wants to see the animation again, she can reload the page. Or if you use the same element in a number of pages relating to each other, she'll get another chance when she moves to the next page.

A few of the animations discussed here loop. You will also see that they may not be the only animated element on the page. One of the reasons this can be done is that the logo is noticed the first or maybe third time and then is understood to be an identity element viewers "know" is moving but don't have to pay attention to and can move on to other information.

The Netscape "N" is a particularly interesting example (see Figure 5.2). The shooting stars tell you the browser is actively obtaining data, so your eyes keep checking in with the logo, and you never forget whose browser you are using. Shooting stars have also been known to lull me to sleep. Clicking the "N" takes you to Netscape's home page. Internet Explorer makes a similar use of its "E" and globe (see Figure 5.3).

figure 5.2

The Netscape "N" links to Netscape's home page.

figure 5.3

Microsoft's Internet Explorer animated logo.

At the AltaVista site, `http://www.altavista.sofware.digital.com`, if you enter the frames section of the site, the lower-left frame displays an animated GIF version of the AltaVista logo (see Figure 5.4). This section of the site uses a mountain from its West coast home, presumably to uplift and inspire us in our searches. The animation brings letters from behind the mountain as if they were on a rotating cylinder, reminiscent of opening movie credits; the letters wrap around the front of the mountain and disappear. This simple and elegant animation loads quickly and gives you something to watch while all the frames refresh. The logo remains in position no matter where the frames take you, so you never forget that you are at AltaVista!

figure 5.4

A series of GIFs forms the AltaVista logo "comin' round the mountain."

The folks at enviromedia aren't into flash and dash. They too believe in meaningful enhancements on the Web, and you can check it out at `http://www.enviromedia.com`. Their logo, a very cool one we think, is organic and still modern with an amusing animated eyelash. Or is it a flower? It's hard to tell which it is, but this animation gives the page an atmosphere that is friendly, growing, and global (see Figure 5.5). This is a perfect accompaniment to the global welcome on the first page of their site (see Figure 5.6). The image loads quickly and is memorable; good stuff for the Web!

figure 5.5

The folks at enviromedia have a clever animated logo.

figure 5.6

The welcome page at `http://www.enviromedia.com`.

Many of the examples throughout these chapters come from our redesign of the dezine café for designOnline, Inc. of Evanston, Illinois. This site has unique challenges because of its design focus. The visitors, including a professional design audience, are very critical of the site's content and design. They are a savvy audience looking to see creative uses of new technology.

The identity mark for the dezine café is the emoticon ˜D]. An emoticon, like the ubiquitous smiley :-), is a way of bringing a tone of voice to informal writing such as email, chats, or newsgroups. Emoticons are an effort to bring the written exchange closer to a human conversation. The logo concept was originated by Kristina Swarner of designOnline, Inc., and we were delighted with its simplicity and impact. Good design solutions can be found everywhere. The purpose of the dezine café site is to encourage intellectual, creative, and human exchange among designers, and the emoticon reinforces our effort to bring the human dimension to the Web. Figure 5.7 shows the opening page of the dezine café and the emoticon in context.

figure 5.7

The opening of the dezine café section at `http://www.dol.com/Root/`. *You can find an abridged version of dol.com on the CD-ROM.*

The curve of steam coming from the cup was animated, not by moving it from side to side, but by building from the bottom up like rising steam. Adding the gently moving steam is like adding the smell of coffee to the sight of a cup. One of the things we must not take for granted is what kind of feel an animation gives an object. Here we made the steam "rise" out of the cup. If we had made the animation wipe "down" it wouldn't have had the same meaning. Think before you animate. The logo is used in a still version on pages where there are other animations competing for attention, but wherever possible the steaming version is used. The animated GIF is only 3.4K and will load quickly no matter what your connection speed. We discuss how we built this in the discussion of animated GIFs later in this chapter in the GifBuilder section.

At `http://www.hotwired.com` the Netizen section discusses how citizens on the Web can participate in the political process and seize the power inherent in common action. The powerful animation of the feature title leaves you in no doubt as to the purpose of the section (see Figures 5.8 and 5.9). It begins with a hand coming up and grasping flashing lightning bolts in a fist. From the fist, the letters that form "Netizen" emerge from both sides of the fist. The font chosen for the type and the style of illustration contribute to the feeling of strength, effectiveness, and power.

figure 5.8

HotWired's Netizen animation at `http://www.netizen.com/netizen`.

figure 5.9

Completed Netizen section title.

Character Animation

Our studio hasn't done much animation of characters; we simply haven't had appropriate opportunities. In preparing this chapter, we searched the Web to find animated characters where it made sense to find them. Not too many available! Where would an animated character be a good idea? Wouldn't you think that the Pillsbury site (`http://www.pillsbury.com`) would have the doughboy doing his thing on the Net? What about Disney (`http://www.disney.com`). Does "The Mouse" move around on its pages? You could check for yourself; things may have changed since this book was published, but as of this writing it doesn't. No moving, talking Mickey on the first page of the Disney site. We thought, "Okay, he's got to be in the guy who takes you on the guided tour of Disneyland." Nope. Now wouldn't you have thought these were natural situations for animation? I'm sorry to tell you that even the home of American animation doesn't have an animated character!

If the client you are working with has a character linked to its product or company, see if you can find a way to use that character in some part of the site. An animated character leading you on a tour of a site, especially a large site, can be an engaging and humorous way of showing everything the site has to offer. If an animated character was part of a classic ad campaign (such as the giggling doughboy), it could be a part of the section recounting the history of the company. Either one of these applications of animation would get me to visit the site, and I would probably tell my friends! This is the kind of interest an animated character can add to a site.

Even characters not well-known and loved can make you chuckle, get your attention, and convey concepts as you will see in the following examples. They will give you an idea of some appropriate uses of animated characters at Web sites. As with any animated element, think carefully how the animation enhances the purpose of the site.

Repeat Loops

Movies that loop indefinitely tie up the processor and slow browser access to the network. This can cause problems for the viewer. We suggest you:

- Only use one animated GIF per page or a series of very lightweight GIFs or Shocked movies

- Program the movie to stop playing after a given number of loops

- Program a way for the user to stop the movie

I found the following ad at one of the search sites; no URL is given because it is not there anymore. The concept is simple; you can get the idea from Figure 5.10. The character's eyes pop open every couple seconds. It captures your attention and draws it to the advertisement because it is a surprise. You are busy checking out the results of your search and pow! This guy's eyes pop open. Cool, simple stuff that does the job.

figure 5.10

*Eyepopping Claris
FileMaker Pro ad.*

At the brilliant site `http://www.cow.com` for cow.interactive communication, there is a wonderful logo that is also a character: a cow built from simple wooden blocks (see Figure 5.11). Using Shockwave for Director, the cow changes into a face (people) and into a rocket ship (technology) when activated (see Figure 5.12). The transitions from one element to another show the blocks, clearly defined in three dimensions, floating through the air and reconfiguring as the new element. It's amazing; the wood looks just like the blocks you built many a highway or high-rise with as a child and the shadow detail makes the reorganization seem like a levitation and magical reorganization. This sounds quite ambitious but it all loads before you have even begun to get impatient. The logo only moves when activated by rolling over the frame, so it does not have the unwanted effect of nagging the visitor for attention. At `cow.com` they describe themselves as a "new breed" of interactive communicators exploring the "open pasture" of the future!

figure 5.11

cow.interactive
communications is
one of the most
elegantly and
creatively animated
sites on the Web.

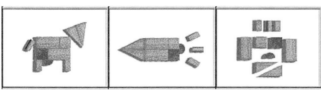

figure 5.12

Here are the cow's
other forms.

Our Web site, `http://www.vizbyte.com`, uses the "bYteguy" character as the little fellow who leads you places throughout the site. We thought it would be great to animate him, as we have done in multimedia presentations. You'll often find him spinning a laser light hula hoop (see Figure 5.13) or falling through layers upon layers of the responsibilities of the designer. We were intrigued that in the comments at the site the bYteguy was mentioned as a symbolic representation of the visitor. Don't ever think that the concept behind a design is not appreciated!

figure 5.13

This bYteguy leads
you to our site:
*http://
www.vizbYte.com.*

Animated Text

Animated text is one of the most intriguing challenges in Web design.
Designers have long been familiar with the power of fonts and type
treatment to give pace, emphasis, and tone to the written word.

Type can become more than the sum of its characters and become a
"visual language." Some graphic designers have taken the emotional
expression of type to such an artistic extreme that its original purpose of
legibility is unfulfilled. See any of the postmodern type designs that are
the mainstay of magazines such as *Emigre*.

Going in another direction, the Visual Language lab at MIT, under the
guidance of the late Muriel Cooper, used only one or two basic fonts, but
words and letters took on an existence of their own. We might compare it
to four-dimensional concrete poetry with time as the fourth dimension.
Words shrink, blur or race by, come toward you or disappear in the
distance, and tiptoe or shout. They deliver an emotional as well as
intellectual message. Even the meaning of the words can be enhanced and
vocabulary increased with visual representation. Fuzzy content is made

clear with text coming into focus. Words shout becoming larger and bolder; italic phrases rush buy.

The most common human experience with animated typography is the television commercial, and this use is relatively new historically speaking. Since the advent of the remote mute button, agencies have consciously designed for a silent medium, increasingly replacing or reinforcing voice over with on-screen text. Have you noticed that it has become common-place to put white text (usually less than six words) alone on a black screen? Recently, however, the new trend is to add animated text to grab your attention by giving the words personality. Words push other words off the screen, some words pull others along, some burn themselves into objects, and yet other words jump off labels and come to life.

The most obvious reason to animate text is to get people to look at it. Something you hear repeated over and over again when designing for a surfing audience is "people don't read." Any designer who has conscien-tiously posted written instructions has had the bitter experience of realizing that the instructions are ignored more often than not. However, when the text teases you by not appearing all at once, you are much more likely to read it as it comes into view. There are three constraints on this positive effect:

- There can't be more than a paragraph or two of text or you may lose your audience's attention.

- It can't have too much motion that makes the text unreadable.

- The text must load at approximately the rate at which most people read.

cow.interactive communications has a very creative approach to this problem. Using the frame interface in Netscape, a very wide horizontal GIF with text appears across the bottom right of the browser and the visitor must scroll, and scroll, and scroll to get to the end of the single line of explaining the company and offering hotlinks to information about its people, projects, and clients. Although this is not animation in the traditional sense, it has the effect of the text appearing a bit at a time. It's hard to explain (Figure 5.14 gives you the general idea), but you should really check it out at `http://www.cow.com`.

figure 5.14

Horizontal scrolling makes text appear at http://www.cow.com.

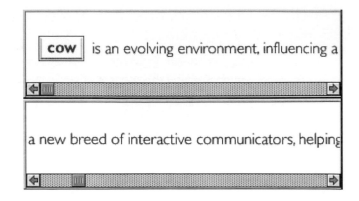

At vizbYte we had the challenge of explaining our company structure and function. There are two divisions of our firm that overlap in many areas including the creative direction. We wanted to present both STELLARViSIONs, a graphic design firm, and bYte a tree multimedia productions. They share the domain name, vizbYte.com, which is built from the two names (see Figure 5.15 and 5.16). The text introduces the "two companies with interwoven intentions" as you can see on the CD-ROM that accompanies this book.

figure 5.15

The entry page of the shared site for STELLARViSIONs and bYte a tree productions.

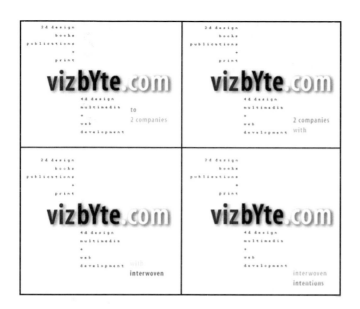

figure 5.16

The progression of
type that appears
at the *http://
www.vizbYte.com*
entrance.

Although not animation in the true sense, our discussion of the power of
type on the Web cannot close without some mention of the vector graphic
capabilities of Shockwave for FreeHand. The technical aspects of this will
be discussed in the last section of this chapter, but the key element is the
capability to "zoom in" or enlarge a graphic live on the Web, just as you
would if you were working in an illustration program on your computer.
Because the FreeHand files are vector graphics, there are no pixels that
get larger and larger, just lovely curves and shapes—including the shapes
of letters.

When we were asked to pioneer the use of vector graphics on the Web for
Macromedia, we searched for a meaningful use for vector graphics and
this capacity to enlarge type. We created an illustration for the Conversation section of the dezine café, in which the visitor followed a "chat" by
zooming further and further in to make the next phrase in the exchange
large enough to read (see Figure 5.17). It could be argued that this is not
animation, but the way the type jumps out at you when you zoom, we're
not sure what else to call it! You can experience it on the CD-ROM that
accompanies this book and see for yourself.

155

figure 5.17

Chat illustration and enlarged sections at `http://` `www.dol.com/` `fhdshock/` `chat.html`.

Animated Navigational Elements

As discussed in Chapter 2, ensuring that visitors can find their way around your site is of paramount importance. Therefore it might be tempting to animate navigational elements that may not be immediately obvious or to let viewers know that they have indeed activated something through their actions. Animated navigational devices are starting to proliferate on the Web. Why is this? The tools are getting better and so are the browsers. With Java applets (freely available at a number of sites) and the Shockwave plug-in, the kind of signals such as rollover color changes previously only available on interactive CD's are now possible on the Web.

There are still a number of drawbacks in using these methods, however. Java can be painfully slow. When using Java, the browser is the compiler and you have to wait for it to do its work. I recently waited for the applet at WebMonkey on the HotWired Network for over four minutes (`http://` `www.webmonkey.com`). This is more than inconvenient because the Java applet must be running to navigate to anywhere beyond the opening screen! Would you wait four minutes or more to get an interactive site menu? A thoughtful design would have at least included hypertext links as a backup to the Java "imagemap."

If you use Shockwave technology, the navigational devices designed in Director for CD-ROM presentations can now be repurposed for the Web. In Chapter 8 we discuss Macromedia's interactive navigational menu at its site.

Experiment and test the interactive navigation you intend to use at a site. You may have a T1 line, but will your viewer? You should test at 14.4 Kbps (unless you know that dial-up visitors are not important to the site). If the wait isn't considerable at that speed, you'll be okay. Remember that with animated GIF files, the browser must register the click on the navigational graphic to take the visitor to the desired location. The animation itself can potentially interfere with the browser's capability to accept the command, resulting in frustrating multiple clicks. Test this carefully!

Simple roll-over highlights and color changes, however, can enhance the clarity of navigation. The Hayden Books site (`http://www.hayden.com`) is an excellent example (see Figure 5.18). This can be achieved using a Java applet that is freely available (it's called GrowButton, and you can find it at `http://www.mbmdesigns.com/macjava/appletgallery/GrowButton/GrowButton.html`)!

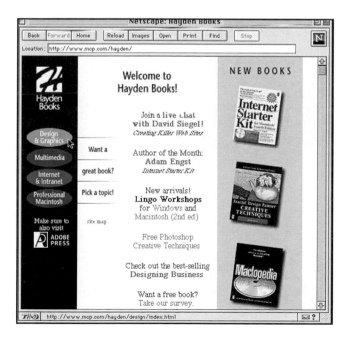

figure 5.18

A simple roll-over highlight.

The frame section of the AltaVista site (`http://www.altavista.software.digital.com`) uses a clever device of three-dimensional balls in little slots that change color and move as you select them and remain in position to help tell you what section you are in (see Figure 5.19). Because of the very tangible look of the beautifully rendered balls, it seems as if you should be able to drag them with the mouse into their new position. That would be well beyond a simple animated navigational element and a more truly interactive experience.

figure 5.19

Navigational
elements at
AltaVista.

You can experience a flurry of animated icons at http://www.sosimple.com, the site for Samsung (see Figure 5.20). Here the designers used a series of animated icons for entry-level navigation. Each animation helps reinforce the text below it. The top of the head in the first icon for the braintrust, for example, opens up to reveal the braintrust. This kind of reinforcement is an excellent use of animation initiating navigation. Check out http://www.sosimple.com firsthand to appreciate the color, simplicity, and activity at this consumer-focused site.

figure 5.20

A flurry of animated navigational icons at the Samsung site.

When we introduced a series of Shockwave for FreeHand illustrations to the dezine café, each illustration corresponded to a section of the designOnline site. Although the illustration pages linked directly to each other, we also wanted links from the main designOnline pages, each to its companion illustration. Because we did not want to distract from the main navigational directions for each page, a small, easily recognizable element seemed the best choice. We choose a simple swirl (created with the Swirl plug-in in Photoshop) and took it through seven steps (see Figure 5.21). On the What's New page we told visitors to follow the swirl if they had the Shockwave for FreeHand plug-in. You have already seen the swirl in context in Figure 5.7.

figure 5.21

The swirl animation. Check it out on the CD-ROM.

Animated Informational Graphics

As corporations begin to put more and more substantial content on the Web, the informational graphics seen in annual reports and marketing material will move from print to the screen. The goal of an informational graphic such as a bar chart, pie chart, line graph, or even diagram is to make a point. A concept that cannot be clearly conveyed in text can often be powerfully illustrated in a graphic. Informational graphics masquerade as neutral presentation of data, but they invariably direct you to draw a specific conclusion from the data.

If colored shapes and lines communicate more powerfully than paragraphs of text, can *moving* shapes and lines be yet more powerful? Of course, in certain situations they can, but there are even more pitfalls to animating representations of data than to animating logos or buttons. Animating the wrong thing can risk not only irritating the visitor or hearing "so what?" echoing across cyberspace, but it can also risk misinforming viewers or distracting them from the primary point of the graphic. The following story helps illustrate this point.

A client handed us a printed brochure explaining investment strategies and basically said, "Bring it to the Web." The client suggested that some of the graphs in the brochure might be animated, if this would add to the clarity of the concept being conveyed. The brochure was replete with pie charts and bar graphs, and we thought we had a chance to really show off. Figure 5.22 is similar to the type of graphic common in the brochure (not the actual content). At first it seemed like a cool idea to have one pie transform into another. Upon reflection, however, we realized that it was misleading to show the animation progressing from growth to moderate growth because they are two separate categories of investors. The entire brochure, in fact, was designed to encourage investors to choose what investor type suited their situation and stick to it. We could, of course, leave the pies separate and just have the slices fill in, but what does this really add except cuteness?

figure 5.22

Animation of these pies would not add to their flavor.

Investment Distributions

conservative growth

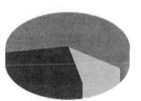

moderate growth

rapid growth

Elsewhere in the printed brochure, there was a graph that used six still images, with time as the horizontal axis, showing return on investments held for different numbers of years (similar to Figure 5.23; again, this does not show the actual content). Here the progression from one graphic to another reflected what actually occurs over time. We indicated the passage of years with a calendar-like counter in the upper left and showed the bar changing dynamically as the years passed. Figure 5.24 shows the first and last image in the animated GIF, which loops three times. We explain how we created this graphic in the description of the animated GIF file format later in this chapter.

figure 5.23

A graphic similar to that in the printed brochure.

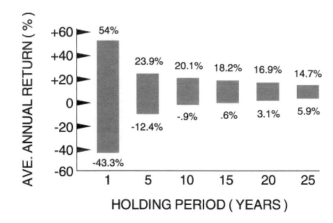

figure 5.24

The first and last "frames" of the animated GIF.

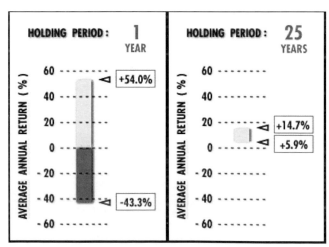

Animations can be informational without being charts or graphs. At the Merce Cunningham site (`http://www.merce.org`), you can select an article about Merce. There are also animated movies illustrating different dance moves created by Merce Cunningham (see Figure 5.25). The series of ellipses used to create the figures enables Merce to choreograph and create records of movement without live dancers. This form of notation is excellent for conveying the movements in the dance.

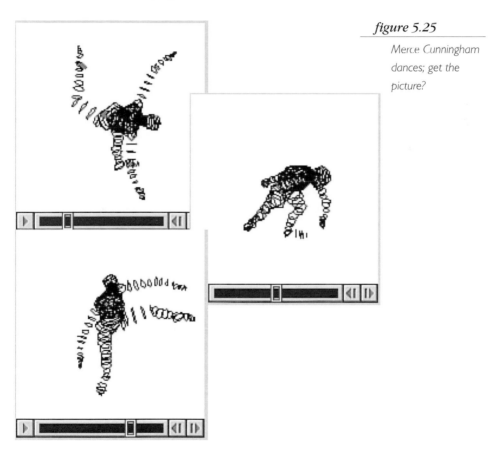

figure 5.25

Merce Cunningham dances; get the picture?

163

A Slide Show of Web Pages

A basic aspect of the World Wide Web is that visitors to a site view a page for as long as they choose and then select from navigational options on the page or in the browser. They may have to wait for bytes to load, but they can choose to wait or surf elsewhere. A dramatic violation of this convention is when a site is set up to automatically load a series of HTML pages in a predetermined sequence and pace. These pages are variously called *splash pages*, *bumper pages*, or *metapages*.

This means that you come across a page and, without any action on your part, the browser goes to another page. If the background and some images are in cache, this will give the illusion of movement or transformation on the part of the image that does change. Timing is tricky for this technique, however, for if the connection is slow for whatever reason, the visitor may be transported to a new page before the original page has completely loaded—a very irritating experience.

The most common use of metapages is for a site's introductory pages to present visitors with key information without requiring them to click through a series of pages. Navigational elements to advance the sequence more quickly can be available for those who are already familiar with the content of the pages or have very fast connections. At `http://www.dol.com`, for example, you see two introductory pages before arriving at the home page (see Figures 5.26 and 5.27). The first page announces the presence of Shockwave and the second gives links to acquire plug-ins; this necessary business is taken care of but does not take up space on the home page.

figure 5.26

The introductory page at designOnline.

figure 5.27

The page that
automatically loads
after a delay.

A very good use of client-pull is the rezn8 site (`http://www.rezn8.com`).
Here a simple slide show runs in a loop until you leave. Clean, simple
page design (and a very cool name) make this a fun site to visit now and
then. Rezn8 updates the images in the slide show based upon newly
completed projects. Using client-pull, the folks at rezn8 make sure that
the complete image has loaded before it moves on to the next one. There
isn't any viewer control over the images at this site, and that's the way
they want it (see Figures 5.28 through 5.30).

figure 5.28

The first of a series
at Rezn8.

figure 5.29

The second of a
series at Rezn8.

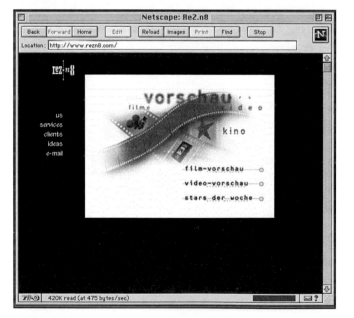

figure 5.30

The third of a series at Rezn8.

Animated Graphics/Special Effects

More than a few corporate giants have chosen to take a whimsical rather than serious approach to their Web sites. One of the most charming is http://www.7up.com (see Figures 5.31 and 5.32). The "carbonate your brain" site uses a bevy of interactive elements. I'll give you a rundown on them so that when you visit a site you have an idea what you are looking at. Two revolving 7up cans serve as bookends to the "carbonate your brain" text. These are 3D rendered illustrations made into looping animated GIFs. They continue their spin as long as you are on the page. Across the page runs a Java applet banner of type letting you know about the latest promotional happenings. This applet can be aquired in many places and is included in Macromedia's AppletAce package. It also runs continually. Ready for more? If you have the Shockwave plug-ins, the illustrated bubbles float up onto the page (with a rock-and-roll riff) and assemble themselves into a series of illustrations.These have rollover interactions displaying text such as "listen up," "speak up," and "what's up."

figure 5.31

It's an up thing.

figure 5.32

The 7up cans spin
and the ticker goes
by.

The Shockwave graphic takes a little long to load; probably because of the
audio. When it is redone with the new Afterburner with audio compression, I'm sure it will show up a bit quicker. Overall, this is a very impressive site without overload despite the range of activity—what can I tell you:
"It's an up thing."

Basic Animation Concepts and Techniques

We have talked a lot about possibilities for the use of animation on the Web. Since many of us come from the world of print design, we thought we would go over some animation basics, discussing the various options for getting your animation on the Web. If you are already producing animation, this section is probably not for you.

You can think of animation as a flip-book of still images (called frames), each subsequent image covering the previous, at a rate giving the impression of movement. There are several keys to this illusion that we will discuss briefly:

- The images must register (line up with each other)

- The difference between one still image and the next must be relatively subtle

- The impression of motion should be reinforced by the illustrative style and quality

Registration

Animators for traditional cartoon animations used (and still use) a technique called "onion skinning." This refers to the technique in which the frame being illustrated is on a translucent sheet of paper attached at one edge to the illustration of the previous frame (which is visible underneath it). The animator flips the paper quickly up and down from one corner to get an idea of how the transition will appear. The edges of the paper represent the edges of the frame and must remain perfectly aligned. If a cartoon character is standing waving his hand, the entire body should align perfectly except for the hand.

This seems quite self-evident when expressed in this way, but in practice it can present some challenges. If your images are not precisely aligned, there will be a jerkiness and jumpy quality to the animation. Therefore there must be a high-tech equivalent to the "edge of the paper" technique. Some software programs have coordinates or registration points to ensure that the images align. Some programs such as the paint window in Macromedia Director have "onion skinning" features in which you can see a grayed image of a previous frame in the background of the one you are creating (somewhat like a template for tracing in an illustration program). If you are using a pixel-based program such as Adobe Photoshop, you can keep all your files the same pixel height and width even if parts of the image itself are "disappearing." The main point is, as you are preparing your animation, be sure you have a reliable method of ensuring that any "motion" from frame to frame is motion you desire, not the result of poor registration.

NOTE

Be careful about using coordinates when the images are not exactly the same size. Say a 3D rendered object is rotating toward you from a broadside to a more narrow edge; the second image will be narrower than the first. Aligning these arbitrarily in the upper-left corner would not work. Even a center alignment system might not always be successful if an image is (or becomes) asymetrical.

Difference from Frame to Frame

The more frames you include to accomplish a particular sequence, the more subtle the changes from frame to frame and the smoother the animation will appear. However, this reaches a point of diminishing return when so many images have to be displayed that jerkiness may be introduced depending on what the viewer's processor can handle. Also, on the Web, the file size gets large quickly as more frames are added.

The amount of change acceptable between frames of an animation is a matter of judgement and testing and also depends on the goal of the animation. For the steaming coffee cup animation discussed in the GifBuilder section later in this chapter, a curve of steam about 60 pixels in height appears in seven increments, which is about 8 pixels per frame. You can judge for yourself on the CD-ROM whether this is smooth enough.

The viewer's brain will interpolate between the frames that are shown (such as the rising steam) and take it in as one motion. This is more difficult to do with more complex motions or ones that are supposed to look "natural." There must be enough information given as actual frames so that the viewer can fill in the gaps without noticing that these gaps exist.

If you are making a major change, such as the color of the background, consider using a transition (such as can be introduced using Adobe Premiere)—unless you are looking for the jolting effect of a sudden change.

NOTE

This discussion is not the same thing as deciding how many frames per second you will use to display your animation. If the jumps from frame to frame are too abrupt, it will not really look like motion, no matter how quickly you run the frames!

Reinforcing the Impression of Motion: Quality and Style of Illustration

Remember the Clutch Cargo cartoons? No, you probably don't, but those of us over 40 were subjected as children to this "animated" TV show. The drawings of the figures were completely static (maybe they were cut-out figures) and they would "walk" across the screen by simple moving from left to right (with a little up and down bounce). None of their limbs moved in any way! I think the lower jaw moved up and down when a character was speaking. Beware of software programs the promise to enable you to "make things move"; sometimes they simply mean you can literally move an object across the screen. Just moving something from point A to point B on the screen usually isn't enough to make the object truly appear to be in motion.

For some things this is not relevant. If you have a yellow ball bouncing above the words to a song, the yellow circle can move (on a smooth curving path!) without actually transforming in any way. If, however, you want a bipedal character to "walk," you must create stills of the various positions of the legs and arms associated with walking (the guys in Clutch Cargo were always behind a foreground screen of underbrush so you couldn't see their legs). If you are not a skilled illustrator, you will not be able to make this seem remotely natural—even the most bizarre cartoon figures are given very natural and organic motion in professional studios or they just simply aren't successful.

In between the simple moving circle and the complex issue of natural organic movement, however, there is a wide range of possibilities and

171

techniques to help create the impression of movement. Consider, for example:

- Changing the scale of an object so it appears to come closer as it moves

- Varying the pace of motion; objects should move faster as they get "closer"

- Changing the shadows so that the animation gives the impression that the object is moving with respect to a fixed light source

- Rotating the object slightly as it moves

- Having other objects or the background "affected" by the motion

- Having the object "affected" by the motion (such as hair blowing backwards)

Animating the Background

Animation involves movement, but it need not be the movement of the foreground objects. When an object or word needs to remain still long enough for the viewer to take in its meaning, consider animating the background in some way to keep the pace of the animation going. The design problem that lead to this insight is described below.

The conversation area of the dezine café encourages interchange among designers. We were searching for a visual element that would be part of the header in this section. Since this is not a traditional face-to-face oral conversation, we wanted to use a metaphor that encouraged the visitor to expand his or her concept of interpersonal communication. We chose to draw from the strikingly visual method of communication of sign language.

We borrowed a book on sign language, got out our trusty QuickTake camera, and shot a series of photos of my hand forming the letters T, A, L, K. On the opening page they were used as still images with the corresponding letters that served to introduce the meaning to those of us who cannot read sign language. We quickly discovered that much of the cadence and emphasis of sign language comes from the movement, comparable to tone and cadence in verbal speech. Four still images just didn't do it.

Animating just the four hand positions did not achieve the desired result either. Each image had to remain long enough for the viewer to register the position, which made it seem like the hands were static; we had to make them speak out loud. Introducing changes in the halo effect around the hand dramatically increased the impact of the images, echoing the emphasis given by a speaker. Now there was a resonance! The result was a simple GIF animation from eight PICT files "weighing" a total of 20K that is used in the heading of all interior pages of the section (see `http://www.dol.com/Root/cafe/talk/rantz`, or see example on the CD-ROM that accompanies this book). We discuss in more detail how this was achieved, and show some illustrations of the process, in the section about animated GIFs later in this chapter. So, when you are looking to add a bit of life to a page but don't want to labor over lifelike animation, consider an abstract approach such as color effects on the foreground or background.

Using 3D Graphics in Animation

When we were looking for software to help us accomplish simple animations, we were surprised to find that almost all the software claiming to create animated sequences is 3D modeling and rendering software. This is a fairly complex discipline in itself, the skilled 3D rendering and animation of images. For a great step-by-step demonstration of the high end of this craft, check out the studio at the Animation House site `http://www.animationhouse.com/main.htm` (see Figure 5.33).

Of course, what is called 3D artwork is not three-dimensional at all; it is displayed on a flat screen like any other artwork. What makes it 3D? Geometry, transformations, attributes, lighting, shading, and textures give the impression that the object has mass and depth.

 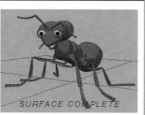

figure 5.33

Animation House explains and demonstrates the 3D modeling and animation process.

The advantage of creating this kind of artwork in a 3D modeling program is that you can then rotate it to any angle without having to redraw it. So even if you are not as skilled as the folks at Animation House in creating a creature, you can create simple shapes that can "spin" (if they must). Tricky calculations such as what happens to the light source and how the shading should be handled are performed for you by the software. This takes us into a discussion of getting some help in authoring animation sequences from software.

Animation Authoring Software

One can, of course, draw each frame of an animation separately in an illustration program. This may not be as hard as it sounds because the magic Save As command enables you to base one image to a large extent on an exact copy of a previous one. Or you can build an animation in layers, for example, in Adobe Photoshop; the various stages in a transformation can be stored separately on layers. In this sense, almost any image software can be used to author an animation. The software discussed here, however, enables you to create more complex animations without actually creating every frame. Note that we are talking about authoring applications for creating animation. The software used to deliver animation to the Web will be discussed in the next section, "Options for Bringing Animation to the Web."

What exactly can software do "for" you? There are two major ways to save a great deal of time and effort by using a software program that can create animated sequences:

- Create a smooth sequence of frames from point A to point B

- See an object from more than one point of view

In the first instance, animation applications create the "in between" steps for you if you provide images for the beginning and end point of the sequence (called key frames). An animation may be made up of a whole series of these sequences, so that a 30-frame animation may have only 5 key frames. The trick is to give the application enough information so that it does a mathematical progression from one key frame to the next. As you view a prototype animation, you may realize you need to add more key frames to give it the quality you desire. Also, when you instruct the application to create a sequence, you must choose how many frames will be needed to have the sequence run smoothly. For the Web, our advice is to start with fewer frames than you think you need and add as necessary.

We have already referred to the second advantage specific to 3D rendering applications, which is that the object can turn in space (or you can seem to fly around the object). The software calculates all the perspective, shading, and lighting (based on variables you specify). The 3D information is stored in the native file format of the application. When you create an animation it renders each frame in the specified orientation, scale, position, and so on, and exports it as a series of still images. Another great advantage is that you can go back and add other movement rather easily working from the original file.

NOTE

> It is misleading to call these kinds of programs "animation software" because their primary purpose is powerful 3D rendering, but they are the best animation applications on the market.

3D/Animation Applications

Here we discuss applications (from lower- to higher-end) that enable you to create 3D artwork and type or add dimension to your existing vector graphics. This is not intended to teach you how to use any of these applications, but to give you some idea of which might be an appropriate investment. First we will outline the general capabilities they all share.

3D applications work within an XYZ axis and generally begin with a wireframe representation of the figure. You can work with the wireframe to save processing all the shading data until you are ready to render a particular view of an object. All these programs permit you to do the following:

- Extrude, revolve, and bevel

- Position light sources at an angle or from behind and choose the intensity of the light

- Choose shading techniques, view objects from multiple positions, and choose perspective settings

- Take a texture, or a piece of artwork, and apply it to the surfaces of the object

This should not, however, give the impression that the applications are all alike; they vary greatly in how sophisticated they are and how difficult they are to learn. The area where the highest-end applications excel is in helping the animator to mimic lifelike motion and organic shapes (the biggest challenge in animation). In other applications everything is basically built from combinations of polygons.

Adobe Dimensions: A Good Starting Point

http://www.adobe.com/prodindex/dimensions/

For someone starting out, we would recommend Adobe Dimensions, especially if you are familiar with the Pen tool interface (used by Adobe Illustrator and other graphics programs). This program is quite reasonably priced and relatively easy to learn. It also has the advantage of enabling you, if you prefer, to work with existing flat artwork and use Dimensions to merely create an animated sequence. If you are working in 3D, you can always go back and edit your original artwork and the changes will be reflected in the extruded form. We can testify to the fast learninig curve because we needed a sequence in a hurry and simply opened the program and figured out how to create it in a matter of less than an hour. Figure 5.34 shows the Dimensions interface, with the XYZ axis and the Sequence dialog box that generates an animated series of still images.

figure 5.34

The Sequence dialog box in Adobe Dimensions enables you to set the number of frames in the sequence.

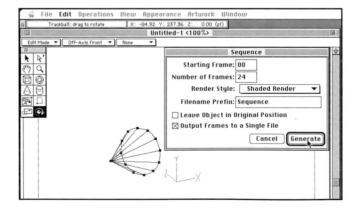

Mid-Range: Infini-D, Vision3d, and Extreme 3D

Specular Infini-D: `http://www.specular.com/products/infini-d/`

Macromedia Extreme 3D: `http://www.macromedia.com/software/extreme3d/`

Strata Vision3d: `http://www.strata3d.com/products/Vision3d/Vision3d.html`

We discuss these together because they are very similar programs in many ways.

- They are mid-level applications

- They enable you to perform "fly-throughs" in which the angle of the viewer changes as if seen from a camera actually flying through openings in the modeled shape (such as an arch in a building)

- They are powerful enough for most multimedia designers to use for work on the Web or CD-ROMs

We prefer the interface of Strata Vision3d, which seems more animation-friendly. It has the added advantage of enabling you to export the animated sequence as a QuickTime movie or PICS file (a file that combines a series of still PICT files in one file). In Figure 5.35 you can see the Advance and Preview buttons for viewing the animation, and to the right of these, the slider showing seconds on the top and frames on the bottom, on which you place events in time. For those familiar with this kind of interface, the Strata program is a good choice.

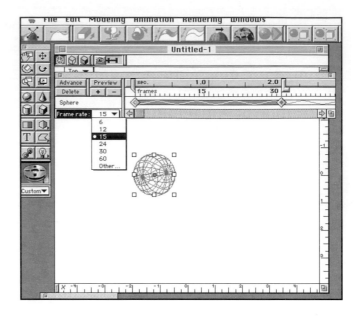

figure 5.35

In Strata Vision3d you can set the number of frames per second and the slider will display the new relationship between frames and seconds.

High-End: LightWave and Softimage

NewTek's LightWave 3D: http://www.newtek.com/

Microsoft's Softimage 3D: http://www.microsoft.com/softimage/

These both are heavy hitters with big price tags. LightWave 3D by NewTek, Inc., has been used in Hollywood productions such as *Babylon 5*, *SeaQuest DSV*, and *Star Trek: Voyager*. We will give you some detail about the second application, Softimage 3D, so that the incredible power of a high-end application is apparent.

Softimage 3D is an animation package that uses NURBS (Non-Uniform Rational B-Splines) as well as polygons to construct a three-dimensional object. Its capability to mathematically calculate surfaces between curves, called a patch, gives an image more plasticity. With five different sets of curves to choose from, there is more control enabling an even smoother, more organic-looking base surface. The problem of broken polygons is eliminated.

Several tools also enable greater exaggeration or accuracy of natural movement and its effects. Weight, gravity, collision, and various other features can all be programmed and assigned to each model to be calculated in during the animation process.

Character animation is accomplished through the use of inverse kinematics. The designer is able to build a skeletal structure within an object, then by manipulating the "bones" of the skeleton, he can create very natural-looking motion. Character animation also enables subtle facial movement and combines with another set of predefined mathematical rules, called expressions, to add quiet detail to movement enabling the animator to suspend disbelief.

Particle physics is built into Softimage as well. Models may be manipulated in varying degrees by breaking them into pieces over a period of time. Effects can be simulated as well, including wind, gravitational forces, elasticity, and friction.

After the designer sets up the physical and environmental characteristics of the complete animation, the program does the math and makes it happen. It eliminates the need to key frame each bounce, jerk, or wink, as well as the speed of a fall, the velocity of a projectile, or the impact of a crash.

Very few software packages provide this level of sophistication in modeling as well as animation. The learning curve for the more advanced features in the application is steep. Simple animations can be achieved in a relatively short time frame, making the learning process more enjoyable.

Other Animation Software

Now let's look at a couple of other programs that can be helpful: Director and Premiere.

Macromedia Director

http://www.macromedia.com/software/director/

Macromedia Director is a multimedia authoring program for interactive presentations that can include animation, sound tracks, and interactivity. Because Macromedia has created Shockwave to deliver presentations on the Web, it is a logical choice for preparing some kinds of animation (see the section "Options for Bringing Animation to the Web" later in this chapter).

NOTE

In the list of multimedia elements that can be contained in a Director presentation, those who have worked with Director may think we have left out video. It is true that Director presentations can contain video in the form of QuickTime movies, but as of this writing these presentations cannot be brought to the Web.

Director is a complex program with a relatively steep learning curve, so to tackle it just for a small animation is ludicrous. However, if you already own and are familiar with Director, you can use it to its full advantage. The most salient reasons to use Director is that you wish to coordinate your animation with some interactivity and/or sound track.

In Director, you bring elements in as cast members that can either be created in Director (using the Paint window) or brought in from other applications. Each cast member appears on the stage at a given point in the drama as a *sprite*. For the purposes of animation, a cast member is a particular piece of artwork. The sprite is the artwork on the stage in a particular position, at a point in time, with a particular scale, rotation, and color. This distinction between cast member and sprite is significant because if what you want to animate are the attributes that can be applied to a sprite, that is much simpler than if you have to use multiple cast members.

In the presentation "Before the Alphabet," for example, which you can see on the CD-ROM or at `http://www.vizbyte.com/livestuff/btab.html`, a Sun-like image rises at the beginning of the presentation. Because this was simply a change of position for the cast members, a technique known as "in-betweening" was used. In Figure 5.36 you see the first position of the elements and the Score window showing the technical recording of cast members 7, 8, and 9. (This gives you some idea of the interface for Director; Macromedia claims it will be vastly improved in version 6.0, eliminating the Score window altogether.) In Figure 5.37 you see the final position of the elements and the In-Between command is selected from the Modify menu. This will now create 36 incrementally different frames between the key frames 14 and 50.

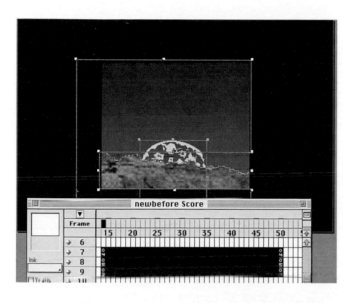

figure 5.36

The first key frame (#14) in the Director sequence.

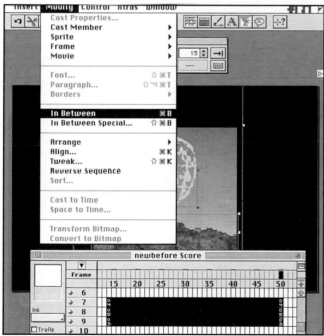

figure 5.37

Choosing In-Between will fill in the empty frames between frames 14 and 50.

Using the more powerful In-Between Special, you could designate a smoothly curved path for the animation, set up a fade, accelerate or slow down the pace of movement, or go from a smaller sprite to a larger one.

Note that in all these situations the same cast member is used; the base artwork itself does not change.

You can also set up a series of cast members (a series, for example, that moves the legs of a figure in a walking motion) and apply that series repetitively over time with a command known as Paste Relative. You can of course place different cast members individually on the stage to show a progression of images. If these images are already a series of numbered PICT files from another animation program, you put them into the score as a sequence with one step.

One other animation-friendly aspect of Director is that in the Paint window you can use an Onion Skinning technique so that you can see a gray image of a previous cast member while you draw a subsequent one (see the discussion of onion-skinning in the "Registration" section under "Basic Animation Concepts and Techniques"). In Figure 5.38 you can see the gray image that is offset from the current image. The Onion Skin dialog box enables you to go forward and back in the cast and toggle onion-skinning on and off.

figure 5.38

A software version of traditional onion-skinning in Macromedia Director.

Another strong feature is the capability to apply transition effects (wipes, and so on) to your animations. Be careful which you choose because some will slow down the animation (such as dissolve).

NOTE

Transitions in Director are stored as cast members, not actually applied to the artwork. Therefore they will be present only if the delivery system is a Director presentaion (or Shockwave). If you decide to export the animation from Director as a QuickTime movie or series of PICT files, the transitions will not be present.

As you can see, Director is not as powerful as the previously discussed animation programs for authoring animations, especially complex ones. If it is just a matter of moving things around, it will do the job, but more subtle movement might be better created elsewhere and imported into Director.

Adobe Premiere

http://www.adobe.com/prodindex/premiere/

Here is another application that is not an animation program, per se; it is generally used to edit video clips. As a matter of fact, you cannot create artwork in Premiere at all. So why are we discussing it here? Because you can bring simple artwork into Premiere and apply impressive transition effects, which can then become part of the artwork in a series of stills (unlike Director transitions). Figure 5.39 shows you the impressive array of transitions, displayed in an animated dialog box, so you see the transitions demonstrated. Note that we have not even begun scrolling in the box.

As with Macromedia Director, this would be an investment of time and money if your studio is not already using Premiere. However, many multimedia studios are already comfortable working in the Premiere environment, so it seems worthwhile to point out ways we have found it useful even for simple animations.

TIP

Premiere can export animations as a filmstrip file (PICS format) that can be opened as one file in Adobe Photoshop. Effects such as gradations can be added that are not available in Premiere. The project is simply saved in Photoshop (keeping the same format) and opened again in Premiere.

figure 5.39

An animated palette of transitions in Adobe Premiere.

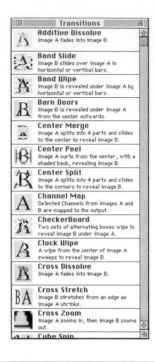

figure 5.40

Applying a Page Peel transition in Adobe Premiere.

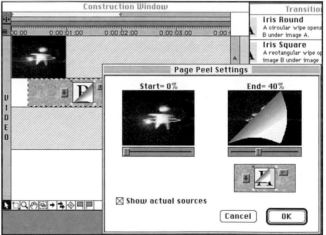

Image Optimization Software

DeBabelizer: http://www.equilibrium.com/

It is essential that the individual graphics you bring into an animation be optimized for the Web. With an animation you usually have a stack of files; how can you efficiently process them? In Chapter 5, discussing graphics for the Web using DeBabelizer was discussed. One of the strongest features of DeBabelizer with regard to animations is that is can batch process a stack of files (so you can get some much-needed sleep).

Options for Bringing Animation to the Web

Our challenge as designers is when, where, and how to use technology to enhance the experience for visitors to the sites we create. The tools we use to create the elements are as important as the results of our work. In this section we will review various technologies available to animate a Web site and discuss their advantages and drawbacks. Our first preference is to choose the simplest option that will accomplish the task.

As can be seen by the case studies discussed, most animation projects go through several steps, each of which involves software choices. As was seen in the discussion of software earlier, each type of application has its strengths and weaknesses. Figure 5.41 shows some of the paths a project might take, whether it is destined to end up on the Web as Shockwave presentation, a QuickTime movie, or an animated GIF file. These three methods of bringing animation to the Web will be discussed in detail in the following sections, and you may want to return to this figure after you are more familiar with the pros and cons of each approach. The primary point of this chart is to emphasize that there is not a cause and effect relationship; because you used certain software in authoring an animation, you must use a particular delivery system on the Web. We usually choose the delivery method that will work best for the goal of the overall animation (does it require sound or interactivity?) and for the goal of the Web site (are we avoiding plug-ins?) and work backwards from there!

TIP

You will notice on the flowchart one example of a project going from Director to Premiere as numbered PICT files (exported from Director). Why on Earth would anyone do that? The answer is: if the desired final format is an animated GIF and there are transitions. Director transitions will not be preserved in the numbered PICT sequence that would be used to assemble the animated GIF. Therefore the project could be brought into Premiere, have transitions added, and exported again as numbered PICT files that are brought into a utility such as GifBuilder to make the animated GIF.

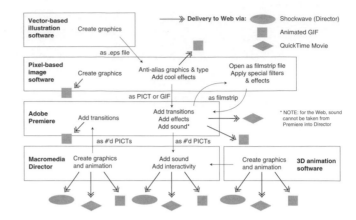

figure 5.41

Some possible paths for projects, with three possible final Web delivery systems.

There are general considerations to keep in mind when making a decision about the final format of your animation:

- Your audience and its browsers

- Your software investment

- Your expertise

Who will be viewing the animation? How much do they really care about this animation? (Are they die-hard fans who will do whatever it takes, or will they be turned off by any inconvenience or delay?) The statistics from your server should be able to tell you the browsers used by most of the visitors to a site, which is an essential piece of information. (If you are not already getting statistics from your server, speak to your system administrator about how to get them.) How experienced are the visitors? Will they have plug-ins or be willing to get them?

TIP

Don't always assume that the most sophisticated viewers will have all the latest plug-ins. At the time of this writing we are running Netscape 3.0 alpha on one machine to be able to check out Java. The plug-ins for Shockwave for the Mac are not yet compatible with Netscape 3.0, so if Shockwave is used on a site we have to make a note and switch to a computer running Netscape 2.0. There is a perpetual catch-up between the browser version and the plug-in version. On the other hand, when surfing with Netscape 2.0 (on a Macintosh) to find cool animations for this book, we were periodically attacked without warning by Java, which the browser could not handle. The

> moral is: always let visitors know what is required and what is optional to view your site. The best sites are programmed to detect which browser you are using and serve HTML accordingly.

What budget do you have available for software? Several wonderful programs are modestly priced or (at this date) freely distributed. You may already own software that you can put to use in ways you had not considered previously. We will discuss programs commonly found in a design studio rather than specialized animation software used by professional animators.

What skills does your studio command? Are you already producing multimedia and want to make the most of bringing those skills to the Web? Do you simply want to add some motion to your Web pages without tackling the learning curve of multimedia authoring programs such as Macromedia Director? Do you already have programming capability using CGI and can step up to Java without full armor? Or are you a coding-phobic creative right-brainer?

With all of these factors in mind, we will discuss the major file formats used for animation on the Web:

- The popular animated GIFs (the GIF87a and GIF89a formats from CompuServe)

- QuickTime from Apple

- Shockwave from Macromedia for both FreeHand (vector graphics with kinetic onscreen effects) and Director (interactive projectors)

- Server-push/client-pull

- Java from Sun Microsystems (discussed in Chapter 8 on interactivity)

- VRML (again, discussed in Chapter 8)

- Other plug-in technologies

Where possible we go through a step-by-step example of how a particular animation was achieved.

NOTE

Early animation on the Web used primarily CGI scripts and server-push/client-pull, which both depend on server and connection speed. How many others were trying to connect to a popular server, the speed of the server itself, and the baud rate at which you are connected also affect the pace of the animation and could make it jerky and ineffective. More recent animation formats download to your computer and play from cache files, just like a still image. Bandwidth affects loading time (actually downloading time) but not the quality of the animation once loaded. If the animation is looped, it will continue to play using the cache.

GIF Animation

GIF animations have become the darling of Web designers, and for good reason. They are simple to understand, simple to make, simple to use, don't require a plug-in, and are platform-independent. These animations can most easily be explained as a digital flip book. A series of still images are compiled into one file, GIF89a enables multiple images to be compiled into one GIF file. This is done using a specialized application such as GifBuilder (for Mac) or GIF Construction Set (for Windows). Figure 5.42 shows the icon that tells you the GIF was created with GifBuilder and is an animated GIF. Animated GIFs are linked in an HTML document just like any still image:

```
<IMG SRC="******.gif">
```

figure 5.42

The icons for animated GIFs from GifBuilder versions 0.3 and 0.4.

GifBuilder0.1 icon

GifBuilder0.4 icon

TIP

We usually put the suffix "ani" before the ".gif" so that internally we know the difference between the still cup.gif and the animated cup.ani.gif.

One of the major advantages of the animated GIF over plug-in options is that if a browser doesn't understand the format, the first GIF in the series will be visible. With some browsers it is actually the last GIF, but in any case there is a real image there from your animation. If you go to a site and don't have a particular plug-in, the entire experience will be interrupted with dialog boxes and empty spaces where the element requiring a plug-in belongs. I hate this and so will your visitors.

GIFs enable up to 256 colors. It's probably not a good idea to use that many, but it's nice to know it's possible. The animations can also be made to loop and create a continuous animation. In this way a designer can make effective use of a few frames. This saves download time and the weight or "K" of the animation.

At our studio we often create a series of images in Adobe Illustrator or FreeHand. We then convert them to PICTs, optimize the palette using Photoshop or DeBabelizer, and assemble the "flip book" using a shareware application such as GifBuilder (on a Macintosh).

The pros of animated GIF files:

- No plug-in necessary

- First GIF in the series fills image space until others load

- Most popular browsers can read the animation (Netscape and Explorer)

- Browsers see a static GIF even if they don't understand the animation

- GifBuilder (for Mac) is freeware with online help and good documentation

- GIF Construction Set (for Windows) is shareware and also easy to get

- The component GIF files do not have to be present on the server; the animated GIF file holds all the information.

- Bandwidth-friendly with use of color palette optimization

- Easiest possible HTML tagging

The cons of animated GIF files:

- No audio (sound)

- No viewer control

- If looped, they can interfere with other images loading

- Animations can be saved to a viewer's hard disk

- When used as a link, GIFs can be difficult to click successsfully without multiple tries

Tools

You need the following tools:

- GifBuilder (Macintosh)

- GIF Construction Set (Windows)

NOTE

> Another promising tool on the Windows side for creating GIF animations is VideoCraft GIF Animator. You can learn more about it at `http://www.andatech.com/welcome.html`.

GifBuilder was written by Yves Piguet (email: `piguet@ia.epfl.ch`) of Switzerland. It can be used manually to collect PICT, GIF, TIFF, or Photoshop images or to convert QuickTime movies, FilmStrip, or PICS files to a series of images housed in one GIF89a file. GifBuilder is scriptable using AppleScript with other scriptable applications such as clip2gif. GifBuilder is freeware, which means it's copyrighted but you don't have to pay anything to use it.

GIF89a gives quite a bit of control over the frames. Combined with Netscape support, version 0.4 enables the designer to specify the pixel coordinates of each frame, the 100ths of a second between frame display, designating a color to be transparent, and interlacing (although this can create poor loading of images during the animation). There have been substantial improvements in the new 0.4 version of GifBuilder. You can now view the animation, for example, within the application rather than having to go into the browser to check on it.

NOTE

Obtain GifBuilder from `http://iawww.epfl.ch/Staff/Yves.Piguet/clip2gif-home/GifBuilder.html`

Get information about GifBuilder from `http://www.adobe.com/studio/tipstechniques/GIFanimation/main.html`

Obtain a plug-in to make still GIF files from Photoshop (Macintosh): `http://www.boxtopsoft.com/`.

Obtain GIF Construction Set from `http://www.mindworkshop.com/alchemy/gifcon.html`

One of the most flexible things about GifBuilder is that it accepts material from many sources and formats. This means animations prepared in just about any application can easily be brought into the GifBuilder. A useful feature to look for is whether your application can export graphics as *numbered* PICT files. This will ensure that the frames come into GifBuilder in order. Although you can create the animation in GifBuilder, moving an image step-by-step, we have found it an awkward environment for that task.

The First GIF Example: Coffee Anyone?

We talked about why we animated the design café emoticon in our discussion of animated logos, now we will tell you how we did it. This is an excellent example of how quickly and easily a very effective animation can be implemented. You can see it at various places at the dezine cafe, including `http://www.dol.com/Root/cafe/wow/events.html`, or on the CD-ROM that accompanies this book.

The logo with its soft drop shadow was created in Adobe Photoshop. Without any special "animation" software, we created a series of still PICT images that would build the steam, beginning from the complete image and working backward in segments. In other words, we deleted a portion of the top of the steam, saved, deleted more, saved, and so on (see Figure 5.43). The canvas size in Photoshop was not reduced and the image was not cropped, so all the resulting PICT files were the same height and width. The key is to have as few PICTs as possible that still give a smooth-looking animation—we only needed eight for the animated steam (see Figure 5.44). It is helpful to save the PICTs with numbers or some system that puts them in the correct forward order (so your first save is the

191

highest number). You can skip numbers if you decide to eliminate some increments.

figure 5.43

Incrementally deleting the steam in Photoshop.

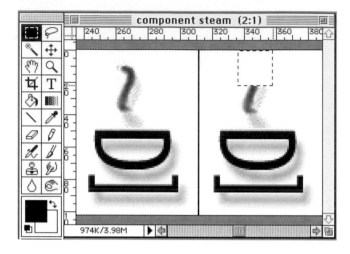

figure 5.44

The pieces of the animated cup logo.

After launching GifBuilder, we selected the files and dragged them into the frames window (see Figure 5.45). Because they are displayed in order, you can select all at once and drag into GifBuilder. You have the option of dragging into GifBuilder one by one to set the order or changing the order in the assembly utility, but it is better to name them consecutively. We tested and adjusted the timing and set the animation to play as a continuous loop. The new GifBuilder 0.4 enables you to play a set number of loops, which was not possible in the earlier version with which we built the steaming cup.

Remember that every pixel counts. The first time we did this animation we used the entire logo. However, because the top half of the logo with the steam was easily cut apart from the bottom, we rebuilt it (in a matter of minutes) working with the steam portion of the logo only. We then placed the animated steam above a still GIF of the coffee cup and presto! One-third the load time.

Frames						
7 frames	Length : 0.70 s	Size : (71x43)			No loop	7/7
Name	Size	Position	Disp.	Delay	Transp.	
steam00.GIF	71x43	(0 ; 0)	N	10	–	
steam01.GIF	71x43	(0 ; 0)	N	10	–	
steam02.GIF	71x43	(0 ; 0)	N	10	–	
steam03.GIF	71x43	(0 ; 0)	N	10	–	
steam04.GIF	71x43	(0 ; 0)	N	10	–	
steam05.GIF	71x43	(0 ; 0)	N	10	–	
steam06.GIF	71x43	(0 ; 0)	N	10	–	

figure 5.45

The steam GIFs being combined in GifBuilder.

The Second GIF Example: T*A*L*K

Earlier we discussed the concept of animating the background of an image in the TALK animation for the dezine café. You can see this animation on the CD or online at `http://www.dol.com/Root/cafe/talk/rantz.html` (see Figure 5.46). Here is some additional detail about how that was done.

figure 5.46

The animation in context on the page.

193

We shot the photos against a cement wall, four shots per position (see Figure 5.47 for an example). We opened the four best images in Photoshop, adjusted the brightness, inverted the color palette, and cut the hands out of the background to maintain the glowing aura. The edges of the image were softened using the Feather command, giving a slight halo effect, and irregular-shaped edges of the background faded into transparency (see Figure 5.48).

figure 5.47

*The trusty
QuickTake comes
through again!*

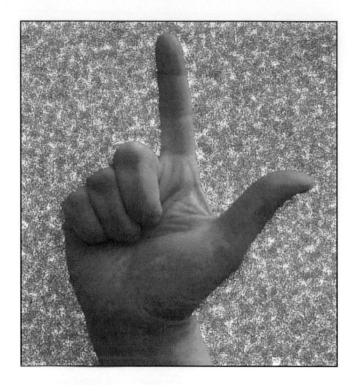

figure 5.48

*The four feathered
backgrounds for one
of the four letters.*

New color backgrounds from the color palette of the Conversation section
of dezine café were added. We created many transitional backgrounds,
playing around with effects in Photoshop, and then chose three or four
for each position to be included in the final animation. The images were
sized to the correct pixel height and width and saved in GIF87a format
(no interlacing), which eliminates unnecessary colors from the file and
reduced the stills from 10K to 2K.

We then brought the GIFs into GifBuilder and adjusted the timing (see Figure 5.49). You can view this animation on the CD-ROM that accompanies this book (see Figure 5.37 to see the animation in context).

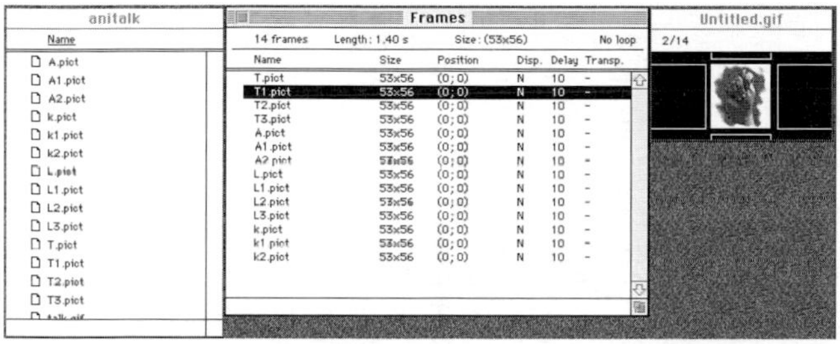

figure 5.49

The project in GifBuilder with the delay set to 10 for each frame.

A Complex Example: The Informational Graphic

Our first two examples of animated GIFs were very simple, showing how much impact can be achieved with relatively few images in a GIF. The informational graphic showing the range of return on investment over a period of years (described earlier), however, was much more ambitious (see Figure 5.24).

We began with a layered Photoshop file as the background that remains unchanged and 58 different individual pieces for the changing images. In the cup and talking hand animations you will recall that we were careful to keep the Photoshop files the full height and width so that the images would position over each other precisely and wouldn't need to be aligned in GifBuilder. With 58 frames, this would have made a very large animated GIF. Therefore, we carefully cropped all the specific elements and brought them into GifBuilder as small segments, but with a consistent size within each series. Each file was saved as an 8-bit indexed color PICT (to retain better image quality than a GIF).

Rather than naming sequentially, we used an alternative approach of displaying the file in the Finder by icon in groups (see Figure 5.50). Then it was possible to select the icons in the correct order to drag them into GifBuilder. This is much easier than trying to rearrange the frames in GifBuilder.

figure 5.50

*The PICT files set up
to drag into
GifBuilder.*

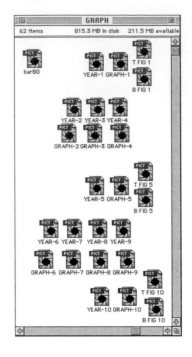

The background image defined the frame size (see Figure 5.51). The small segments were positioned on top of the background in GifBuilder using the "frame position" x and y coordinates. The Disposal Method, which controls whether the image in the previous frame remains in position or is "disposed of," was set to Do Not Dispose, so the background remained and the sections were able to be layered on top of one another (see Figure 5.52).

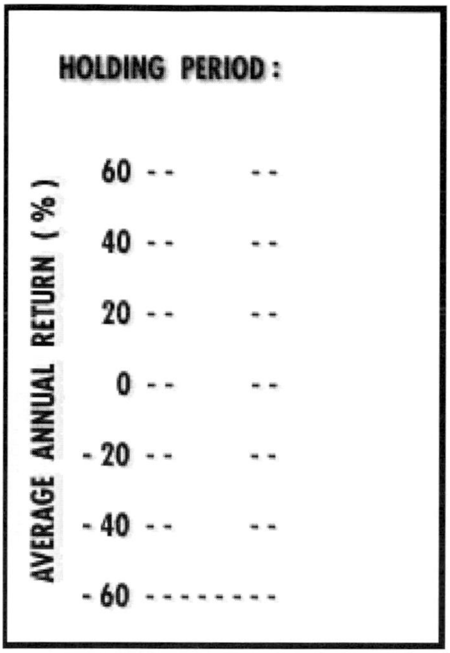

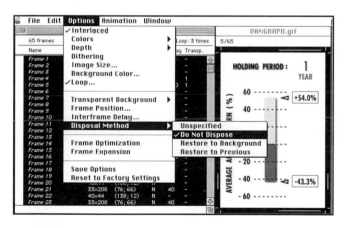

HOLDING PERIOD:

AVERAGE ANNUAL RETURN (%)

figure 5.51

The background
image.

figure 5.52

Setting Disposal
Method in
GifBuilder.

The only segments that were given transparency were the boxes containing the +/-% information; these were assigned transparency "Based on First Pixel" to enable the dashed lines to show through the indicator arrows (see Figure 5.53).

figure 5.53

Setting the tranparent areas to be those that match the color of the first pixel.

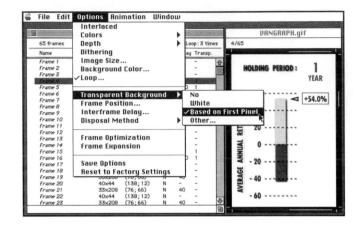

To simulate simultaneous appearance of each section of the animation, "as fast as possible" was chosen from the choices of Interframe Delay. After the first set of images appeared, a pause was needed to present the information. An interframe delay of 400/100ths (4 seconds) was set for the last object in the first group (see Figure 5.54).

figure 5.54

Setting the interframe delay.

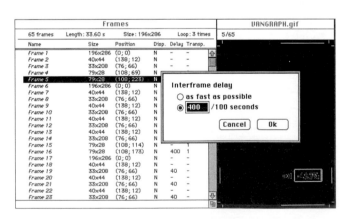

After this pause, the background was reintroduced, which wiped the stage clean. The intermediate year numbers and corresponding graphs were introduced in pairs with "fast as possible" interframe delay between the two, and 40/100ths interframe delay between each pair. This achieved the effect of the year numbers and the graphs changing in unison. When a major landmark was reached at which new +/-% data came in, another four-second interframe delay was set so the viewer can peruse the information. The rest of the animation was built in this way, consecutively, and then the animation was set to loop three times. The Frames window in the application tells you the name of each frame, its size, position, disposal method, and transparency (in that order) (see Figure 5.55).

Frames					
65 frames	Length: 33.60 s		Size: 196x206		Loop: 3 times
Name	Size	Position	Disp.	Delay	Transp.
GRAPH-6	33x208	(76; 66)	N	40	–
YEAR-7	40x44	(138; 12)	N	–	–
GRAPH-7	33x208	(76; 66)	N	40	–
YEAR-8	40x44	(138; 12)	N	–	–
GRAPH-8	33x208	(76; 66)	N	40	–
YEAR-9	40x44	(138; 12)	N	–	–
GRAPH-9	33x200	(76; 66)	N	40	–
YEAR-10	40x44	(138; 12)	N	–	–
GRAPH-10	33x208	(76; 66)	N	–	–
T FIG 10	79x28	(108; 122)	N	–	1
B FIG 10	79x28	(108; 157)	N	400	1
barBG	196x286	(0; 0)	N	–	–
YEAR-11	40x44	(139; 12)	N	–	–
GRAPH-11	33x208	(76; 66)	N	40	–
YEAR-12	40x44	(138; 12)	N	–	–
GRAPH-12	33x208	(76; 66)	N	40	–
YEAR-13	40x44	(138; 12)	N	–	–
GRAPH-13	33x208	(76; 66)	N	40	–
YEAR-14	40x44	(138; 12)	N	–	–
GRAPH-14	33x208	(76; 66)	N	40	–
YEAR-15	40x44	(138; 12)	N	–	–
GRAPH-15	33x208	(76; 66)	N	–	–
T FIG 15	79x28	(108; 127)	N	–	1
B FIG 15	79x28	(108; 152)	N	400	1
barBG	196x286	(0; 0)	N	–	–
YEAR-16	40x44	(138; 12)	N	–	–
GRAPH-15	33x208	(76; 66)	N	40	–
YEAR-17	40x44	(138; 12)	N	–	–
GRAPH-17	33x208	(76; 66)	N	40	–
YEAR-18	40x44	(138; 12)	N	40	–
YEAR-19	40x44	(138; 12)	N	–	–
GRAPH-19	33x208	(76; 66)	N	40	–
YEAR-20	40x44	(138; 12)	N	–	–
T FIG 20	79x28	(108; 126)	N	–	1
B FIG 20	79x28	(108; 150)	N	400	1
barBG	196x286	(0; 0)	N	–	–
YEAR-21	40x44	(138; 12)	N	–	–
GRAPH-21	33x208	(76; 66)	N	40	–
YEAR-22	40x44	(138; 12)	N	–	–
GRAPH-22	33x208	(76; 66)	N	40	–
YEAR-23	40x44	(138; 12)	N	–	–
GRAPH-23	33x208	(76; 66)	N	40	–
YEAR-24	40x44	(138; 12)	N	–	–
GRAPH-24	33x208	(76; 66)	N	40	–

figure 5.55

The Frames window in GifBuilder 0.4.

199

WARNING

You will notice that the frame names in Figure 5.42 preserve the PICT filenames that correspond to each frame. If you close the application and relaunch to work on it again, all the filenames are lost! The frames will simply be "frame1," "frame2," and so on.

This graphic now runs over time, just as the information is conveying the return over time, and the years are going by in the corner of the frame! This animation is on the CD-ROM ("informational graphic") accompanying this book, but not online live anywhere because it is just a prototype example based on a fictitious situation.

QuickTime

Most designers are quite familiar with QuickTime. They might not be sure what it does, but they vaguely know it is a part of the Macintosh system somewhere and they know the logo. Because it is primarily concerned with video, we will discuss QuickTime more thoroughly in a section just like this in the Chapter 7, which discusses video.

Actually, it's a system extension that was developed by Apple Computer—originally for the Mac and now available in a version for Wintel computers. This software adds an enormously exciting function to any operating system. It makes it possible for the designer to view and edit video, animation, music, and other dynamic information without extra hardware while providing very reasonable image and sound quality. During its short life QuickTime has rapidly extended its capacity to broadcast quality, full-screen, and full-motion when combined with fast computers and powerful hardware; however, this is not recommended on the Web because it would take too long to load.

QuickTime is often considered a "movie" tool because it brings "movies" to the digital environment. A movie is the audio and moving visuals combined. This is a powerful combination to bring to any Web site whether the visuals originate as video footage (see Chapter 6) or a series of stills. The possibility of adding sound is the most powerful advantage over animated GIFs because even subtle sound increases the impact of an animation (see Chapter 7).

Apple expanding QuickTime technology for the Web and its new QuickTimeVR plug-in will certainly be a boon to interactive enhancement on the Web (see Chapter 8).

QuickTime in HTML makes use of the EMBED tag calling on a .mov file. You can see more about the parameters that can control looping options, etc., in the QuickTime section of Chapter 7. Here we will just say that the HTML document must include:

```
<EMBED="******.mov">
```

NOTE

The EMBED command is a Netscape tag that is supported by Internet Explorer. Explorer has a separate approach using an image tag with a DYNSRC (dynamic source) instead of SRC. See http://www.microsoft.com/ie/support/revguide/ for more information. As far as I know, Netscape is not yet supporting this DYNSRC attribute.

The pros of animation with QuickTime:

- Can incorporate audio and/or video

- Efficient built-in compression scheme

- Supported by Macintosh and Wintel platforms

- Viewer on/off control

- Plug-in packaged with Netscape

- Supports palindrome looping (start to end, end to start, and so on)

- Begins to play when 90% downloaded

- Relatively easy HTML tagging

The cons of animation with QuickTime:

- Browser plug-in necessary

- System extension necessary (for viewers and developers)

- Not supported by Internet Explorer 2.0 (just 3.0)

- Not as bandwidth-friendly as animated GIFs

With Netscape as the browser, there are two ways to view a QuickTime movie. The visitor may set up the appropriate helper applications for either Mac (MoviePlayer) or PC (Media Player). That way when the browser encounters a QuickTime movie (.mov) file, it responds by opening up a separate window showing the QuickTime controls outside the browser environment. After the movie is viewed, the file may be closed and the viewer goes back to the browser.

The more elegant way uses QuickTime as a plug-in rather than a stand-alone application. Since Netscape now has an embedded QuickTime plug-in, the movies can be created to seamlessly integrate into the viewer experience. You have the option of displaying the controls (see Figure 5.56). QuickTime was designed to be friendly, and its graphical interface toolbar has familiar controls much like a tape player or VCR. Alternatively you can give the viewer information on how to click or double-click to start and stop the animation.

figure 5.56

QuickTime control bar.

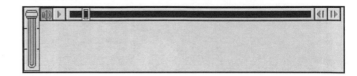

Tools

There are essential tools for working with QuickTime:

- QuickTime extension
- Internet Movie Tool
- MoviePlayer (Mac) or Media Player (Windows)

While Microsoft's AVI (Audio/Video Interleave) format is widely used by PC owners, QuickTime has more encompassing cross-platform capabilities and is growing in popularity. To work with QuickTime movies you need to have both the QuickTime extension for either the Mac or PC as well as an application that plays QuickTime. The extension adds the functionality to the hardware, whereas the application plays the movie file (MoviePlayer for Mac or Media Player for PC).

Apple's Internet Movie Tool prepares movies for the Web and also enables the plug-in to present the first frame immediately. Now the movie can begin to play before it has been downloaded completely. This is terrific! Any tool that enables a placeholder to show up so that the experience for the visitor is not disturbed is great stuff for a designer.

Not essential, but useful if your images are not optimized well to begin with, is Movie Cleaner Pro from Terran Interactive at `http://www.terran-int.com`. This utility helps reduce file size. However, if you start with well-optimized images, you may find, as we have, that it actually increases the size of the .mov file!

NOTE

QuickTime is free at http://www.QuickTime.apple.com.

A great place for QT information is http://www.QuickTimeFAQ.org:8080/. It includes:

- The QuickTime FAQ (Frequently Asked Questions)
- QuickTime software (including some exclusive stuff)
- Other QuickTime resources
- Late-breaking tools for developers

A QuickTime Example: bYte a tree Xmas Greeting

We have already introduced our little "bYte guy" that has become popular at our site. We thought he would be the best messenger of holiday greetings when that season rolled around last year (see Figure 5.57). You can view the message on the CD-ROM with this book or at http://www.vizbyte.com/livestuff/xmas.html, but here we will tell you how it was done.

figure 5.57

Here is our guy in Photoshop with his hat.

203

The character was originally drawn using a Wacom Tablet in Adobe Illustrator. He then lived primarily in Adobe Photoshop and traveled among many images for the site. For the closing credits on our multimedia work he was given a glowing hula-hoop that spins around him—the animation cells (just four) were created in Photoshop. We found him there and decided to add appropriate seasonal headgear of a red floppy hat in four positions (see Figure 5.58). These images were brought into Adobe Premiere.

figure 5.58

Here is our guy in Photoshop with his hat.

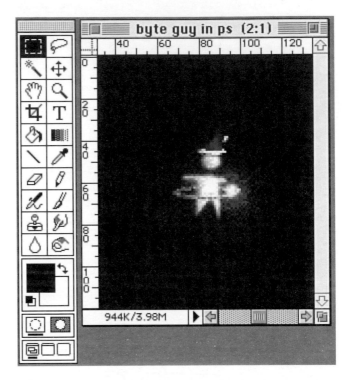

Type for the words "Season's Greeting from bYte a tree" was set and positioned precisely in Adobe Illustrator, saved as an EPS file, and opened in Adobe Photoshop with anti-aliasing enabled. The key frames were created by working backward from the completed message, deleting some letters, saving, deleting more, and so on (see Figure 5.59).

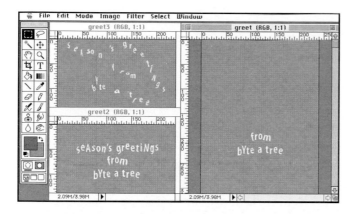

figure 5.59

The letters in Photoshop for the greeting.

Three key PICTs were brought into Macromedia Director and then cut apart to make separate cast members for each letter. In Director the letters were animated to fall, at different rates, like a gentle snow against a blue screen that could be easily knocked out to create a black background (see Figure 5.60). Smaller white "flakes" were drawn in Director to create a feeling of depth. The movie begins with the tiny white dots falling, then larger letters falling, and then a pause inserted so that the letters line up (more or less) to be read. Then one by one they start to slip, like a snowball on glass, and fall away.

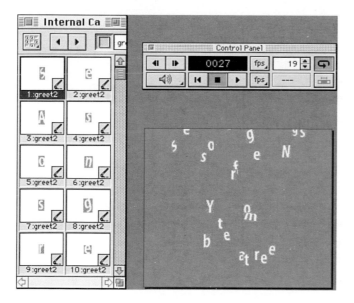

figure 5.60

The falling letters in Director.

205

The presentation was exported from Director as numbered PICT files and brought into the Premiere movie, where the byte guy with the hat is still spinning. Premiere was the best choice of software giving the finest control in adding the music and setting it up so that it could loop seamlessly (see Figure 5.61). In Premiere the Make Movie command created a QuickTime movie. In the Compression Options we chose Animation, which prevents certain distortions that video can tolerate in the compression process but animated stills cannot. We felt the music was integral to the impact of the greeting, which eliminated the option of the animated GIF. If the completed piece had been a Director presentation, we might have considered Shockwave more carefully, but since it ended up in Premiere, the Make Movie was the simplest course (and we prefer staring at the QuickTime logo during loading instead of the Macromedia logo).

figure 5.61

Letters meet the bYte guy in Premiere.

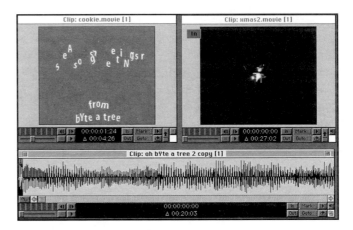

Shockwave (for Director)

If you are already creating projects in Macromedia Director or in FreeHand, you are on your way to porting interactivity and vector graphics to the Web. Macromedia has made a commitment to the Web in a big way with its Shockwave plug-ins. Shockwave helps make anything you can make in Director, Authorware, and FreeHand applications ready for the Web. A designer can use applications she is already familiar with to easily create an illustration or Director movie and then use the Macromedia Afterburner application to compress and make the file ready for access within your browser on the Web. Plug-ins are available or in the works for Netscape's Navigator and Microsoft's Internet Explorer. We will be discussing the FreeHand aspect later on; here we are concerned with bringing presentations from Director to the Web. There is more discussion of Shockwave and Director in Chapter 8, which deals with interactivity (Director's strong point).

Shockwave comes in two parts:

- **Afterburner** is a Tool Xtra for Director movies that compresses and makes them ready for uploading to an HTTP server. Movies are compressed through Afterburner and use a .dcr extension for identification. The "c" in .dcr identifies a movie as a compressed Director movie. Afterburner is a compression device. It is not necessary to use it for the plug-in to recognize the movie. However, movies get large quickly when you want to add interactivity or sound. As we say here at bYte a tree, "just
  burn it!"

- **Shockwave Plug-In for Director** enables movies to be incorporated into the page layout of an HTML document. The plug-in also recognizes Director movies with a .dir extension (a standard Director movie) or a .dxr extension (protected movies that can be played but not opened in Director). The plug-in recognizes the Director file extension and enables the movie to play within the browser window.

TIP

207

Although Afterburner is a great compression program, and we recommend using it to make even a small presentation smaller, this should not be taken to mean that Afterburner can take any Director file and make it ready for the Web. Presentations originally intended to run off hard disks or CD-ROMs should be carefully reviewed to save bandwidth whereever possible. Also, if there are QuickTime movies in the presentation, this is not yet supported by Shockwave.

You must configure your HTTP server to recognize and handle shocked Director movies. Most servers are Unix-based platforms, although there are also servers that use Mac and Windows platforms, such as MacHTTP and WebStar. To configure the MIME type for Shockwave movies (which is application/x-director), see Appendix B.

The pros of Shockwave for Director are as follows:

- True visitor-initiated interactivity

- Excellent compression (using Afterburner for Director)

- New audio SWA (Shockwave Audio) sound compression and streaming audio

- Relatively easy HTML coding using the EMBED tag

- Bandwidth-friendly if you are not carried away

- Can control color palette of HTML page from Director movie if desired

- If you're not afraid of Lingo, you can build in URL links

The cons of Shockwave for Director are as follows:

- Plug-in needed

- Entire animation must load before it will play

- A white box (the size of your presentation) shows up no matter what color background

- Expensive application required for creation

- Relatively steep learning curve

- Poor documentation (improved in 5.0)

- Support for QuickTime within the presentation is under development

- Requires server configuration

Tools

Essential tools for working with Shockwave for Director are:

- Macromedia Director

- Afterburner for Director

Shockwave makes use of the EMBED tag in HTML.

Here's a sample of HTML that shows an embedded director movie.

```
<EMBED SRC="mypresentation.dcr">
```

For more information about parameters, see the Shockwave section of Chapter 8

We suggest you check `http://www.macromedia.com/shockwave` for the most current information.

A Shockwave Example: The bYte Gun in the Toy Box

At `http://www.vizbYte.com` we have a section called the toy box. The idea here is to give people things they can take home (download) and have as a souvenir of our site, things that are fun and stupid that they are likely to show all their friends—and of course promote our firm. We originally created the bYte gun as a self-contained Macromedia Director player file that could be downloaded. With the improved compression of the new Afterburner, we decided to put it live on the Web so that visitors could check out what they were getting (see Figure 5.62).

Browsers Currently Compatible with Shockwave

Internet Explorer 2.0 (Mac only) and 3.0

Netscape Navigator 2.02 and 3.0

Attachmate's Emissary

Netmanage's WebSurfer

Platforms that Support Shockwave

Macintosh Power PC: Authorware, FreeHand, Director 5

Macintosh 68K: Authorware, FreeHand, Director 5

Windows 3.1: Authorware, FreeHand

Windows 95: Authorware, FreeHand, Director 5

Windows NT 3.5.1: Authorware, FreeHand, Director 5

Windows NT 4.0—Not yet supported

figure 5.62

You can check out
this toy on the CD-
ROM or at `http://`
`www.vizbyte.com/`
`livestuff/`
`bytegun.html`.

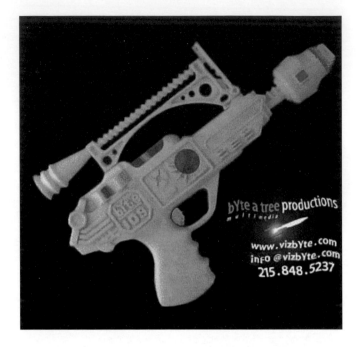

210

The gun was photographed with the Apple QuickTake camera, touched
up in Photoshop, and saved as a PICT. This was brought into Macromedia
Director and hot spots were set up where the cursor would change and
various things would happen. For areas of the toy to flash and light up,
areas of color were overlayed on top of the image of the plastic gun. You
can see the various cast members in Figure 5.63. It was saved as a compressed .dcr file using Afterburner.

Shockwave was the logical choice for delivering this to the Web because it
required both sound and interactivity.

Shockwave for FreeHand

Vector graphics on the Web! Zoom in to 25000%, no ugly pixels! We are
used to taking our drawings from an illustration program into a pixel-
based application such as Photoshop or Xres before they can be viewed
on the Web. No longer! Shockwave for FreeHand enables the browser to
display native FreeHand graphics. At this point these are not animated

graphics in the usual sense, but kinetic art is-created by the refresh of the screen when zooming or panning. This can be used to create some exciting and dynamic graphics.

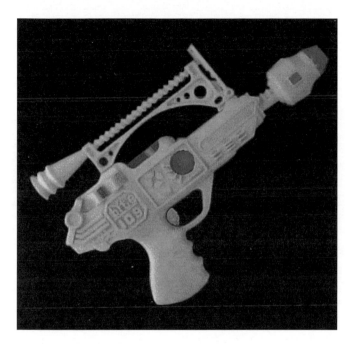

figure 5.63

The bYte gun is a Director movie. Different "hot spots" cause the cursor to change and indicate an area that will make a different sound.

The Shockwave for FreeHand files enable live panning and zooming activated by tools in a special palette. This is a huge improvement over the previous version where the viewer had to remember specific key combinations to zoom in, zoom out, and pan.

Shockwave for FreeHand comes in two parts:

- **Afterburner for FreeHand** contains the URL Manager and Afterburner Xtras that you can install in FreeHand. The URL Manager Xtra lets you add URL hot spots to FreeHand graphics of any shape (a map device) and the Afterburner Xtra enables the importing and exporting of compressed FreeHand files. Afterburner for FreeHand is available for Macintosh and for Windows; it requires FreeHand 5.0 or later. Afterburner is a compression device. It is not necessary to use it for the plug-in to recognize the movie.

211

- **Shockwave Plug-In for FreeHand** enables native FreeHand documents to be incorporated into the page layout of an HTML document. The plug-in recognizes FreeHand documents with a .fh5 or .fhc extension.

The pros of Shockwave for FreeHand:

- True vector graphics, not bitmapped or pixel-based
- Viewer can zoom in or out and pan, creating cool kinetic effects
- Zoom enables layering of many details in a small area
- Relatively easy HTML coding using the EMBED tag
- Excellent compression using Afterburner for FreeHand
- Navigational links can be easily built-in using URL Xtra

The cons of Shockwave for FreeHand:

- Not true animation
- A white box the size of your illustration appears while graphic is loading
- The entire illustration must load before anything is seen
- Expensive (though common) application required for creation
- No audio
- Plug-in required
- Requires server configuration

Tools

- Macromedia FreeHand
- AfterBurner for FreeHand
- URL Manager Xtra

Available at `http://www.macromedia.com/Shockwave`

A Shockwave for FreeHand Example: The designOnline Cup Hunt

For designOnline we created a series of vector graphics we mentioned before in our discussion of the "chat" graphic (see "Animated Text" and Figure 5.17 earlier in this chapter), in which the viewer zoomed and zoomed to see more and more text. There were two other illustrations that have a deliberate kinetic or "animated" effect that we will describe briefly. To experience the effect, you must browse the files on the CD-ROM; a screen shot in the book cannot reproduce it.

One illustration is the designOnline logotype with overlapping color layers and shapes that are stepped within one another smaller and smaller. This gives the effect, when zooming, of ripples of outlines radiating out from the screen. You really feel as if you are going deeper and deeper into the logo. This illustration was very simply built in FreeHand. Remember, the fewer points, the simpler the illustration and the smaller the file. We found that we could have many, many simple polygons (a circle is four points) rather than one letter converted to paths or one traced element. In this case we made an entire layer of progressively smaller shapes on green and then on top of that repeated the effect in purple. Therefore you get a flash of green under the purple as the screen refreshes.

The size of the document in FreeHand determines the size of the area into which the illustration will load in the browser (unless you change this by using a different height and width in the HTML). Be sure to set up your document size so that it works well with the illustration. We found that it was good to have some white space around the image itself so that the viewer could enlarge the graphic without any cropping effect. The FreeHand file is saved with a .fh5 suffix, and it is ready to go into the HTML.

WARNING

Although the strength of the vector graphic is that it displays smoothly, this will not happen if the viewer's computer does not have the font you use! Always use Times or Courier or convert the type to paths. Converting to paths increases file size dramatically, more than any other single factor.

To take even more blatant advantage of the screen refresh, we actually hid messages under shapes in a file we called "subliminal." When the viewer clicks, a word will flash onscreen and be covered up by the next color layer (see Figure 5.64). You can zoom in and out until you are able to read the type (actually a disadvantage for those with faster processor speeds). This was an illustration that corresponded to the "inspiration" section of the dezine café commenting on the elusiveness of inspiration.

figure 5.64

A series of screen captures of the FreeHand files with simulated zoom.

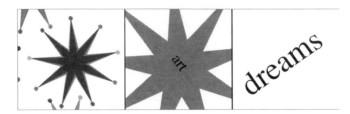

Server-Push, Client-Pull, and CGI

Using server-push and CGI (Computer Gateway Interface) scripts requires more technological knowledge than the plug-in technologies. The designer has to learn how to talk to the site server. The designer must also take into consideration Net traffic, how long it takes instructions to travel to the server, and how long it will take to receive the reply. Using these interfaces requires a knowledge of server traffic.

214

NOTE

By the way, once upon a time, server-push was the *only* way to do animation on the Web. Up until several months ago, designers had no choice but to deal with CGI.

These days, when the Net is clogged up with newbie Net surfers and the constant sending of graphic files, our studio prefers the options that download and do not depend on the server any longer. With plug-ins and Java, why bother with this clunky stuff?

The efficiency of Net communications is based on the fact that you are only connected to a server as long as necessary. Keeping a connection open is a serious burden on any server. If you are visiting a site on a dial-up line, you often will not experience what a designer had intended. An example of this is Rezn8 (see Figures 5.24 through 5.26)

With server-push, the server sends down a chunk of data; the browser displays the data but leaves the connection to the server open; whenever the server wants to, it sends more data and the browser displays it, again leaving the connection open; at some later time the server sends down yet more data and the browser displays it; and this continues until the script is completed.

An HTTP connection is held open for an indefinite period of time, usually until the server knows it has completed sending the data to the client, a terminator command is sent, or until the client interrupts the connection. In client-pull, HTTP connections are never held open; rather, the client is told when to open a new connection and what data to fetch when it does so.

In contrast to client-pull, server-push takes advantage of a connection that's held open for multiple responses. In this case the server can send down more data any time it wants. The major advantage is that the server has total control over when and how often new data is sent. The downside is that the open connection consumes a resource on the server side while it's open. By the way, server-push has two other advantages: a server push is easily interrupted (you can just hit Stop and interrupt the connection), and the complete image loads before switching pages.

The pros of server-push include the following:

- The server sends data when previous data is complete

- Many creative possibilities

- No plug-in required

The cons of server-push include the following:

- Dependent upon open connection to server; can be slow or intermittent

- As programming goes, server-push is relatively difficult

- Completely at the mercy of the server

- No support for sound

- Works only with Netscape

215

With client-pull, the server sends down a chunk of data, including a directive (in the HTTP response or the document header) that says something such as "reload this data in 10 seconds" or "go load the next URL in 20 seconds." After the specified amount of time has elapsed, the client does what was asked of it, either reloading the current data or getting the specified new data.

The results are accomplished by using a variant of the MIME message format that lets a single message (or HTTP response) contain many data items. In client-pull, it is accomplished by an HTTP response header (or equivalent HTML tag) that tells the client what to do after some specified time delay. For details, check out `http://www.np.ac.sg:9080/~piaweb/class4/meta.html`.

The pros of client-pull include the following:

- As programming goes, client-pull isn't too difficult

- Many creative possibilities

- No plug-in required

The cons of client-pull include the following:

- Dependent upon open connection to server; can be slow or intermittent

- Is a "timer" device, so a page can change before all the data has loaded

- Works only with Netscape

Tools

Server-push requires writing a CGI script and using appropriate programming tools (or simply "borrowing" a server-push script someone else has written).

Client-pull is done simply by adding code to your HTML files, so all you need is your favorite HTML editor.

An Example of Client-Pull: dezine café Opening Pages

Earlier we discussed the opening pages of the dezine cafe (see Figures 5.26 and 5.27). You can also browse these pages on the CD-ROM. You'll notice that the document switches pages after 10 seconds. What's happening? We're using the META tag (a standard HTML tag) for simulating HTTP response headers in HTML documents:

```
<META HTTP-EQUIV="Refresh" CONTENT="12; URL=/Root/home1.html">
```

TIP

You should make sure the META tag is used inside the HEAD of your HTML document. It must appear before any text or images are displayed as part of your document.

FutureSplash Animator

FutureWave Software, Inc. `http://www.futurewave.com/`

FutureSplash Animator is for creating small, fast, vector-based drawings and animations that are then played by the proprietary (free) FutureSplash player. FutureSplash Animator has features for creating fully animated cartoons, logos, technical drawings, and interactive buttons.

Animation sequences created with FutureSplash Animator are streamed onto Web pages, so the animations play as they are downloaded. Sequences using this multimedia application's vector-based format can be played at any color depth and are scaleable to any size. FutureSplash Animator supports a variety of other Import/Export file formats for drawings and animations.

Features include the following:

- Multi-platform—FutureSplash Animator takes full advantage of Macintosh, Power Mac and Windows 95/NT platforms.

- Good value—A vector-based drawing and animation tool for about $250 (street price).

- On the Web—View FutureSplash Animator drawings and animations on the Web using the free FutureSplash Player.

- Built-in anti-aliasing—Eliminates the "jaggies" on-screen

- FutureSplash Animator—Export files in the FutureSplash Player format for streaming vector animations.

Java

The Java programming language is hot stuff, about the hottest stuff next to the use of animated GIFs. It's not as easy or as stable, however. I've read that the name was chosen during one of numerous brainstorming sessions held by the Java team. They wanted to come up with a name that evoked the essence of the technology—"liveliness, animation, speed, interactivity, and more." "Java" was chosen as a reminder of the hot, aromatic stuff that many programmers like to drink a-plenty.

For a discussion of the power of Java, see the Java section in Chapter 8.

An animation applet is a much more elegant implementation of inline animation than Netscape's clunky server-push/client-pull gimmick previously mentioned. If the animation graphics are small, download time is minimal and the animation is smooth. Since it cycles through the images on the client's machine, the loop doesn't start running until all of the images are downloaded and ready to go. There are configurable options such as how many times to loop, pauses, and so on.

Beyond the animation of characters and highlighting menu bars, there are ways to animate headlines, rotate 3D models, and so on.

After it sees an APPLET tag, a Java-capable browser will download the code for the program described therein and attempt to compile and run it on the client's machine. All Java distributions and, one would assume, future implementations of the language include standard libraries, an interpreter and compiler, and several precompiled examples of applets.

What Browsers Support Java?

Netscape Navigator 2.0.1 and 2.0.1 Gold for Windows

Netscape Navigator 3.0 for Windows and Macintosh.

Sun's HotJava

Microsoft Internet Explorer 3.0

What if the visitor to the site doesn't have a Java-savvy browser? Actually, it's not all that bad: non-Java-enabled browsers will ignore the APPLET tag and its corresponding PARAM tags. Java-enabled browsers will ignore any tags between the APPLET tags that are not PARAM tags. So, you can place any HTML, including references to Shockwave movies or animated GIFs, between the last PARAM tag and the closing APPLET tag. Non-Java-enabled browsers will take note of the other HTML, and

Java-enabled browsers will ignore it, instead displaying the applet according to the parameters specified in the PARAM tags (which pass information along to the Java applet. This is actually one of the most flexible aspects of implementing a design that is multiple-browser-capable. Here's example HTML of a Java applet with a backup GIF:

```
<APPLET CODE="GrowButton.class" CODEBASE="graphics" WIDTH=80
HEIGHT=32>
<PARAM NAME="image1" VALUE="mac/graphics/mac-button1.gif">
<PARAM NAME="image2" VALUE="mac/graphics/mac-button2.gif">
<PARAM NAME="image3" VALUE="mac/graphics/mac-button3.gif">
<PARAM NAME="link" VALUE="http://www.mcp.com/hayden/mac/
index.html">
<A HREF="mac/index.html">
<IMG HEIGHT=32 WIDTH=80 BORDER=0 SRC="mac/graphics/mac-
button1.gif" ALT="Professional Macintosh">
</A>
</APPLET>
```

When a designer is given the opportunity to prepare options for the viewer, the experience at the site is enhanced.

Don't forget that you will need to configure your server to handle Java applets. Check with the server administrator before going ahead with plans you may not be able to support.

The pros of Java include the following:

● Don't need a continuous connection to the sever to run the applet

● If you're good enough, there are infinite creative possibilities, since it's a programming language and you can create whatever you want

● No plug-in required

● Can incorporate audio and interactivity with animation

● Universal, for all platforms

● The specifications for the language are free

● AppletAce and other graphical authoring environments to create applets are being developed rapidly

● Tons of public domain applets available for your use

The cons of Java include the following:

- Requires programming knowledge; very steep learning curve

- Few Macintosh development tools available at this date

- Browser-dependent; must be Java-savvy

- Programming abilities necessary

- Can be a threat to server security or a burden on the server

- No audio

Other Animation Options

Want more choices for adding animation to Web pages? There are plenty. Most of the following proprietary technologies require people to download plug-ins. But they're worth a look.

Sizzler

Totally Hip Software Inc.
`http://www.totallyhip.com`

Sizzler is a software package that streams animation for playing on the Internet in real time. Sizzler comes in two parts: a converter and a plug-in. The plug-in provides the necessary software to view animation on the Web (when the animation is created with the Sizzler converter). The converter enables you to create and play animation on your Web site by converting PICS files, QuickTime movies for Macintosh, or AVI or DIB list file formats for Windows converter into animation. Remember, you must know how to animate and have the necessary animation tools first, such as WebPainter.

The current beta release of Sizzler plays only animation, but the folks at Totally Hip are planning on enhancing Sizzler's capabilities to include streamed delivery of other media types such as sound and interactivity.

They're also working on better compression ratios, increased support for more media types, timing control, scripting, transparencies, and multiple animations.

And More...

- Enliven (`http://www.narrative.com/`). Interesting server solution for streaming animations with audio. Windows 95 only.

- Electrifier (`http://www.electrifier.com/`). Animation and vector graphics in remarkably small files. Mac only.

- Emblaze (`http://www.Geo.inter.net/ebz/ebz.htm`). Full-motion, streamed animation. Windows and Mac.

- mBED (`http://www.mbed.com/`). Animation files with added interactivity features. Windows and Mac.

- WebAnimator (`http://secure.deltapoint.com/animate/`). Not only animation, but full-fledged multimedia. Mac only (for now).

chapter

6

 *by Stella Gassaway*

Audio: An Earful of Atmosphere

As designers, most of our work has been accomplished in a still and silent

world: a quiet and comfortable two-dimensional place where we have

control…until now. The world may be smaller, but it is not flat. Clients are

looking for multidimensional solutions. An enhanced tool set offers us new

opportunities to enter a vibrant four-dimensional space. An atmospheric

place.

So how's the weather?

Well, for most designers it's pretty stormy. Thinking about making things move may be intriguing (see Chapter 5); adding sound is another story. Audio is not being used to its full extent in Web design, and for good reason: most of us started as print designers and we aren't familiar with the use of audio. It's time to get over that if we want to create the right atmospheric conditions. Remember: We create it, enter it, and become part of it.

Our primary concern, of course, is design. The information in this book serves one purpose: to demonstrate the possibilities. We don't have to learn the intricacies of audio design and mastering. We do, however, need to know enough to do the following:

- Ask the right questions

- Make our job easier

- Design with a knowledge of the tools and devices being used

Until recently the interface we created with audio was awkward and the technology for delivery on the Web weak. The ability to integrate audio into a Web page is just arriving. Even those of us who thought of ways to integrate sound into our sites didn't have many tools to work with until now. Downloading and playing audio outside the browser is a disruptive way to experience a Web site's enhanced elements. Even when the sound is an enhancement rather than an integral part of the site, it's a pain when a helper application launches, opens a not-so-cool-looking control bar, and either plays the sound when you didn't expect it or waits for you to initiate the sound when you thought it would play.

Plug-ins, a relatively new technology, are a plus for the designer and viewer. There are limitations to plug-ins; it's not a perfect world, but at least you can play sound and music from within the browser. As browser developers enable new technologies to be integrated more conveniently, viewer (or auditor) and designer win. The key to delivering rich media on the Web is compression technologies. With the new QuickTime plug-in bundled with Netscape and available for cross-platform use, new opportunities for quality, integrated audio are possible. The most recent release of Shockwave audio compression increases the possibilities with even greater compression.

This chapter has three sections.

- Design issues for integrating audio into a site: the various purposes it can serve and the forms it can take (music, sound effects, and voice).

- The basics of audio: includes scary terms such as digital recording, MIDI, file formats, and some of the more popular applications for working with audio files.

- How to bring audio to a Web site: the technological options, compression schemes, and blow-by-blow examples of how we created audio experiences for the Web.

Integrating Audio into a Site: Design Issues

It's intriguing to think about adding sound to an environment you are creating. You want to set the right mood, integrate sounds with interaction, instigate activity, and reinforce the metaphors that make visitors to your site comfortable travelers.

I always imagine sound in the work I design. I imagine walking through brochures I've designed as if they were buildings to be explored, and I hear the sounds of a fold opening as if it were a door. In our studio we are aware of the silence and space sound can fill. These are our considerations when bringing audio to the Web. Each sound effect, piece of music, or voice-over must enhance the experience. If sound isn't important, leave it out. This is important not only for aesthetic reasons but for technical reasons, too. Sound adds considerable "weight" (file size) to a site. File size demands more bandwidth and clogged bandwidth slows down everything you are trying to do.

It's important to consider what happens if the sound doesn't work. Have a plan B in mind, incorporate more than one way of conveying the information. Redundancy is a good word when it comes to the technical aspects of bringing multimedia to the Web; you need alternate ways around potential barriers. When you add enhancements, several scenarios must be considered. If the sound doesn't load, will the viewer know what to do? How can you let them know what to do without the use of sound?

Absorbing what we observe in the world around us adds richness to our design solutions. It is what enables us to speak to others. On the opening page to the bYte a tree section of the vizbYte site (see Figure 6.1), for example, the bYte guy is surprised by the glowing bYte a tree sign. The sign flickers on and off to get the viewer's attention much like a neon sign. What else would signal us that the sign was glowing if we weren't looking at it? What would get our attention? I closed my eyes and thought about it. Of course, the sign would have an electrical humming sound.

figure 6.1

The bYte a tree sign at *http://* *www.vizbyte.com/* *byteintro.html*. You can almost hear the buzz.

Audio is another one of the multimedia frontiers where designers must dig deep, learn new skills, access our abilities, and learn to blend our abilities with new and exciting members in the design partnership: musicians and audio engineers.

Integrating Music

Music is one of the richest atmospheric options discussed in this section. Music triggers emotions and memories; it can instigate, intimidate, or exhilarate. Music creates an atmosphere that takes hundreds of words to explain.

Setting the Mood

A romantic setting: the right wine, perfect lighting, and maybe kd lang's steamy Ingénue. Yes, this definitely counts as understanding how music can set the mood. Having a party? Got a theme? Searching for the music to keep everything cruising? You've already integrated music into a situation and you didn't even know it. As designers we're designing the space we're in all the time. We can't help it.

We use music often at bYte a tree because we like music and find it easy to work with. Plus, we have a musician among us and can create our own music, which keeps our multimedia fresh. Being able to create our own music is safer and easier as far as permissions and the legal stuff goes.

Don't get carried away with an opus; music files get very large before you notice it. Technically you can compress sound to death, but that's just what you'll do: kill it and your efforts at creating an atmosphere. Poor audio quality will make a negative impression on your visitor. Short riffs that can be looped are most effective. We'll talk more about that in the technical section.

[e]mersion, an intro movie about the birth of our new media division, is about creating the right atmosphere; setting the right mood. It is fast-moving, digital, dark, and organic. The movie is atmospheric without any music, but the addition of chanting voices and overriding percussion combines the organic and technological aspects of our studio's vision. Out of the darkness comes the light, bYte a tree productions (see Figure 6.2). You can play this from the CD-ROM that accompanies this book, or view it live at `http://www.vizbyte.com/livestuff/mersion.html`.

Before the Alphabet is a type demo for Alphabets, Inc. to promote a typeface of the same name designed by Manfred Klein. Here the visual mood is set with earthtones. The font is modeled after cave paintings and petroglyphs, and the music is spiritual and primitive (see Figure 6.3). Our musician partner composed a piece to create a Southwestern or Native American atmosphere, adding many layers of sounds. With a hand-crafted Native American flute he was able to play not a melody line, but notes to evoke a ceremonial environment. You can experience this on the CD-ROM that accompanies this book or see it online at `http://www.vizbyte.com/livestuff/btab.hmtl`.

figure 6.2

The moody
[e]mersion movie.

figure 6.3

Four frames of
the movie Before
the Alphabet.

Samples of Songs

Some of the hottest sites on the Web are music sites. Independent labels and small bands thrive in this new and inexpensive Web environment. Independent labels and small bands are given distribution power and have music clips available on the Web, whereas before they had to depend on a deal with a record company to get the word out. Music clips may be found in online music magazines, too.

The big guys in the industry all have Web sites. Everyone from MTV to Geffen Records has clips to push of well-known artists and lesser contracts. For example, at `http://www.geffen.com/cowboyjunkies/` you can check out the Cowboy Junkies latest release (see Figure 6.4). The section includes remarks by the band members and audio clips of selected cuts from the CD. Figure 6.5 shows the link to a clip and the player window that opens up to play the clip. Often the clip auto-starts, but sometimes you have to start the clip.

figure 6.4

This page starts with empty chairs and gradually the artists become visible!

figure 6.5

A clip of Lay It Down being played from the LiveAudio player.

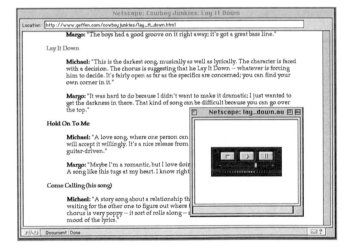

Some music sites to check out (there are many more) include the following:

- `http://www.sony.com`

- `http://www.geffen.com`

- `http://www.EMI.com`

A site does not have to be related to the business of selling music to integrate songs effectively. At `http://www.retroactive.com/rafiles/rodgers.ram`, songs of the Old West come alive for our listening pleasure in their RetroRadio (see Figure 6.6). Explore more of this site, which discusses many topics in an interesting historical context. There would have been little point in discussing the songs without being able to play them.

figure 6.6

The Old West sings to us at retroactive.com.

In general, when you are putting material that previously existed in print on the Web, keep an ear out for songs or musical themes relevant to the material. Obviously, these were not included in the printed material (do you hear this book singing?) and so are a part of culture often overlooked.

Integrating Sound Effects

Our studio's sound dude and myself are inspired by early radio. Yeah, that stuff before the top forty, alternative rock, punk, hip hop, and grunge: radio shows that told a story, where people in the studio put fans, sheets of metal, and lots of other strange things in front of the microphone to transport us to the event taking place. You forgot you were listening to people standing in a radio studio.

A dandy example of radio ingenuity is "War of the Worlds," where the "aliens coming out of the space ship" sound was created by opening a jar in a toilet. In the awe-inspiring game Myst, the huge clock sound was made by hitting a large 7/8" Craftsman wrench with another wrench to get the sustained, reverberating sound, which was then lowered in pitch. Using this kind of ingenuity, you can create sound effects that come across powerfully on the Web because they tolerate compression better than musical effects. Don't think you have to invest in special equipment to generate sounds; look around you and open your ears! There is a difference between hearing something and listening to it; pay attention to what you hear and develop your listening skills.

Supporting the Metaphor

What happens when you close a door, turn on the shower, take an elevator, or slam on the breaks? Simple sounds that support the metaphor help us reinforce the atmosphere we want to create. Sound effects let visitors know something has been activated or something is about to happen. Applying sound to Web sites helps visitors relate to the actions they perform.

The most overused (but usually appropriate) sound is the click sound that goes with "click here" instructions. The click sound is used in tutorials to reinforce that you have indeed "clicked" and initiated a result. We're not very fond of the click at our studio; we are always looking for alternative ways to say "click."

Typing is often required in interactive demonstrations. Even though typewriters aren't used much anymore, the sound of keys being struck on a typewriter is often used to support the interaction.

In one of our most recent interactive pieces, a QuickTime puzzle at `http://www.dol.com/puzzle/`, the goal is to stop all the QuickTime movies so that they add up to the dezine café emoticon (see Figure 6.7). While clever, this puzzle seemed somewhat lifeless until we added the ticking of a clock, which created a sense of urgency and game atmosphere. You can hear this for yourself on the CD-ROM or online (we discuss the interactive aspects of the puzzle in Chapter 8).

figure 6.7

Here is the cup puzzle unsolved and solved.

Webmonkey (`http://www.webmonkey.com`) should certainly be in every Web designer's bookmarks. It's a great place to find out what's new for your design and development toolbox. We mention the site here because the menu selector is a wrench the monkey turns to your selection in the main menu (see Figure 6.8). A "chunk" sound plays as the wrench clicks into place. This helps support the action and informs viewers that they have indeed selected something. Click and you are off to one of the sections.

figure 6.8.a

When Webmonkey pulls the wrench, you hear it.

233

figure 6.8.b

The wrench
continues to move.

An amazing thing about adding sounds that feel like a "natural" consequence of an action (either by an animated character or the visitor) is that the sound sometimes goes almost unnoticed; it draws attention not to itself but to the animation or interaction.

Getting Attention, Generating Surprise

When trying to get the attention of a visitor at a site, we make an effort to add sound as an element of surprise. We'll let a sound file load while we distract the visitor with text, the fastest-loading element, and images. Using sound successfully at a site requires excellent compression of the sound for quick loading and a bit of magician's skill to make it appear seamless.

Integrating Voice

One of the most familiar sounds is the human voice. Depending on how it is used, it can be reassuring, instructive, or irritating. Here we will discuss three uses for voice on the Web: voice-over, narration and storytelling, and interview clips.

Voice-Over

There is probably nothing more friendly or more disturbing than a human voice coming from nowhere. It can be quite a surprise. At bYte a tree we use voice-overs to give instructions or get someone's attention. Nothing wakes you up from a doze in front of the old tube faster than a loud "ahem" as used in the opening to our interactive introduction to bYte a tree productions (see Figure 6.9). You can see how this works at `http://www.vizbyte.com/byteatreeintro.html` or on the CD that accompanies this book. We essentially set an alarm with the interactive elements we use; the interactive element waits a designated amount of time and then if there is no response, the alarm is a voice saying something like, "Excuse me. Ah, pardon me, had you intended on moving along?"

figure 6.9

Here we ahem! for attention in text and audio.

Using voices on the Web adds an organic point of view, an intervening human element. Verbal commands are helpful when other attention-getters don't work. The bYte a tree introduction is self-running for the first section and then the viewer is invited to explore the screen. We tried using written instructions but found the audience had relapsed into passive mode during the self-running portion, and many folks would just stare at the screen waiting for something else to happen. We found that a voice saying, "Ha! And you thought we were going to do all the work, now it's your turn…" was by far the most effective way to shift the audience back into active mode.

At `http://www.m-ms.com`, the M&M site, there is an incredibly perky voice-over inviting you to join the cartoon M&M's in a tour of the site: "Keep your hands inside the vehicle," and so on. This is fully in keeping with the humorous but sticky-sweet atmosphere of the site.

Narration and Storytelling

A story, by its nature, requires more than a brief of audio. When discussing music we recommended short looped clips; this strategy would obviously take a story nowhere. Luckily, the sound of a voice is the most crunchable recorded audio data. Therefore, adding narration to a Web site doesn't take up a bunch of space since voices can be used effectively at much lower quality than music.

In discussions of audio on the Web, the comparison to television and radio often overshadows other models. Suppose the publication you are browsing at the dentist's office could talk to you? With streaming audio and plug-ins such as RealAudio, a site such as `http://www.word.com` becomes more than a magazine. To enhance the experience in its feature short stories, Word often uses RealAudio clips (see Figure 6.10).

figure 6.10

A short story at `http://www.word.com/machine/vanderbilt/` and an audio sidebar is activated by clicking the dashboard radio.

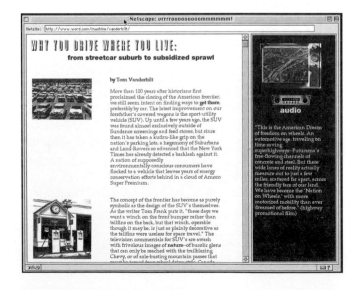

Interview Clips

Don't think that a small audio clip accompanying an interview or article isn't an important addition to the visitor experience; it enhances the news story. Interview clips add the same impact to a story on a Web site that a photo does to a story in print. The text gives the sound a context, and then the audio clip can extend the viewer experience with the speaker's tone of voice, the tension or comfort in the voice. When the Presidential support plane crashed in Wyoming, CNN Interactive had an interview clip of President Bill Clinton expressing sorrow over the crash. The impact of that emotion could not be carried by reading the written quote (see Figure 6.11).

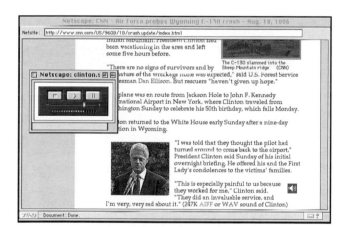

figure 6.11

Present Clinton's clip at http:// www.cnn.com after the crash of an Air Force Cargo support plane expressed what the written quote could not.

237

Radio on the Web: National Public Radio

We couldn't resist discussing this site, `http://www.npr.org`, because it is the most ambitious use of continuously streamed audio on the Web that we know (see Figure 6.12)! Going to the National Public Radio site is like tuning in on the radio; the quality of the sound is pretty close to what you get on a small transistor. However, with a radio, you are stuck with what they are playing at the moment. We all know how frustrating it is to tune in in the middle of an interview with your favorite world leader. At the NPR Web site you can choose what you want to listen to and read a little about the content before you listen (see Figure 6.13). This site updates the news every hour, and the rest of the programming stays pretty current also (the time that the report was broadcast is noted). This incredible audio quality for long sound files is possible through a technology called RealAudio (see the RealAudio section at the end of this chapter).

figure 6.12

The NPR home page, `http://www.npr.org`.

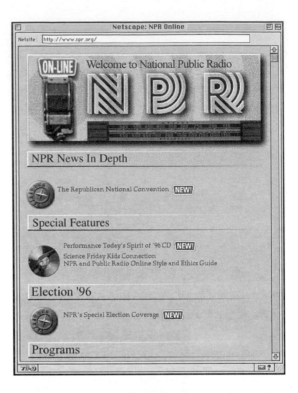

figure 6.13

Here's where you choose the sound files you want to listen to at the "station."

Audio Basics

As designers we're not familiar with audio development. How can we change that? Well, for starters, you're reading this section of the book, aren't you? We can also hang out with our musician friends and ask them questions, or better yet add a partner to your studio who is a musician (ours is also a professional photographer, so we get two multimedia folks wrapped into one). Most of the information in this section is based on the knowledge and skill of our musician partner at bYte a tree productions.

Some of the information that follows will test your will to learn about audio. Don't worry, there isn't a quiz later! Just Zen a bit, read it, and let the Force be with you. Besides, we've come up with a cool analogy to the two-dimensional world of graphics just for you!

If you are interested in really diving into this topic, we recommend *The Incredible Sound Machine* by Mark Andrews from Addison-Wesley (for Mac users).

Digital Audio

Most sound you hear on the Web is from a digital audio file. The sound the human ear receives is *analog* sound. The digital life of a sound, as far as we're concerned, is a silent one. Therefore there are two critical steps at the beginning and end of the sound design process: The analog-to-digital conversion of sound into the computer (or other digital recording device such as a DAT recorder) and the digital-to-analog conversion enabling sound to come back out of the speakers in your computer. In between the digitized audio can be transferred, edited, manipulated, compressed, decompressed, stored, and so on, with all the flexibility associated with digital data.

About Digitized Sound

Analog recording on tape (or vinyl records, if you remember them) is continuous in nature. When sound is digitized by a digital recorder it is broken down into discrete units, from which several issues arise. Designers must have a basic grasp of these concepts to make intelligent design decisions about the use of audio. (Take a deep breath because some very technical stuff will be thrown at you here.)

The digital recorder grabs samples of sound at set intervals. There are three factors involved in this sampling process:

- The number of samples taken per second

- The amount of information contained in *each* sample

- Whether the recording is stereo or mono

The more samples taken per second, the closer to continuous the recording will be. You don't actually hear gaps in lower-quality digital audio, but something is definitely lost. The more samples taken, the more information in the resulting audio file and the larger the file size. High-quality audio files are very large indeed. Samples per second, or *sampling rate*, is referred to in kilohertz (KHz) and called *frequency* (22,000 samples per second = 22 KHz).

NOTE

> While it is common practice to refer to sampling rate as the frequency of a sound, it is not the same thing as the frequency of an analog sound, which is the number of cycles per second of a sound wave.

The amount of information each sample contains, or the *bit depth,* also affects sound quality and file size. We are working with computers that break down everything into sets of 0's and 1's, or *bits*. A simple yes/no, on/off, 0/1 is not enough to describe even a brief millisecond of sound. Therefore a group of bits is needed; the larger the group, the more detail captured. In addition, the variation permitted between the softest and loudest sounds in the piece (the *dynamic range*) is increased as the bit depth is increased. The two standards are 16-bit sound (at high sampling rate; this is CD quality) or 8-bit sound (typical on the Web).

The variable of sound recorded in mono or stereo (or beyond) is sometimes referred to as *channel depth*. In stereo you have two parallel sets of sound data, and, subsequently, twice as much data.

Table 6.1 shows you comparisons of file sizes at various sampling rates, bit depths, and channel depths (mono/stereo). You can play all these files from the CD-ROM that accompanies this book and hear the difference in quality for yourself. It should be noted that this chart reflects the final size of the file. Audio files should begin with as much information as possible and only be simplified to save file size at the end of the process. The only exception is a voice or sound effects file, where you're not going to use it for any other purpose other than the Web. In that case, begin at the desired final bit depth and sampling rate.

TABLE 6.1

File Sizes at Various Bit Depths and Sampling Rates

FILENAME	BIT DEPTH	SAMPLING RATE	MONO/STEREO	FILE SIZE
emersion16-44	16-bit	44 Khz	Stereo	3,040K
emersion16-22	16-bit	22 Khz	Mono	1,536K
emersion16-11	16-bit	11 Khz	Mono	800K
emersion8-44	8-bit	44 Khz	Mono	1,536K
emersion8-22	8-bit	22 Khz	Mono	800K
emersion8-11	8-bit	11 Khz	Mono	416K

NOTE

This digital recording process and the digital audio files described have similarities to the CD-quality audio you hear on music CDs, but they are not identical. The process used for music CDs is digital but more sophisticated and higher-quality.

Digital Recording

In the beginning, a digital audio file begins its life as a digital recording as

- A conventional (analog) recording

- Sound, voice, or music through a microphone

- Music played on an electronic instrument connected to a digital recorder

To convert an existing analog recording to a digital audio file, you need a device (such as a tape deck) connected to the computer. Never try to play a recording through speakers and in through a microphone! Your CD-ROM drive can read an audio CD directly, and with the correct adapter you can plug a stereo or DAT tape into the microphone port of your computer.

WARNING

Do not use existing recordings without express written permission of the copyright holder!! Even if you think you have permission from the composer, there are performer's rights and publisher's rights. The music labels do not take this lightly; it does not have to be for commercial use for you to be taken to court! For detailed information, go to `http://www.copyright.org`.

When recording, be sure you use a quality microphone, not the one that comes with your computer. It is best to use a microphone connected to a digital recording device rather than go through the intermediary step of analog recording—unless there are advantages such as taking the microphone somewhere the computer cannot go. If a composition can be played on an electronic instrument, such as a musical keyboard, the ideal is to have the instrument connected to a digital recorder. You get the idea; the stuff should go through wires, not through the air, if possible. After a piece of audio is digitized, however, there is no degradation in transferring digital information from computer to computer.

As mentioned above, the original sound file should hold as much information as possible. 16-bit/44.1 KHz is the generally accepted standard. Always record at this setting for music. In addition, adjust your microphone or internal controls in the digital recorder so that the fullest sound (full dynamic range, softest to loudest) is captured. However, be sure your volume is not too high or distortion will result. Many tests may be required to get the input levels set correctly, but if your recording procedures are consistent, they shouldn't have to be reset. In Figure 6.14 you see a visual representation of the recorded sound as it's displayed in Macromedia's SoundEdit 16. The visual wave should take up at least half the available space; otherwise, you don't have as many options in the editing process.

Basic Audio Hardware

In the music industry, recording is done in a sound studio into a multitrack tape deck or DAT recorder and then mixed using high-end equipment that costs tens of thousands of dollars. This can be overkill (and over budget) for simple sound effects and voice-over, especially when the sound is destined to be played back from a computer speaker on someone's desk.

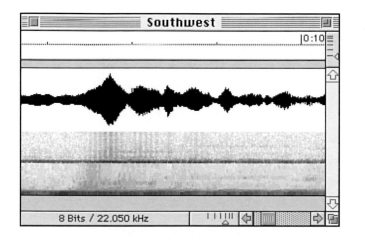

figure 6.14

The visual representation of a sound in SoundEdit 16.

This is a brief discussion of what basic equipment is necessary or useful if you want to create your own sound, music, and voice recordings for use on the Web. This is not to discourage the wise practice of using a professional sound studio where appropriate, for example, to record the performance of a musical piece. We also reveal what equipment we used in our examples.

Music Keyboard or Synthesizer

The keyboard is one of the most versatile, common, and easy-to-use digital instruments. However, other electronic musical instruments, such as an electric guitar, can also be played into a digital recorder. There is no point in purchasing any instrument unless you have someone in your studio with the talent to *play* it. This may seem silly, but we know of a firm that dutifully bought the "necessary" equipment for multimedia, and its keyboard is gathering dust because there are no musicians on staff.

The basic requirement for a keyboard (or other instrument) is a "sound out" jack that enables digital sound to travel to the computer or other digital recorder. This is a dramatic quality improvement over playing a keyboard and trying to catch it on a microphone. The drawback of less-expensive keyboards is that the keys are small and difficult to play for a musician accustomed to playing a piano. Increasing the price of a keyboard is the number of "voices," the electronic approximations of instruments such as piano, trumpet, drum, and so on. Our keyboard, a Yamaha

PSR-510 (mid-range), has 128 voices and the capability to program MIDI internally. Other brands are Roland, Hammond, Kurzweil, Casio, Kawia, Korg, Fatar, and E-MU, and prices range from a few hundred dollars to several thousand.

Microphone

The important thing to look for in a microphone is its capability to record only what you intend it to record—the more expensive the microphone, the less background noise and hiss you get. If you use the microphone that came with your computer, even the better-than-average Macintosh microphone, you get unavoidable background noise. Even if you think you are in a quiet place, something such as the air conditioning or heating system in the building will come across as background noise that is painfully difficult to edit out. Our brains filter out background noise, even though we are not aware of the process; a microphone has to be designed to act in the same way. It is worthwhile to invest in a studio-quality microphone that plugs into your computer or recorder or mixer. Some well-known brands are Shure, AKG, Audio Technica, and Breyer Dynamic and prices range from under $100 to a few thousand dollars.

WARNING

Do not plug a powerful microphone into the jack on your computer unless you know that it was intended for that purpose. The "silver dollar" microphone jacks on many Macintoshes, for example, cannot handle a standard microphone; damage to the microphone or computer may result.

Recorder/Mixer

You can record into a computer using digital recording software; however, there are advantages to recording into an analog recorder/mixer. A small 4-track cassette recorder and mixer gives you more control over the microphone, enabling you to adjust the treble, bass, and increase the recording level. 4-track refers to the fact that you can record four separate sounds that are stored side-by-side and can be played back together. The advantage of the hardware mixer is that you can take the microphone physically away from the computer and use multiple microphones to record ambient sound, record an event, or record in a quiet location (such as a closet). You also can record several layered tracks of sound or music, work with them until you are pleased with the result, and then digitize them as a single track editor into a sound editing program. This avoids taking up a lot of your hard disk space with the multiple tracks. Our model is a Tascam Porta One 4 track cassette recorder and mixer. Some other brands to consider are TEAC, Fostex, and Korg.

NOTE

Many of the functions performed by this recorder/mixer can be accomplished using a software equivalent such as Deck II or Session, but you can't carry these away from your computer.

WARNING

Using analog tape increases the danger of hiss. You can minimize this by using high-end noise reduction units such as Dolby or DBX, but these are costly.

Computer Hardware

You need a "microphone in" jack and a 16 bit sound card. The Macintosh is the most audio-friendly system because even low-end machines can record into the computer. If you are purchasing a 16-bit audio card, look for these features:

- A jack that enables a microphone to plug into the card

- Additional input channels (for multiple audio sources)

You need a minimum 16MB of RAM and plenty of hard disk space. When running high-end programs such as Session or Deck II, be sure your hard disk is optimized so that your sound files do not become fragmented.

We use a Power Mac 8100/80 with 48MB of RAM and a 1GB hard disk.

Speakers

Although it is good to have high-quality speakers to listen to during the sound design process, always test sound on the lowest-quality speaker available to hear what most of your visitors will hear. There are special speakers (with their own power source) to use with computer equipment that are shielded. Be sure not to put traditional speakers near your equipment because they contain magnets and the magnetic field will erase your hard disk and disrupt the calibration of your monitor! Some reliable computer speakers are Koss, Altec, and Sound Blaster.

TIP

Headphones are the best audio output option when trying to edit and "tweak" the sound. Headphones protect you from all the external sounds of your environment.

MIDI

Even though the discussion in this chapter refers primarily to digital audio, it is significant to introduce the topic of MIDI, mention its strengths in terms of the Web, and explain how it differs from digital audio in essential ways. We use the word "essential" deliberately; MIDI files are different in their *essence* from any recording (digital or analog). MIDI files are a set of instructions, not unlike the score for a musical composition.

Why Is MIDI Important?

As we have often seen, file size is critical for multimedia experiences on the Web. A MIDI file is exponentially smaller than its digital audio counterpart. We mention this at the outset because the promise of tiny files is what prompted us to understand what this MIDI stuff was all about.

MIDI stands for Musical Instrument Digital Interface. "Instrument" is the key word. MIDI is a way of storing and coding music, not recording it. Unlike a recording that can be played on a any boom box, a MIDI file requires an intelligent instrument (such as an electric guitar, drum machine, or synthesizer) or a MIDI software player to "read" the code and play the piece. Although there is unique MIDI encoding for specific instruments (such as Korg Model X synthesizer), used by musicians during composing, General MIDI is a standard that enables communication among different electronic instruments and computers. For each note General MIDI specifies one of 128 instruments (or "voices") as well as the pitch, duration, and volume of the note. MIDI contains information about what notes should be played when, with no limit to how many are hit simultaneously; you don't have to be an octopus or an orchestra to create complex compositions. Since General MIDI is the only type of MIDI

relevant to general use, all further discussion refers to MIDI that conforms
to the General MIDI standard.

> Although many use the term "MIDI" to mean General MIDI,
> there are musicians who work in their own worlds, so when
> asking your genius friend for a brilliant original composition, be
> sure that it is indeed in General MIDI.

With MIDI the sampling rate and bit depth agony is bypassed. You don't
have to sacrifice audio quality, there is no chance of background noise or
hiss, and you don't have to worry about compression and decompression.

So, What's the Catch?

Unfortunately, visitors to your site are unlikely to hook up a musical
keyboard to their computer to play your MIDI files. Therefore the "instrument" they will hear is a software application that approximates the sound
of the instruments and plays the piece (Arnold's MIDI player, for example,
as seen in Figure 6.15). Although the *audio* quality is not degraded, the
musical quality may be lacking because of the primitive nature of the
playback device.

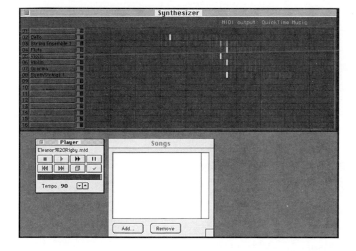

figure 6.15

Arnold's MIDI player,
available from
http://www.
hitsquad.com/
smm/.

247

Also, General MIDI encodes only the most basic elements making up a
musical composition. Any nuance subtleties are not preserved. You
cannot edit MIDI files in the way you can edit digital audio files. You can

combine them, you can change the tempo, and you can remove notes, but that's about it. You also cannot convert a MIDI file into a digital audio file. An instrument (such as a keyboard) must play the MIDI composition and the result must be recorded.

TIP

You can edit a composition using the built-in MIDI sequencer on your keyboard to lay down different tracks. When you're finished, the result is played (by the keyboard) into the digital recorder to become a digital audio file. This saves you from working with multiple large music files on your hard disk.

We have been talking about music here, not voice or sound effects, because MIDI handles only the standard 128 instruments and cannot encode the human voice. You can use the instruments (especially percussion) to make sounds rather than musical compositions—a brief "plunk," for example.

Leaving aside the high-end specialized options, there are two ways to create MIDI files. The first is to play a composition on a musical keyboard/synthesizer using its internal sequencer. You then "dump" or transfer the MIDI coding from the keyboard to the computer using software such as D-SoundPro (shareware available on the CD-ROM with this book). Alternatively, and this is our preferred method, you play the composition on a musical keyboard/synthesizer, which sends the signal through a hardware interface device (such as Opcode MIDI TranslatorII) through the printer port of your computer into sequencing software such as Master Trax. Simpler still, you can download one of the many MIDI clips available on the Web, from, for example, `http://www.midifarm.com/`.

NOTE

You can get information about MIDI software and hardware at `http://www.opcode.com/`.

There are many cross-platform MIDI plug-ins, but the most promising is the MIDI player included in the QuickTime that comes with Netscape 3.0. The LiveAudio plug-in also calls on QuickTime to play MIDI files. There is even a control panel with QuickTime 2.5 giving you the option of sending sound out through a port to play on a keyboard synthesizer. This is an important application for sites dedicated to music enthusiasts, but perhaps less expensive devices will become available that serve this purpose. (See the discussion of QuickTime later in this chapter.) An excellent resource for software, plug-ins, players, editors, and so on is the Shareware Music Machine at `http://www.hitsquad.com/smm/`.

MIDI versus Digital Audio: A Graphic Analogy

Here's an analogy to help explain the difference between digital audio and MIDI to visual designers: MIDI is like a vector line drawing, and digital audio is like a scan of that line drawing. This is illuminating if you think about image and sound quality or resolution and preservation of artistic character.

Image/Sound Quality and Resolution/Sampling Rate

We are all familiar with the garbage in/garbage out rule for scanned material. A client sends you a business card with a poorly printed logo half an inch high and wants it enlarged on the cover of a binder. Similarly, if you have a poor-quality recording, it is difficult to "touch it up" and improve the quality of the sound.

When scanning, an image is divided up into tiny squares (pixels) that approximate the original image. A resolution must be chosen, with improved quality (number of pixels per inch) weighed against larger file size. When recording, sound is broken up into tiny chunks strung to-gether to approximate the sound. A sampling rate must be chosen, with improved quality weighed against larger file size. When scanning, it is important to not pick up unwanted background or dirt; the same is true of recording. When discussing bit depth, our example is actually a direct parallel rather than an analogy; both kinds of information (a pixel or a sound sample) must be described by groups of bits; the more bits in the group, the more options available for description. Hence 8-bit sound, like 8-bit color, is a basic "palette."

In PostScript language, lines and curves are described by a complex coding process from the act of drawing on the computer. MIDI language describes the notes in a coding process from the act of playing a MIDI-capable instrument.

249

The joy of a PostScript line drawing is that it is resolution-independent. There is no debate about how many pixels per inch is enough. Similarly with MIDI, you do not have to choose a sampling rate or weigh 8-bit versus 16-bit; the code contains all the information. A line drawing might be a 100K file; a scan of a similar drawing might be 3MB. Everyone has redrawn logos rather than use scans in order to have a cleaner and smaller file. A MIDI file of a 49-second composition is 17K. When that same piece is recorded as digital audio at 16-bit/44.1 KHz, it was 4.5MB, and at 8-bit/22 KHz, it was 1.2MB!

Preservation of Artistic Character

The artistic restrictions of drawing in the vector environment are analogous to the limitations of the MIDI code, which only hold specific information and not the nuances of sounds or performances. We find ourselves wondering if today's limitations of MIDI are analogous to early computer drawings spurned for lack of artistic character. If we had a line drawing by Picasso or Miro, we would hesitate to try to redraw it in the more efficient vector world just to save file space. Similarly, if you want to present a performance by an artist, it must be recorded and played, not coded in MIDI and re-created. You won't find any MIDI files at the music industry sites that promote their musical artists.

Music, Sound Effects, and Voice: Special Considerations

The previous discussion does not take into account the different issues that apply depending on the nature of the sound being worked with. Voice, for example, can tolerate much lower bit depth/frequency than a musical piece.

Music

Musical performances on conventional instruments (and singing) should be recorded professionally in a sound studio. If a client gives you music to use that is not first generation (an audio tape or, even worse, a video tape), attempt to get the final mix on DAT tape from the originating sound studio. If you have the talent in-house, or a musical collaborator, play a composition on an electronic instrument (usually a keyboard). For music, you usually can't go below 8-bit/22 KHz without adding intolerable hiss and degradation of sound. If you are planning to bring the music into a QuickTime movie consider using QuickTime Musical Instruments to bring a MIDI file into QuickTime (for more information go to `http://www.quicktimefaq.org/`).

Voice

When trying to economize, especially for self-promotional projects, everyone thinks they can do voice-over in-house. How difficult can it be?

All it takes is hearing the same project recorded by a professional and the difference is night and day. Professionals possess a quality of voice that records well, known as vocal tone, in addition to talent. Professionals can control the pacing and inflection of the speech both for dramatic effect and for good sound quality. Amateurs may drop their voices, slur their words slightly, or run their words together. (How many times have you poorly recorded your voice mail greeting?) Combating these faults often leads to an unnatural and self-conscious pattern of speech.

You can get away with lower bit depth/sampling rate for voice files than for music: 8-bit/11 KHz is typical. With voice, the rule about starting at a high bit depth and sampling rate and coming down does *not* apply. The dithering process can create problems in voice files. Record at 8-bit/11 KHz from the beginning. If you already have a higher-quality file that needs to be brought down, send it out to an external device and redigitize it at the proper settings.

Sound Effects

Our sound guy makes all kinds of noises with different materials and tests how they sound when recorded. We were looking for the sound of pouring coffee, but it turned out liquid poured into a coffee cup sounded too much like water into a glass. Something that sounded "thicker" was needed. The true action is not as important as a *sound* implying that action. Remember using potatoes for ice cream in a photo shoot? Improvise! We have a recording room set up in a bathroom (good for reverberating sound) away from ambient studio noise. We generally record at 16-bit/44.1 KHz and end up with an end result at 8-bit/22 KHz or even 8-bit/11 KHz.

Editing Sound

There are many sound editing programs available. The minimum operations you need to perform are:

- Normalizing
- Limiting of peaks or spikes
- Reduction of sampling rate
- Reduction of bit depth (dithering)

Other editing techniques include fade in, fade out, amplify, reverb, equalize, and noise gate. If you don't know what these are, you shouldn't be doing them. Be aware that combining several sounds into one file can increase the amplitude; the combined sound is louder than any of the individual sounds. You may need to adjust for this. You should do all editing to create the sound you want before preparing the sound for the Web as described in the upcoming section, "Bringing Audio to the Web."

Referring to the figures when reading the following paragraphs is helpful, as the descriptive language of sound editing generally refers to the visual representation of the sound. Sounds for the Web are destined to become 8-bit, so the sound must be optimized so that as little as possible is lost when conversion, or dithering, occurs. Dithering is comparable to taking the resolution down in a pixelated image.

Normalizing enables you to increase the entire waveform as much as possible without cutting off any peaks (clipping). Figures 6.16 and 6.17 show the effect of the Normalize command in SoundEdit 16. If the sound levels were set correctly during the recording process, this may not be necessary. Normalizing is generally recommended; there are times, however, when Normalizing will lose crucial subtleties in the sound. This should be the last part of editing before the sampling down.

figure 6.16

A sound before normalization in SoundEdit 16.

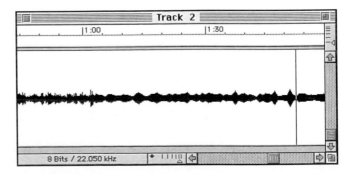

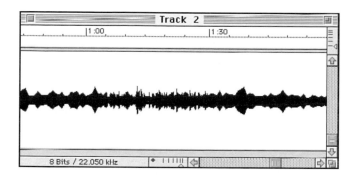

figure 6.17

A sound after normalization in SoundEdit 16.

TIP

The L1 filter, a tool available from Waves Technology, converts files to 8-bit/22 KHz, making adjustments for optimum results. This works with Adobe Premiere and most audio programs.

Applying the Normalize command sometimes seems to have no effect. Because Normalize does not enable any area of the sound to be cut off or clipped, if there is a peak in the waveform, the sound cannot be boosted (see Figure 6.18). The peak or *spike* defines one end of the dynamic range (softest to loudest). Because the dynamic range is limited, especially in 8-bit sound, the rest of the sounds are crowded at the low end of the range. The best idea here is to re-record the sound, avoiding the spike. However, if you are stuck with a poorly recorded sound from another source, edit the peak to bring it down. Beware, though, that over-editing, especially if you are not an expert, can do more harm than good.

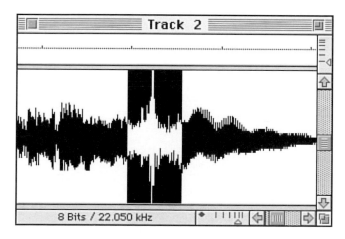

figure 6.18

An example of a spike.

Be sure you perform all desired editing, combining of sounds, and tweaking before you perform the last two steps of sampling down and dithering (reducing bit depth). Figures 6.19 and 6.20 show how these operations are performed in SoundEdit 16; other applications have similar commands.

figure 6.19

Bringing down the
sample rate.

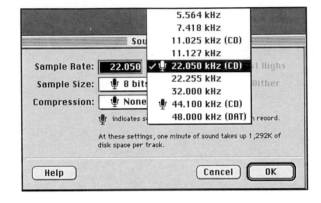

figure 6.20

Bringing down the
bit depth to 8-bit.

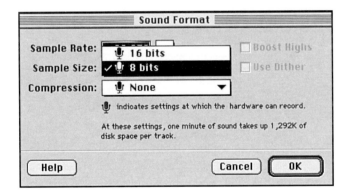

Always keep a copy of your final mix at the higher bit depth and sampling rate. If you need to go back in and make changes, do it to the larger file.

Audio Software

We mentioned earlier that traditional sound studio equipment to record, mix, and edit audio costs tens of thousands of dollars. Luckily there are applications that run on almost any desktop computer and do an acceptable job for most purposes. These programs are moderately priced when compared to graphics programs and other multimedia authoring tools. In addition there are small shareware programs that fill many specific needs.

SoundEdit 16 Version 2

Macromedia

http://www.macromedia.com/software/sound/

SoundEdit 16 is a cross-platform product offering a large array of audio editing capabilities at mid-range cost. A SoundEdit 16 file's icon (on Macintosh) is shown in Figure 6.21. Version 2 works specifically with AfterBurner audio compression for use on the Web. This version also offers more efficient disk usage and an easier user interface (see Figure 6.22). One of SoundEdit 16's downfalls is the length of time required for processing effects.

figure 6.21

Icon for sound file created by SoundEdit 16.

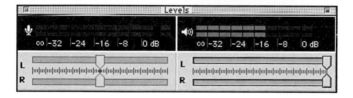

figure 6.22

Recording levels in SoundEdit 16.

DECK II 2.5

Macromedia

http://www.macromedia.com/software/sound/

This powerful, reasonably priced audio software originally from OSC was created for the Mac. DECK II was designed for serious creators and educators who don't have the luxury of large corporate funding. It has an excellent reputation for its multiple features that enable easy manipulation of detail. You can record layered tracks and use the software sound mixer to create effects, fade in and out, and so on. Version 2.5 includes numerous features that make DECK II appealing to the Web designer. It ships as a part of Macromedia Director Multimedia Studio. DECK II's downside is its interface, which has a "harsh" feeling to us, and the documentation is relatively mediocre.

Sonic Foundry Sound Forge

Macromedia
`http://www.macromedia.com/software/sound/`

This is the Windows option for Deck II 2.5 in the Macromedia Director Multimedia Studio package. Sonic Foundry Sound Forge enables you to play and record sound on any Windows-compatible sound card, edit channels in stereo files, and apply effects. You can also change the bit depth and sampling rate of sounds.

ProTools

Digidesign
`http://www.digidesign.com/`

This Digidesign program is considered by many sound professionals to be the premier digital audio editing software of choice. Originally created for the Mac as a hardware-based digital editing system, recent advances in the Power Mac architecture eliminated the need for additional external hardware. All the original power and tools of the program are now available for the desktop. ProTools features non-destructive editing and cross-fading (combining different samples with no noticeable seams). It has the capability to create a single sound file out of many sound files and to create mono files from a stereo sound file. With ProTools all audio editing is done within the program and the files are saved as digital files on the computer before they are placed on a server for users to download.

Session

Digidesign

`http://www.digidesign.com/`

This cross-platform digital sound studio application is by Digidesign. Session gives you much of the power of a high-end studio at a fraction of the cost. It is similar in many respects to DECK II, but the interface is friendlier and more intuitive. Figure 6.23 shows you the major panels for the application: the control panel on the right, the editor in the center, and the mixer on the right. Session is designed to work with Digidesign's Audiomedia II sound card, which enables multiple input channels.

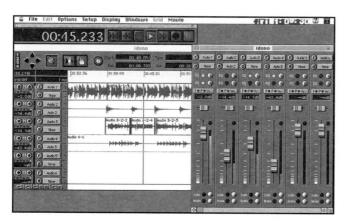

figure 6.23

The control, editor, and mixer panels in Session.

Adobe Premiere

Adobe Inc.

`http://www.adobe.com/prodindex/premiere/`

If you do not have a separate audio editing program, you can handle basic functions within Adobe Premiere. Audio can be captured with a microphone using Capture/Audio from the File menu. You can layer separate audio tracks (up to 99), control the volume of each, and apply faders to each as a primitive mixing environment. You can export audio only as a QuickTime movie (not as an AIFF, .wav, or .au file).

Shareware Audio Software

D-SoundPro enables you to do the basic minimum editing (normalize, limit peaks, reduce sampling rate, and bit depth).

SoundApp is a recorder only; you cannot use it for editing.

These programs and many more are available for both Mac and Wintel at the Shareware Music Machine at `http://www.hitsquad.com/smm/`.

File Formats

The most popular and most common cross-platform audio file formats are AIFF (Audio Interchange File Format) and WAV. These audio file formats were initially developed for the Mac and PC, respectively. The file extensions are .aiff (for Mac, .aif for Windows) and .wav. A file with the extension .aifc is a compressed AIFF file for Macintosh.

Other audio formats include μ-law (pronounced moolah), which use the suffix .au and so are often called AU files, and MPEG audio (suffix .mpeg for Mac, .mpg for Windows). AU files are not found on the Web very often; they were an early file format for the UNIX platform, and the sound quality is not as good as more recent formats. MPEG is an awkward file format because it not native to any platform, and you must have specific hardware (an MPEG card) to create the sound and specific software to play it.

RealAudio, which is described later in this chapter, takes files such as AIFF or WAV and encodes them into .ra files that work in the RealAudio environment.

MIDI files are not audio files, but they contain the data played as a piece of music. These files use the suffix .midi (for Mac) or .mid (for Windows).

Bringing Audio to the Web

If you haven't been around long in Web years (they're a lot like dog years), you might wonder what the big deal is about streaming audio. In the old days visitors to a site transferred an entire sound file to their own hard drives before they could hear it. The audio file was downloaded from the server, using FTP or email, then another program (such as SoundBlaster, SoundMachine, or MoviePlayer) launched to play the file. Recent browser developments offer a new option: inline plug-ins that enable sound files to be played without leaving the browser and start playing before the entire file is downloaded (streaming). Many browsers can now read embedded sound file formats or you have the option of using QuickTime, Shockwave, or RealAudio systems to deliver your sound.

The last section of the chapter reviews the following:

- How to embed sound files into your HTML, and how browsers play them

- Using QuickTime, Shockwave, and RealAudio

- The pros and cons of using each of these methods

- A case study where the technology was used

Sound Files in HTML

Here we are discussing taking a sound file in its original format, which could be AIFF, AU, WAV or MIDI, and getting the browser to call upon and play the sound. How the file is played within a browser depends on the browser, browser version, how it is configured, and so on. (Netscape 3. 0, for example, has the LiveAudio plug-in built in, and it plays all of these formats. Internet Explorer can play them as well.) Therefore, the actual playing of the file is out of the control of the designer.

The Pros and Cons of Sound files in HTML

The pros include the following:

- Cross-platform support; many plug-ins and helper apps will play these sounds

- No special server configuration needed

- Easy HTML syntax

- Most players enable the listcner to stop, start, and pause the sound playback

259

The cons include the following:

- No control over what player is used

- No streaming; sound must download completely to play

- No sychronizing with animation or video

- Sound plays automatically (unless triggered by JavaScript)

Having no control over what player is used is especially significant to designers when we don't want the look of the page disrupted by a player control panel. You can eliminate the player (at least in Netscape 3.0) by specifying a very small height and width for the file in the HTML; there simply isn't room to display the player. Then, however, your visitor will not be able to stop, start, or pause the playback.

To embed sounds in the HTML, you use the EMBED tag as follows:

```
<EMBED SRC="mysound.wav">

<EMBED SRC="mysound.au">

<EMBED SRC="mysound.mid(i)">

<EMBED SRC="mysound.aif(f)">
```

The parentheses indicate the fourth letter of the suffix used on the Macintosh platform only. After the filename, before the closing bracket, you can specify several factors (choose either TRUE or FALSE):

- `AUTOSTART=TRUE/FALSE` (to begin automatically/wait for user)

- `LOOP=TRUE/FALSE` (to loop/not to loop)

- `CONTROLS=TRUE/FALSE` (to show control panel/not)

Note that EMBED is a Netscape tag, but Internet Explorer supports it.

Explorer recommends you insert sound files by using its Background Sound tag:

```
<BGSOUND SRC="mysound.au>

<BGSOUND SRC="mysound.wav>

<BGSOUND SRC="mysound.mid(i)>
```

You can set a loop for a certain number of repeats or continuous:

- `LOOP=3` (to play three times)

- `LOOP=4` (to play four times)

- `LOOP=INFINITE` (to play continuously)

AIFF files are not supported by Internet Explorer's BGSOUND tag, and it remains to be seen if Netscape adopts this tag. We would recommend a "wait and see" position.

QuickTime

QuickTime is becoming more popular as a delivery mechanism because it combines video (or animation) and audio. The QuickTime plug-in required to see (or hear) multimedia files is becoming more widely distributed, often being packaged with browsers. Its greatest advantage over the methods discussed in the previous section is that you can synchronize the sound with animation or video. Even if you are not seeking this combination, you might use QuickTime to take advantage of the option it provides of a viewer-initiated click on/off interface, choosing only between autoplay or a controller. When you make a sound file into a QuickTime movie, it is no longer a standard audio file but a .mov file.

> **NOTE**
>
> A full discussion of QuickTime can be found in the QuickTime section of Chapter 7, which discusses bringing video to the Web.

The Pros and Cons of Using QuickTime for Audio

The pros include the following:

- Can synchronize audio with video or animation within a movie

- Can use looping and palindrome (forward, back, forward, and so on) sound within the EMBED command in HTML

- You have the option of showing the controller or not

- Sound can play or wait for initiation by visitor

- Plug-in comes with Netscape 3.0 for Windows and Macintosh and is available for all major platforms

- Can include MIDI files that work with QuickTime Musical Instruments (better quality than MIDI out of other browser players)

- No special server configuration needed

The cons include the following:

- No sound compression; must take down file size prior to making it into a QuickTime movie.

- 90% of sound must be loaded before sound begins to play

- You must have plug-in to hear sound

- Interactivity is limited to stop and start

Embedding QuickTime in HTML

For the CD-ROM accompanying this book, we wanted to present sound files of different bit depths and sampling rates so that you could compare the quality for yourself (refer back to Table 6.1). Although most of these files are too large to deliver efficiently over the Web, we embedded them into HTML for easy browsing on the CD-ROM. We chose to make these files, which were originally AIFF files, into QuickTime movies (.mov files) and embed them into an HTML page. This was primarily because we are not fond of the player windows that open in the browser with LiveAudio and the like. Here we will review the process.

Open each file in MoviePlayer (on Windows you would use MediaPlayer). Choose Save As and then choose Make movie self-contained (see Figure 6.24). This saves the file as a QuickTime movie, but you must add .mov as a suffix to the filename. Open the file in Internet Movie Tool to alter the file's coding sequence so that the movie plays correctly on the Web (see the QuickTime section in Chapter 7 for more details).

figure 6.24

*Making a sound file
into a self-contained
QuickTime movie in
MoviePlayer.*

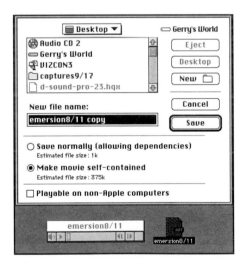

NOTE

Internet Movie Tool's interface looks like a simple Open File dialog box (see Figure 6.25). Choose the file and click Open. The interface here is rather confusing because absolutely nothing happens at this point; you still have the same dialog box with a choice of Open or Cancel. Internet Movie Tool has indeed performed its function, and you can cancel or go on to the next file. Luckily you can drag and drop the files onto the Internet Movie Tool icon.

figure 6.25

This is the only
dialog box or
window in Internet
Movie Tool!.

Your files are now ready, so it's on to writing the HTML. Here is a simple example:

```
<EMBED SRC="emersion16-44.mov">
```

However, you can control many attributes using the QuickTime approach, more than with the straight audio format files. You can decide whether the control bar appearst...

```
CONTROLLER=TRUE/FALSE
```

whether the sound starts automatically...

```
AUTOPLAY=TRUE/FALSE
```

whether the sound will loop...

```
LOOP=TRUE/FALSE
```

or whether it will play forward, back, forward, and so on (palindrome)...

```
LOOP=PALINDROME
```

263

All of these should appear within the brackets of the EMBED tag. See Chapter 7 for a complete description of syntax for embedding QuickTime movies (including Explorer alternatives to the EMBED command).

WARNING

One setting you should avoid is PLAYEVERYFRAME=TRUE, which turns off the audio track of a movie.

A QuickTime Example: SoundbYtes

Because original sound design is one of our strengths at bYte a tree productions, it made sense to display some of our talent at our own site.

You have heard how we think of sound as an atmospheric condition. We decided to allow visitors to create their own atmosphere live on the Web. If at all possible, you should browse the SoundbYtes file on the CD-ROM, or visit the site before reading the discussion below. It will make a lot more sense.

The page consists of 10 colored squares that are QuickTime movies (see Figure 6.26). The movies are audio-only (the visual of the colored square does not change). Instead of the sounds playing automatically, visitors need to click each sound on and off (instructions are given for Mac and Windows). Using the on and off clicking, visitors can activate as many of the sounds as they choose to play simultaneously.

figure 6.26

The final Web page of SoundbYtes accessed from `http://www. vizbyte.com/ sound/.`

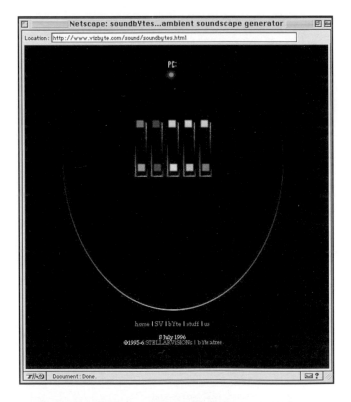

The sounds we chose needed to be as small as possible, and had to work well with each other in all kinds of combinations. Most were embedded into HTML with the PLAY=LOOP command, so they had to loop smoothly to achieve a "seamless" effect. The most time-consuming part of the project was selecting sounds that worked well and could fulfill different roles in creating chaos, serenity, city, country, and that irritating pay phone that won't stop ringing. Our favorite was the combination of an organ grinder, the monkeys, and then the "stamp" played at once.

TIP

Looping is an excellent way to make a short sound have a much longer duration; however, the joint between the repeats should not be audible!

Because the sounds were not musical pieces, the sampling rate was brought down to 11KHz and the bit depth to 8-bit. This was necessary to have the sounds load quickly because QuickTime does not compress sound. The associated degradation was acceptable as long as the sounds were still recognizable and had the desired effect. Other sounds were eliminated because they could not withstand the degradation and maintain their desired effect.

Normally when building a QuickTime movie, we work in Adobe Premiere. Premiere's smallest frame size, however, is 100 pixels and we wanted a small visual image to reduce loading time. We decided to build the file in Macromedia Director using a 16×16-pixel stage (see Figure 6.27). All sounds were imported into one Director file (see Figure 6.28). For each sound file, the color of the 16×16 pixel background was changed. Each color and sound was exported as a separate QuickTime movie. Each movie was embedded separately into the HTML. When we got to 12 sounds, the movie was too slow to load, so we eliminated two but could not part with any others.

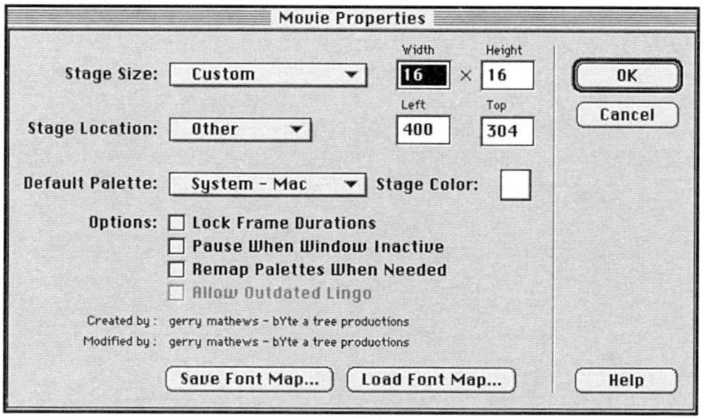

265

figure 6.27

Setting up the 16×16 pixel stage in Director.

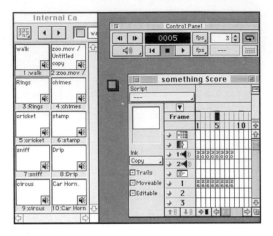

figure 6.28

All 10 sounds were combined in one Director file.

TIP

One sound was not looped; it plays forward and backward (we call it the "stamp"). This was achieved by setting LOOP=PALINDROME in the EMBED tag.

Shockwave: From Macromedia Director Files to the Web

A detailed discussion of using Shockwave to bring Macromedia Director files to the Web is in the Shockwave for Director section of Chapter 8, discussing the strong point of Shockwave and Director: interactivity. However, it is worth discussing separately here because the new version of Shockwave released in July of 1996 brought high-quality audio at low baud rates with its Afterburner compression. The hype accompanying the release proved to be accurate as long as the quality isn't too high and the baud rate isn't too low. You can compress audio up to 176:1, which is pretty impressive. So, the biggest advantages to using Shockwave are interactivity and excellent sound compression and audio streaming. The biggest disadvantage applies only if you don't own or aren't familiar with Macromedia Director; then you have a learning curve and expense between you and Shockwave.

The Pros and Cons of Using Shockwave for Audio

The pros include the following:

- Stream audio

- Audio compression with AfterBurner brings down the size of files considerably

- No special server configuration needed

- Plug-in comes with Netscape 3.0 and Explorer

- Integration into an interactive animated Shockwave presentation

The cons include the following:

- Shockwave plug-in required for Netscape 3 and Explorer 3

- Must create separate paths for each connection speed that you wish to address (ISDN, 28.8, 14.4, and so on)

- Server must be configured for Shockwave movies

A Shockwave Example: The bYte Gun

We mentioned in Chapter 5 that we have a "toy box" at `vizbYte.com` to give site visitors small presents to take home and play with. The bYte gun began as a downloadable Macromedia presentation, and with the improved Afterburner compression we brought it live to the Web. You might want to browse the HTML page with the toy on the CD-ROM or live before reading this discussion, or see it online at `http://www.vizbyte.com/livestuff/bytegun.html`.

Sounds in this toy are a reward for finding the right hot spot (since the toy comes with no instructions), and we wanted something goofy that would put a smirk on visitors' faces. One of the sounds we call "Yea!" consists of game-show-contestant-style "winner music," but instead of a crowd of clapping fans, there is an unenthusiastic audience of one.

The bars of "contestant winner" music were played on a keyboard and recorded into SoundEdit 16. The clapping and "YEA!" were recorded with a studio-quality microphone through the mixer into SoundEdit 16. The two sounds were pieced together one after the other. To save memory, the result was formatted in SoundEdit 16 to 8-bit/22 KHz using Save As to keep the original (SoundEdit 16 adds "copy" to the filename). We imported the sound into Macromedia Director and wrote a Lingo script (which you can find on the CD-ROM) calling upon the sound when the mouse clicked the "hot spot" (see Figure 6.29).

figure 6.29

Lingo script in Director calls upon sound when the mouse clicks the hot spot.

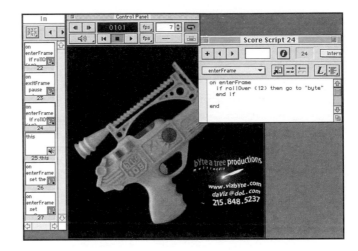

Another sound reward was "bYte a tree, bYte a tree, bYte a tree productions." This script was typed into SimpleText, selected, and using the "whisper" voice that comes with the new Macintosh system, we had the Macintosh "read" the script aloud. We sent this sound out from the Macintosh to the mixer/recorder. It was played back and recorded into SoundEdit 16, coming full circle. Using layers and pitch controls in SoundEdit 16, we distorted the sound to be even stranger than it already was.

All sounds were brought into Director as AIFF files and each had its own "hot spot." To take advantage of the great audio compression of Shockwave we set the compression rate in Director. Selecting Audio Compression Under from the Extras menu enables setting the compression for specific connection speeds (28.8 or 14.4 bits per second) (see Figure 6.30). The actual compression takes place when you "burn" the file, but you must set the audio compression in advance.

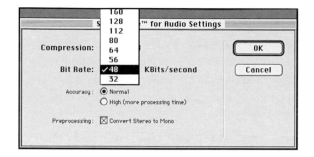

When the presentation was completed and saved, we chose Afterburner from the Xtras menu (in Director 5), which converts the movie into a compressed (ready for the Web) presentation with a .dcr suffix. The movie was then called upon in the HTML as follows:

```
<EMBED SRC="bytegun.dcr">
```

Refer to Chapter 8, the Shockwave section, to read about various attributes that can be specified for a Shockwave presentation on the Web.

RealAudio: The Stand-Alone Format

```
http://www.realaudio.com
```

Made by Progressive Network, Inc., RealAudio utilizes an interactive system between the RealAudio Server and the RealAudio Player for real-time audio delivery over the Net. When a visitor/listener clicks a RealAudio link on a Web page, the audio buffers and begins to play, all within a few seconds. This is true streaming. This gives impression that the RealAudio file is linked directly to the Web page.

When writing HTML documents, links to other documents are shown as URL addresses. Because RealAudio files are live on the RealAudio Server and must be retrieved by the RealAudio Player, extra steps must be taken to complete the network path linking the audio file to the viewed page. When the user clicks the RealAudio link, a metafile (extension .RAM) is activated that sends the location of the RealAudio file to the RealAudio Player. The file is requested and returned in a matter of seconds. Pretty darn cool. The biggest drawback is the price of the RealAudio Server (which is going down all the time).

RealAudio comes in two parts:

- **RealAudio Player 2.0** is available for Windows, Macintosh, and UNIX platforms and requires a 14.4 Kbps modem or better. When you click a RealAudio link in the Web browser the RealAudio Player appears and plays the sound without download delays. RealAudio Player has controls like a CD player. You can pause, rewind, fast-forward, stop, start and adjust the volume (See Figure 6.31). It also tells you how much time is left in the broadcast.

figure 6.31

This is the control panel for the RealAudio Player.

- **RealAudio Plug-In** enables designers to integrate RealAudio into their Web page layouts. Interactive components such as play, pause, fast-forward buttons, and volume sliders can easily be placed anywhere on the page with the same control that HTML offers for graphics using the IMG tag.

270

Configure your HTTP server to recognize the .RPM extension as the MIME type audio/x-pn-realaudio-plugin. Web servers are configured in different ways. Follow the instructions for configuring for .RAM files, and add an additional entry for a .RPM file and audio/x-pn-realaudio-plugin. For more information on MIME types, see Appendix B.

The Pros and Cons of Using RealAudio

The pros include the following:

- Audio-on-demand over 14.4 Kbps and faster Internet connections

- Streaming enables long playtime

- Live cybercasts, including concerts, breaking news, and other live events.

- You can link to RealAudio files on a RealAudio Server

- Optimal sound quality for your connection speed

- Firewall support

- Ability to embed URLs in the .RA files to trigger the loading of new Web pages.

The cons include the following:

- RealAudio is server-based, so you need to buy the RealAudio Server

- Requires server configuration

- Metafiles are required to point to RealAudio files

- Music-quality audio requires a 28.8 Kbps or faster connection

- You can't customize the look of playback controls.

NOTE

Viewing pages that use plug-ins requires Netscape Navigator 2.0 or later. The RealAudio plug-in is installed by the RealAudio Player 2.0 setup program if Netscape is detected.

The HTML

The EMBED tag describes plug-ins in HTML pages, much in the same way that the IMG tag describes images. Many options are available to customize your pages; however, the basic EMBED tag for RealAudio contains only the three attributes shown below:

Syntax: `<EMBED SRC=source_URL WIDTH=width_value HEIGHT=height_value>`

Example: `<EMBED SRC="sample1.rpm" WIDTH=300 HEIGHT=134>`

The WIDTH AND HEIGHT attributes specify the size of the embedded component. Unlike images, plug-ins do not size automatically. The WIDTH and HEIGHT can be specified in pixels (the default) or percentage (WIDTH=100%).

TIP

It is best to choose a size in pixels; however, if you want to stretch the control to fit the entire browser window, use a WIDTH=100% tag. This option is effective with the Position Slider and StatusBar.

The following attributes are specific to the RealAudio plug-in.

With the CONTROLS attribute, the following values enable you to embed individual controls from the RealAudio Player into your HTML layout. You can use multiple EMBED statements to construct a custom interface made up of individual controls.

- CONTROLS=All embeds a full Player view including the ControlPanel, InfoVolumePanel, and StatusBar. This is the default view if no CONTROLS attribute is specified.

- CONTROLS=ControlPanel embeds the Play/Pause button, the Stop button, and the Position slider (same as the Player application with none of the options on the View menu checked).

- CONTROLS=InfoVolumePanel embeds the information area showing title, author, and copyright with a Volume Slider on the right-hand side (same as the panel displayed by the Player application when the Info & Volume option on the View menu is checked).

- CONTROLS=InfoPanel is similar to InfoVolumePanel. It embeds the information area showing title, author, and copyright *without* the Volume Slider.

- CONTROLS=StatusBar embeds the Status Bar showing informational messages, current time position, and clip length (same as the panel displayed by the Player application when the Status Bar option on the View menu is checked).

- CONTROLS=PlayButton embeds the Play/Pause button.

- CONTROLS=StopButton embeds the Stop button.

- CONTROLS=VolumeSlider embeds the Volume Slider.

- `CONTROLS=PositionSlider` embeds the Position Slider (scroll bar).

- `CONTROLS=PositionField` embeds the field of the Status Bar showing Position and Length.

- `CONTROLS=StatusField` embeds the field of the Status Bar displaying message text and progress indicators.

NOTE

> Adding an `AUTOSTART=TRUE` attribute to an `EMBED` tag tells the RealAudio Plug-In to begin playing when the page is visited. Use this feature to begin a narration or play background music.

To create RealAudio files, you must have the RealAudio Encoder, which compresses the files into RealAudio format for delivery over the Web (suffix .ra). For more information, see `http://www.realaudio.com`.

The RealAudio player interface is quite large and sometimes seems a bit cumbersome, but it is customizable in the number of fields you show. Here the title, author, and copyright information is available. As a designer who is concerned that intellectual property is protected, this is a welcome part of the interface. Fair warning is given; those who listen to and download sounds should be aware if those sounds are in the public domain.

273

Other Audio Options

If your audio toolbox isn't full already, there are other options for bringing audio to the Web, though most of these require the user to download a plug-in or the Webmaster to buy a proprietary server add-on. But if your needs require something else, the following options might be worth a look.

- Crescendo Plus (`http://www.liveupdate.com/crescendo.html`). For streaming MIDI. Mac and Windows.

- EchoSpeech (`http://www.echospeech.com/plugin.htm`). High-quality compressed speech files. Windows only.

- Koan (`http://www.sseyo.com/`). For music files created with Koan Pro. Windows only.

- ListenUp (`http://snow.cit.cornell.edu/noon/ListenUp.html`). Speech recognition technology. Power Mac only.

- RapidTransit (`http://monsterbit.com/rapidtransit/`). Another highly compressed streaming format. Windows 95 only.

- ShockTalk (`http://www.surftalk.com/shocktalk/`). Speech recognition add-on for Shockwave for Director. Mac only.

- Speech (`http://www.albany.net/~wtudor/`). For making your Web page "say" the text on it. Mac only.

- Talker (`http://www.mvpsolutions.com/PlugInSite/Talker.html`). Another plug-in for making Web pages talk. Mac only.

- ToolVox (`http://www.voxware.com/`). A streaming format like RealAudio. Windows and Power Mac.

- TrueSpeech (`http://www.dspg.com/plugin.htm`). A streaming audio player for Netscape. Windows only.

chapter

7

 *Stella Gassaway*

Video: Frame by Frame

We've heard it said that with video the Web will become more and more

like television. At hYte a tree this is a frightening thought. As designers we

have a responsibility to be a force that prevents the dumbing down of a

medium with so much promise; a promise of truly interactive, educational

and informative media where entertainment is only part of the equation,

not the sum of the parts.

Television is passive. The promise of the Web is that it demands interaction. (We will talk much more about the positive effects of interactivity in Chapter 8.) The television-like aspects of the Web, however, become much more obvious with the introduction of video. Our vigilance ensures we are using video in a Web-like way and not giving viewers the impression that they might as well be channel surfing.

The primary limitations of video use have been and continue to be technological, but these barriers are being lowered daily, with much accompanying hype. As Web designers we are now promised smoothly running video of indefinite length, improved image and sound quality, and short download time. What makes this possible? Compression, better compression, and *clever* compression. Although still primarily targeted to the high bandwidth, powerful CPU crowd, the elitism of video is being eroded week by week. Web designers are now being offered a serious, high-powered multimedia tool.

The race to deliver quality video from within Web pages has been driven by an obsession for moving images. Designers expect the Web to be more than text and links. Technology is being driven to meet the demands of the site designers. The primary focus of this chapter, therefore, will be design considerations and general principles of incorporating video into a site. In addition we will briefly outline basic concepts of the medium of video (especially compression), mention some software for working with video, tell how to bring it to the Web, and discuss two case studies.

There is a fine line between video and animation. Live-action footage is video; a series of illustrated characters is animation. But what if the drawn characters are moving on a background of manipulated still photographs of real locations? Or what if it is not drawings but type and effects from Photoshop flying past you? Our [e]mersion movie (see Figure 7.1) on the CD-ROM, for example, we have called video, not animation, but there is no live footage in it whatsoever! (see the Case Study section at the end of this chapter for how it was done.) Check out the opop movie (see Figure 7.2) on the CD-ROM; is this video or animation? In general, if there is a clearly "drawn" feeling to the images, or if there is a very limited number of frames in the series (like the animated hand at dezine café), we have classified them as animations.

figure 7.1

The feeling of film in [e]mersion without live footage.

figure 7.2

The drawn quality of the opop movie is obvious in this figure.

Design Challenges

I can remember that even when I was only eight years old I wanted to make my drawings move. I would make multiple pages like a flip book and as I flipped them made accompanying sounds. I made the animals talk and airplanes roar. When I was in high school I made story boards for what of course was my invention…music videos. I wanted to create images that illuminated the story the music told. My generation experienced the first "theme" record album, the Beatles' Sergeant Pepper's Lonely Hearts Club Band, and *Woodstock,* the documentary with split-screen movies and the evolution of video walls. The idea of "mixed media" has been in my mind for quite some time.

The more sophisticated the multimedia elements we choose to use, the greater the design challenge. More than any other multimedia element, video has the capacity to be disruptive and distracting at a Web site. While audio or animation can be more easily used with a light touch to enhance the site, video is much harder to introduce gently. As long as there is a movie on-screen, the visitor is unlikely to pay attention to any other content.

At bYte a tree productions, our goal is to integrate elements into the site, making the interface as transparent as possible. To us this means navigating and activating multimedia elements with ease. The viewer will "know" how to make a movie play because we have worked hard to anticipate the viewer's reactions and needs.

Whether or not to integrate video in the main browser window or to open another independent staging area depends on the interface, how the movie should be viewed, and whether the viewer will have control over playing the movie.

The big tip we can give you about video is to use it judiciously. The size of files, even for a few seconds of video at the standard 160×120, is large. Add audio and you are going to have to work hard to keep 16 or so seconds below 2 megabytes. However, if the video is informational and very important to your audience, make it available to them. Let them choose to wait or not.

Another way to cope with making video available is to create a menu that shows a screen grab from the video clip and notifies you of the estimated download time. We suggest notifying the visitor to the site about any elements that require plug-ins or waiting time in advance. Don't leave the visitor wondering how long it will take.

It is very disconcerting to have new windows popping up without knowing it's going to happen. To soften the blow, control the size of the new window. Your viewers will thank you for it.

We will review some sites using video in different ways and see what advantages are gained by asking two questions:

- How does the use of video enhance the purpose of the site?

- Is the Web the sensible way to view this video?

Promoting Movies

Video clips on the Web can be used effectively to promote mainstream or alternative films.

In the same way that record labels were among the first to introduce audio clips to promote their artists, sites belonging to major and independent movie studios have chosen the Web and video to promote movies. Most of the clips available are trailers shown on television or as previews at movie theaters. Some are clips from the films or scenes reviewers have spoken highly about when reviewing the movie. At the popular `http://www.missionimpossible.com` we were actually less interested in trailers for the movie itself than in their wonderful archive of clips from the original TV show (see Figure 7.3). This was a great use of video because:

- This footage is not generally available

- Even those with slower connections (if fans of the show, like us) are willing to wait for the download.

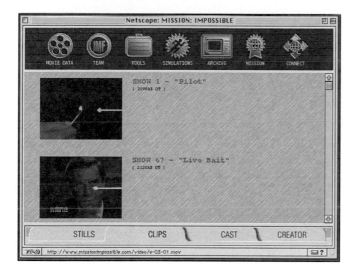

figure 7.3

The archive section at the Mission Impossible site at `http://www. missionimpossible. com/g/index- frm.shtml.`

The use of video at this site is smartly integrated into the interface with the use of screen captures to help identify content and file sizes to notify the viewer of download time expectations. An excellent enhancement to the content at this site, video is one of many interactive experiences and toys.

Our only objection to the interface was experiencing an additional large empty Netscape window popping up with the much smaller movie frame in the middle of the blank page. Specifying the size of the browser window that pops up to neatly fit your movie size is a friendlier way to handle the situation; we resized our window to view the clip (see Figure 7.4). We must have watched the opening credits of the pilot Mission Impossible show (complete with music) at least a dozen times. Then as all good fans do, we cleverly clicked the image and chose Save Movie As so we can show it to our friends!

figure 7.4

The opening credits of the original Mission Impossible TV show.

Keep in mind copyright infringement. Check information at the site or `http://www.copyright.org`.

> **WARNING**
>
> Because anyone can download your movie, play, and copy it, be sure that you (and your client) are comfortable with this before you put it on the Web. Obviously, anyone who steals clips for use in their own work is breaking the law, but keeping a favorite clip for future viewing is a commonly accepted practice.

Because I Am (`http://www.becauseiam.com`) is a movie site for an independent documentary film. A winner of the Apple QuickTime Web Challenge, it incorporates four video clips from the film, a compelling story about a woman living with AIDS. This site is an online media kit for the film that has five sections: movie, credits, publicity, distribution, and production notes. The use of video clips is essential because the site's goal is to sell and find a distributor for the film.

A few things to take note of at this site: The interface confused us. When we arrived at the site using Netscape 3.0 a new frame opened, leaving an open browser window empty on our desktop. Nothing else becomes active in that space during the entire visit. The interface does inform you of the size of the clips; it isn't that obvious, however, what the clips are about even after reading their titles. In Figure 7.5 you can see the interface and the elements used to navigate through the site. As the movie is playing the control bar enables you to replay, stop, and adjust the volume. Throughout the site there is information about the video project and the goals behind it (see Figure 7.6).

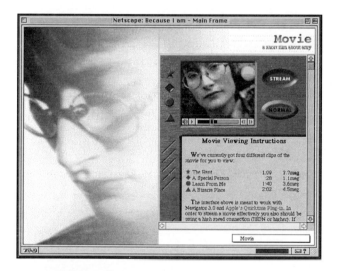

figure 7.5

Movie clip section of the Because I Am site.

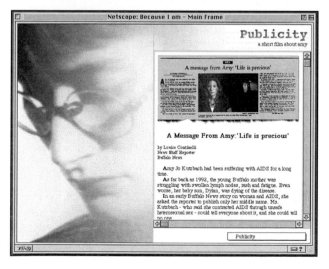

figure 7.6

Publicity screen explains more of the story behind the movie.

The movies are large but worth the wait. The story is compelling, so you'll find yourself downloading all of the clips to see as much of the story as possible.

Journalism

CNN: `http://www.cnn.com`

MSNBC: `http://www.msnbc.com`

c|net: `http://www.cnet.com`

ABC: `http://www.abc.com`

At these interactive network news sites, we see the possibilities opened up by incorporating the best of television, radio, and print: headline news, sound bites, and video footage. The short, fast-paced power of television is combined with the capability for immediate updates, not unlike radio. Substantial columns of text give in-depth stories—the best of print coverage. And, of course, hyperlinks to related subjects are the unique Web contribution.

CNN and MSNBC seek to enhance their stories with still images accompanied by audio clips. You listen to the President while looking at a still picture of him talking. How much would it really add to see his lips moving? The voice carries the emotion and inflection, and unless his face is extremely expressive, it doesn't seem worthwhile to introduce video. However, what about footage of the explosion at the Olympic Centennial Park?

Why would you "watch" the news on the Web instead of on your television? How many of us sit through inane news stories and advertisements waiting for the one topic that is of importance to us? On the Web you can skip stories that bore you or skim the text and skip the video. Also, you can play and replay the video (as well as read and reread the text). Often we don't realize we are interested in a news story on television until the last sentence, and then it is too late to go back and pay attention to the first part where they said *where* the plane crashed!

In Clement Mok's book *Designing Business* (published by Adobe Press) there is a discussion and prototype screen shots of "television on your computer"—Intercast. Intercast is where television and the Internet meet. This is the exciting hybrid that networks are looking forward to; the dovetail of digital information and broadcast signal. The new challenge for designers will be to visualize the transmission of these technologies in a way people will understand and be able to access. We can look toward this future.

So far the use of video clips has been sparing, but as the technology improves, the television news folks will be among the first to translate their video expertise and timely footage to the Web on a regular basis. This appears to be the premise (and promise) of MSNBC.

These small clips and interface efforts are training wheels for designers. We can experiment in these primitive environments and prepare for the future, which is closer than we think.

In Figure 7.7 you see a screen shot from a recent "front page" for `http://www.cnn.com`. The top story is an exclusive interview with the president. Links take you to the full story, a sound clip, or you can view the interview using VivoActive streaming video. If you select the link to the video interview, you are taken to another domain at the CNN site (`http://allpolitics.com`) where you find links to the VivoActive player CNN is using to create "streaming" video.

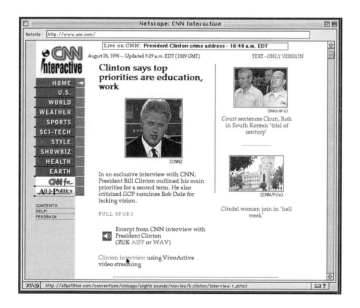

figure 7.7

A recent "front page" at `http://www.cnn.com`.

In this example the movie is integrated into the page. The movie begins to stream immediately.

The quality of this video is poor and the streaming, although it's supposed to be fine at 14.4bps, chugged when viewed. The audio was played way ahead of the video and reminded us of poorly dubbed foreign films. CNN's page is a pioneering effort but isn't very effective, although it supports the goals of the site (see Figure 7.8). The interview was broken into four segments, four separate clips from the interview. The visitor who chooses to see the interview automatically gets the first segment and then can choose to go on to the second or skip to the third or fourth. This is a nice mix of giving the viewer some choice but also being sure that the main point is achieved (through the first clip). Also, breaking the interview up into four segments, rather than one long clip, minimizes the impatience of the visitor waiting for something to happen.

figure 7.8

Clinton interview at http:// allpolitics.com.

Commercial Product Promotion

The Nice site (`http://www.benice.it/english/`) is another winner of the Apple QuickTime Challenge. The movies (see Figure 7.9 and 7.10) at this site have been repurposed from television commercials to movie art in a theme clip. The viewer has the opportunity to see each of the commercials and get an overall look at the site. Here you see the planning and creative thought of an ad campaign. This site will become a full-fledged marketing space for this company's watches.

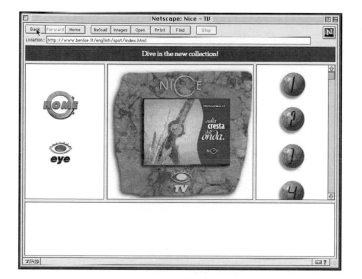

figure 7.9

First access to Nice video promotional clips.

figure 7.10

Promotional clip in context.

Creating postage stamp size images didn't work for me. The changes in the images were so subtle that you had to play them a few times to see what the theme of the commercial was. I think the movies would have been much more successful at twice the size. Download considerations are what probably lead to the small image size, however. The technical constraints due to bandwidth are a big deal when it comes to video, especially if they include audio. There are very few situations for which it is worthwhile to put up video for viewing. Promotion for movies or music videos are probably the best choices right now. Then again, if you are putting the video up on an intranet, say for training or a message from the CEO, it makes sense. But then again, by the time you buy this book there could be considerable changes that make video viable.

As always, know your audience. Will visitors have high-bandwidth access? Maybe then you'll want to get some clips up on the Net. Maybe your site will be used by service staff at a warranty repair center who want to see a video clip of how to replace a part. They'll probably wait a while for a movie to download.

Political Propaganda

Okay, it's a political year, so I couldn't resist. The Clinton/Gore re-election site uses the capabilities of video for propaganda purposes at `http://www.cg96.org/main/d/video/` (see Figure 7.11). Here edited clips of presidential stump speeches as well as policy speeches are available for download. The opening page for video clips uses television shaped images with a frame from the movie inside to give the feel of the video. Below is a caption with file format and size. A clean, well-thought-out presentation.

figure 7.11

Menu page for the video clips.

We downloaded a movie (see Figure 7.12) that appeared in its own window. The designers made clever use of a campaign button for the first frame. The quality of the video clips is pretty good, but the audio often goes up and down in volume. The editing of the clips is a bit rough, too. Still, this is a good use of video. Its integration into the site adds to the depth of information available.

figure 7.12

First frame of
the movie.

Remote Experience of an Event or Live Feed

The Web enables us to connect from remote geographical locations and share experiences to a greater or lesser extent. Most of the sites that have "cams" and show "live" shots are actually periodically updated stills from a video camera. (Remember the famous "fish cam" that had surfers flocking to see what the fish was doing? Well, it was a novelty at the time!) Corporate intranets, where the connections can be very fast, use video conferencing and live video feeds to save the plane fare of sending personnel around the globe.

At `http://live.apple.com/` Apple uses QuickTime Videoconferencing to host live events on the Web. At the 1996 Macworld event, Apple showed some of the speakers (in Figure 7.13 it was promoting the Cranberries live on September 27th). What is intimidating about preparing to view the site is the wide array of tools required (see Figure 7.14). As a ground-breaking novelty, to prove it can be done, it makes sense for Apple to present this site. Our advice is to visit it periodically to see how smoothly the latest technology works before you consider hosting something similar!

figure 7.13

Check out what
Apple is showing
live.

figure 7.14

All the tools that
you have to collect
to experience in the
live broadcast.

When is a live broadcast a good idea? Well, despite the fact that it seems like a huge technical challenge and a major expense to bring live video to the Web, it is less daunting than arranging a live television broadcast. Everything is relative! If you are talking about an event in which people are passionately interested, and the audience is connected at high bandwidth, then perhaps a live broadcast is just the thing to catapult your site into the stratosphere of popularity. The key is to promote the event well in advance so that you actually have an audience for the broadcast! If you do not already have high traffic at the site, consider promoting it in other media as well. Even if the live broadcast is the draw, there should be substance to the site if a broadcast is not occurring, as well as background on the subject of the event.

If, however, you have a good proportion of dial-up users in your audience, do them a favor and don't subject them to live video! Clips and highlights can convey the essence of many events; do we *really* need to hear that speech in full? Until we have more residential viewers connected through cable, this will remain primarily a business and intranet option.

Installments of an Event

Our studio is moving to new quarters that consist of 4,000 square feet of space. As of September 15, 1996, this was raw manufacturing space. As part of an effort to inform clients, peers, vendors, and friends about our progress, we created an event online. The online experience was supported for our mailing announcing the move, which gave the Web address for updates. We took a camcorder to the new studio to shoot a "before" pan of the space, which you can experience on the CD-ROM (see Figure 7.15 for a still example). This was put up at the vizbYte site updating the transformation of our studio. (See how we created this clip in the case study section at the end of this chapter.)

The challenge in creating this transformation was creating an interesting visual space and leaving room for the incorporation of additional movies. We didn't want the viewer to wait for one huge movie to load, so we decided to do a series of movies. The viewer could then play them in sequence to see the changes in the space. We also agreed that we would create a final movie of combined parts of the sequence that would include music and effects. This would replace the sequence of movies after the move was complete.

289

figure 7.15

Check out how
much progress we've
made since this at
`http://www.`
`vizbyte.com/`
`newspace.html`.

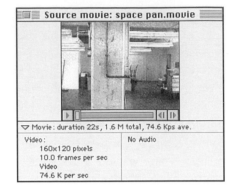

This movie would be the first in a series of projects to give visitors to the site a sense of our space and the people that are STELLARViSIONS | bYte a tree. We plan to add QuickTime VR and a walkthrough of the space. This will be one of the areas inviting visitors to return and see what's new. See how we created this clip in the case study section at the end of this chapter.

Informative Video

Here is one of the most enjoyable and well-designed examples of combined media on the Web. It begins on the first page of the Merce Cunningham Dance site (`http://www.merce.org`). The core page shows a map of images to many media examples that you can choose to experience (see Figure 7.16). A feast of online dance—where should we go first?

figure 7.16

The Merce
Cunningham Dance
opener.

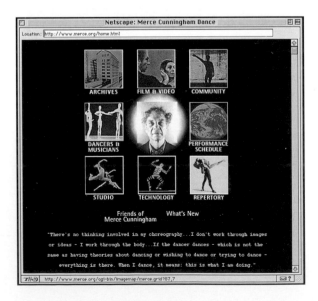

Being interested in how dance is "drawn" and designed, we chose to visit the Merce Cunningham living sketchbook by clicking the wireform figures labeled Technology. The sketchbook is physically located in the archives of the online publication HotWired. At `http://www.hotwired.com/kino/95/29/feature/` (see Figure 7.17) you can see the text and an illustration pertaining to a dance video available for viewing. When you touch the illustration, the size of the video file appears, so you know what you are getting into before you link to a page that holds the appropriate video. A video clip is an excellent choice to illustrate a few steps of a whole dance. With live dance accompanied by sound, you'll feel as though you were actually in the studio watching a rehearsal.

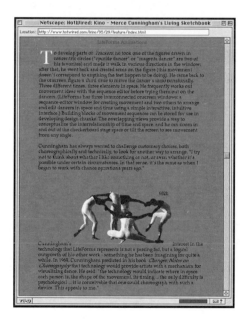

figure 7.17

A page from Merce Cunningham's Living Sketchbook.

This is a great way to create an archive of performances for public view that hasn't been available before. Not unlike music and movies, dance has a place on the Web, too. There are also animated sketches created from concentric circles available at the site. They are discussed in Chapter 5.

The use of video to illustrate moving art was the most appropriate choice at this site, and the clips have been carefully chosen to be adapted to the Web (see Figure 7.18). The folks there continue to inspire with the combination of intriguing content, excellent screen design, and creative interfaces. At first glance the sketchbook seems like a one-dimensional article; the movie clips, however, add another visitor-initiated dimension.

figure 7.18

Three captures from one dance.

Basic Video Concepts

As with audio, video is an area that requires professional expertise and experience. As multimedia designers and producers, we have to know what is possible and team up with the right collaborators.

This section outlines basic video terms and concepts.

NOTE

> If you have already been incorporating video as a component of digital multimedia work, you can skip this section!

A video signal begins as *light*, is translated into *electrical energy*, and is then digitized into bits of *data* that create a display on a computer monitor perceived by the eye, once again, as *light*.

NOTE

> This discussion assumes that the final viewing monitor for video delivered over the Web will be a computer monitor. There are substantial differences between computer monitors and video monitors (such as television sets) that raise thorny issues in desktop video production. While it may become common in the future to surf the Internet through your television monitor, today's standard for the Web is a 72-pixel-per-inch, 256-color (8-bit), RGB (red, green, blue) computer monitor.

When you're evaluating the quality of video, the quality of the *signal* is the key question. Therefore it is essential to understand the parts of a video signal:

- Luminance (contrast and brightness)
- Chrominance (red, green, blue plus saturation)
- Sync (timing control)

When these are kept as separate channels of information, the signal is called a *component* signal; when they are combined, the signal is *composite*. Composite video takes less memory, but when you duplicate it a great deal of quality is lost with each successive duplication or generation. (The original is first generation, the duplicate is second generation, a duplicate of the duplicate is third generation, and so on.) One great strength of component video is that it will stand up well for three to five generations without showing loss. Whether you have a component or composite signal depends upon the camera and tape used in shooting the video.

As with audio, you always want to begin with the highest-quality signal you can obtain, then you can pick and choose what to sacrifice on the bandwidth altar. Component video taken with a better-quality camera using better-quality film (Betacam, for example) yields substantially better results than a home VHS camcorder. In general, tapes and equipment fall into the three categories.

- Home use

- Industrial use (for corporate videos and the like)

- Professional or broadcast use

Hiring camera operators and renting equipment is often a practical solution, but it may be worth investing in a higher-end "home" camcorder to play around with, do tests, and explore possibilities.

NOTE

Interestingly enough, many television shows are shot using film. This is partly because the range of brightness film can capture is 100 to 1, and video's range of brightness is only 30 to 1 (the human eye can see a range of 1000 to 1). This is why even amateurs sense that video feels "flat" compared to film.

If you are given an existing tape, it is should be as few generations from the original as possible. If it is a VHS tape, a dupe is practically worthless because of the "drop out" and digital noise that makes it difficult to edit (to isolate an object or figure from the background, for example) and difficult to compress effectively. Better-quality tape and, especially, component video, stand up to duplication much better than VHS.

Examples of a Capture Card

The Perception capture card is one member of the Advanced Digital Video Workstation family by DPS. Considered mid-range in price, the Win32bit, PCI-based digital video disk recorder system has 10-bit video encoding, integrated SCSI controller, and video component In/Out. The Win32bit requires a Pentium 75 PC with 16MB RAM or DEC Alpha with 32MB RAM running Windows NT (or 95 on Intel chips). It has extremely high video quality, especially for its cost. Originally used for the playback of animation, the Win32bit is extremely fast. With the use of a good audio card, it can do full-blown video and audio editing with the addition of an external software package such as Adobe Premiere. The board includes an AVI conversion utility so that it works directly with the perception codec (see the section on video compression).

Other cards include Imagine 128 by Number Nine, a high-performance PCI card, moderate price for either Mac or Wintel. ATI is a reliable manufacturer of low-cost cards for either platform. In general, the cost of these cards is going down rapidly!

Once you have a video tape, the next step is to get the darned stuff into your computer. For this you need special hardware (unless you are lucky enough to have a Power Macintosh 8500 or other multimedia station with a built-in video digitizing card). The video capture board is a substantial investment; you would need to be doing more than home movies on the Web to justify the purchase! Be sure the board is QuickTime-compatible. The digitizing card compresses the video using hardware compression, which leads us into the discussion of the crucial issue of compression.

Video Compression

Unlike still images, compression was a huge issue for video long before the Web even entered the picture. The hard disk space required by large video files is only one aspect of the need for serious compression. Think for a moment about the file size of one 640×480-pixel, 24-bit color image. Think of how long it takes to appear on your computer screen. Now think about a series of these images being called up onto your screen one after another, 30 images in rapid succession in the space of one second. That is what would be required to play broadcast-quality video on your monitor!

Obviously, no desktop computer can process data at that rate. Even if bandwidth was unlimited and you could send that 30MB file through the Web instantly, your viewer's CPU would choke on the processing required. Since work with video on desktop computers began, compression/decompression schemes—called *codecs*—have been improved and specialized for different purposes.

In this section we will:

- Review steps to reduce file size

- Introduce the concept of data rate

- Compare lossless versus lossy compression

- Compare spatial versus temporal compression

- Discuss codecs: compression/decompression algorithms

- Give you a shortcut you won't be able to resist!

Reducing File Size

A codec always has two ends: compression and decompression. There are three other ways to drastically reduce file size that do *not* follow this model:

- Reducing color bit depth

- Reducing frame size (number of pixels)

- Reducing frames per second

We are discussing these issues here even though they are not compression *per se*, having no corresponding decompression, but the issue of trading off desired smaller file size against quality is the same.

Reducing 24-bit color to 8-bit is a logical sacrifice when bringing your video to the Web because chances are many of your viewers will have 8-bit monitors unless you have a very specialized audience. Reducing the color to 8-bit also improves how efficiently the file can be compressed, as you will see in a moment.

The frame size also has a large impact on file size. Generally, 640×480 pixels is referred to as "full-screen" and 320×240 pixels as "quarter screen." Even at Web sites that cater to higher bandwidths, I have never seen a video frame this large. The most common size for the Web is 160×120 pixels or 120×90 pixels. The key issue is whether the viewer can actually see anything at these small sizes! Figure 7.19 shows you the various proportions of these frame sizes.

TIP

It is crucial that there be plenty of light available when a video is shot if it is destined to become as small as 160×120 pixels. Dark movies become very difficult to see at a small frame size.

figure 7.19

Different

frame sizes.

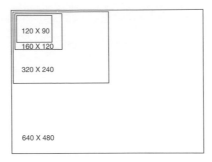

A third way to reduce file size is to reduce the number of frames per second. The standard rate in video is 30 frames per second. You have the option of setting your frame rate to 15 or even 10 frames per second (with visible loss of quality, check out the example on the CD-ROM called "video frame rates"). These are the only three frame rates that will work well with video captured with a standard camera (30 frames per second). On the CD-ROM accompanying this book you can see a video of young Elroy at 30 frames per second and at 10 frames per second, and see the difference in loading time and video quality. This 17-second clip is 2,800K at 30 frames per second and 990K at 10 frames per second.

NOTE

The rate 30 frames per second is standard for National Television Standards Committee (NTSC) video used in the United States and Japan; Europe uses PAL and SECAM, which have a rate of 25 frames per second. These can be reduced to 12.5 or 6.25 frames per second.

You set the frames per second in your video production software. In any QuickTime-friendly application, such as Adobe Premiere, you enter the frames per second in a standard compression dialog box (see Figure 7.20). The pop-up menu restricts you to recommended settings, but you can override these if you want (for some unusual reason).

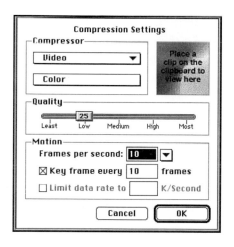

figure 7.20

The frames per second is set to 10 frames per second.

Kilobytes per Second: The Data Rate

We have been talking of reducing file size, but actually a key goal is to reduce the rate data must be processed at to a rate most desktop computers can handle comfortably. If you are planning to stream video over the Web (have it play while it is still downloading), the data rate is even more crucial. The formula for data rate is simple:

```
file size / length of movie = number of kilobytes / number of
seconds = K/sec
```

The Clinton/Gore campaign mini-movie (frame size 120×90 pixels), for example, is 1.9MB and plays for 31 seconds. That gives it a data rate of 66K/sec, which is really low! Generally movies on the Web are between 400K/sec and 800K/sec. If you are using MoviePlayer on the Macintosh, you can avoid math and see the data rate for any movie by choosing Get Info on the Movie menu and selecting General from the resulting pop-up menu(see Figure 7.21). Download a few and check them out!

297

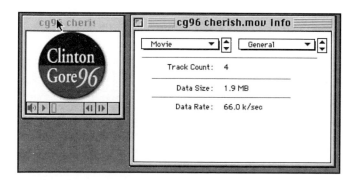

figure 7.21

The General Info window in MoviePlayer tells you the number of tracks in the movie as well as the file size and data rate.

You could theoretically stream video, as is done with audio, for minutes at a time if the data rate was such that the bandwidth, server, and CPU could handle it. This could not apply to dial-up users, however; a 28.8 baud modem transmits data at about 2K/sec. And we said 66K/sec was really low! Also, in the real world there are other demands on a computer's and server's attention that would interfere with streaming for much more than a 30-second clip. If you are making a clip available for download, you will be okay if the data rate is under 800K/sec. You want to watch the length of your clip to avoid long download time for your visitors.

Lossless versus Lossy Compression

Now we will begin to explore the miracle of compression. Consider these two descriptions of a fictitious series of objects:

- The first is green with white dots and smells bad, the second is green with white dots and smells bad, and the third is blue with white dots and smells bad.

- The first is green with white dots and smells bad, the second is the same, as is the third except it is blue.

You will notice that although the second description is shorter, it contains exactly the same information! This gives you a glimpse of how data describing pixels in an image (or a series of images) can be compressed *without losing any information*. This type of compression is called *lossless* compression. Video files must be compressed to be managed in a desktop computer environment, and the first type of compression used is always lossless compression. Video capture cards use lossless compression; if they didn't, you'd be starting with lower-quality video at the beginning of your work!

This compression, however, is not usually enough to get files small enough to be delivered on the Web. There is a more drastic kind of compression that tries to delete "nonessential" data; data that might not even be missed. This is called *lossy* compression, and the idea is to always leave enough information to get the point across! Here is where judging how much sacrifice of quality is acceptable really enters the picture.

A commonly used analogy for lossy compression is a sentence with the vowels left out. Try to read the following two lines:

①   Cn y rd ths sntnc?

②   Cn yu rd ths sntnce?

The general idea is that your brain will fill in the missing parts from context, and from the familiar patterns of the words, and barely notice what is missing. These examples give an idea of how delicate a process this is. The first effort is not entirely successful; the rigid application of a "no vowels" system leaves most readers puzzling at least momentarily. The strategic addition of a bit more detail in crucial places, in the second line, makes it much easier to read without effort. With lossy compression, the algorithms are incredibly "intelligent" and are designed to work well with specific types of material (see Table 7.1 later in this chapter for a full listing of codecs).

WARNING

Never apply a lossy codec to a video file more than once. It should be your last step before putting the movie on the Web, and always save a precompression version!

The key to codecs is that unlike utilities such as StuffIt or Zip, you don't go through a single step of decompression and then possess a full-size file. Every time you play a movie, each frame decompresses, and then it compresses again as soon as the frame is off the screen. This process has to be very efficient and without hiccups!

When selecting a codec, it is not simply a matter of selecting either a lossless or lossy compression scheme. In the compression dialog box displayed by all QuickTime-compatible applications, you are given a slider to set the quality from least to most compression (see Figure 7.22). In general, it is best to leave this set at Medium. Many codecs can be lossy or lossless, depending on the level you set.

Some effects of poorer-quality video will be:

- "Blockiness"—multiple pixels that should be different colors show up as the same color

- "Choppiness"—the sequence of frames does not succeed in simulating smooth motion

- Fuzzy or blurred objects

figure 7.22

The slider for the
level of quality the
codec is required
to preserve.

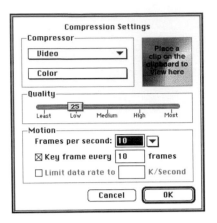

Spatial versus Temporal Compression

Another variable to keep in mind when choosing a compression scheme is that compression can either reduce the amount of data *within* each frame or take a *series* of frames and delete redundant data. The first is called *spatial* compression and treats each frame in isolation, as if you had a whole series of graphics and used the JPEG format to reduce file size for each one.

Here is where the benefits of reducing from 24-bit to 8-bit color are not just less data for each pixel. When spatial compression algorithms look for pixels of identical color to substitute "ditto" for the RGB description, the fewer unique colors, the more compression you get.

The second approach is *temporal* compression, which compares each frame to the one that came before it. So, if the background is constant for a few frames, the data is not repeated in the subsequent frames. Basically, only the pixels that change, or are moving, need to be noted.

TIP

Zooming and panning, those two favorite techniques of the MTV age, create a situation in which every single pixel in the frame is "moving." This means that you get very little benefit from temporal compression. A steady camera (on a tripod is best) and an immobile background (no waving fields of grain) will compress the most efficiently.

When employing temporal compression, it is best to require that a complete frame be described periodically, once per second is generally recommended. This is called specifying a *key frame*. The key frame is a reference point for digital video, a foundation for the compression of the frames that follow the key frame. In Premiere you set the number of key frames in the Compression window, which is standard for all QuickTime-compatible applications. Note that the frame rate is 10 frames per second, so that specifying a key frame every 10 frames results in one key frame per second. This makes it easy to remember:

```
x frames per second requires a key frame every x frames
```

> QuickTime will require that a frame be a key frame if it detects
> that 90% of the pixels have changed from one frame to another.

If the codec you choose employs temporal compression, the word "Quality" above the slider in the QuickTime compression should change to the word "Temporal," which enables you to set the quality of temporal compression separately from spatial compression (as in Figure 7.23). This is a relatively new feature not supported in all programs yet, but we did find it in Movie Cleaner Lite by Terran Interactive. If the codec uses both methods, hold down Option (on the Macintosh) or Alt (for Windows) before selecting the slider to change the slider from Quality (for spatial compression) to Temporal.

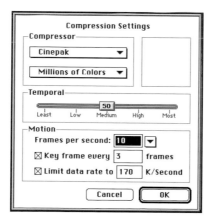

figure 7.23

The slider for the
level quality the
codec is required
to keep when
using temporal
compression.

Codecs: Choices, Choices, Choices

You can see in Table 7.1 that there are many video codecs. The choice is dazzling, even if you look only at the ones that work with QuickTime! When reviewing the table, remember the following:

- Some codecs can be either lossy or lossless depending on quality setting selected

- Many codecs use both spatial and temporal compression

- Many codecs can handle multiple file formats and all these listed are cross-platform except MPEG.

- Many codecs have particular restrictions or strengths

- Codecs that decompress quickly take longer to compress

The most highly recommended codec for the Web is Cinepak, particularly for it's extremely fast decompression speed, the speed at which a compressed file will open and begin to play. To achieve this takes a bit longer in the compression process, but some waiting in the authoring process is worth it if the viewer gains in faster display! For computer generated images, rather than live footage, the Animation codec is often recommended, but we have had better results with Cinepak or Apple Video.

TABLE 7.1
Some Attributes of Common Codecs

CODEC	FORMATS	COMPRESSION TYPE/RATIO	DATA LOSS
None	QT 2.5	None	Lossless
Photo (JPEG)	QT 2.5	Spatial only [up to 100:1]	Lossless at 15:1
Animation	QT 2.5	Spatial & temporal [up to 25:1]	Lossless at "most" quality
Graphics	QT 2.5	Spatial & temporal	Lossless at "most" quality
Apple Video	QT 2.5	Spatial & temporal [up to 25:1]	Lossy at lower quality settings
Cinepak	QT 2.5 & AVI	Spatial & temporal	Lossy at lower quality settings
Component Video	QT 2.5	Spatial only [2:1]	Lossy at lower quality settings
Intel Indeo	AVI	Spatial & temporal	Lossy
MPEG	MPEG, QT for Windows	Spatial & temporal [up to 200:1]	Lossy at lower quality settings

MovieCleaner and Web-Motion

If you are working on a Macintosh and the preceding chart has left your head spinning, there is relief in sight. Terran Interactive has two versions of a utility called MovieCleaner: the shareware version (Lite) and the commercial package (Pro) (`http://www.terran-int.com`). This is a QuickTime compression utility with a built in "Movie Expert" that gives you advice! In Figure 7.24 you see the Easy Settings (of Lite), where the Expert asks you some questions about your movie. Based on your answers, the utility will recommend a codec and settings to use.

Figure 7.25 shows the advanced settings of Movie Cleaner Lite, which are suggested if you already know something about compression. Note that the data rate is displayed in the left panel and the environments in which the movie will play acceptably are listed. You adjust the settings on the right until you achieve the data rate at which you are aiming.

RESTRICTIONS	STRENGTHS	COMPRESSION/ DECOMPRESSION SPEED
Not for final delivery	Reducing 32 bit to 16 or 24 bit	1:1
Minimum frame size = 16x16	Photos/still images	1:1
Not for videotape capture	Fast decompression of computer-generated images	3:1
Slow decompression	High compression ratio	16:1
Minimum frame size = 4x4	Digitized video - compression speed	7:1
Movie size must = multiple of 4 for best quality	high compression ratio - constrain playback rate option	192:1
Compression only 2:1	Storage solution - editing - image quality	1:1
Requires additional video	Live action footage - high compression ratio	192:1
requires hardware assistance	best compression available	200:1

figure 7.24

The Movie Expert
interviews you and
then recommends
compression settings

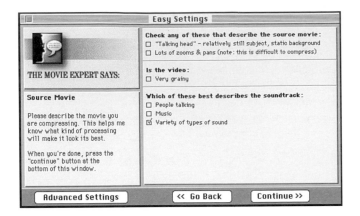

figure 7.25

The Advanced
Settings enable you
to adjust settings to
achieve the data
rate that will play
well in the intended
environment.

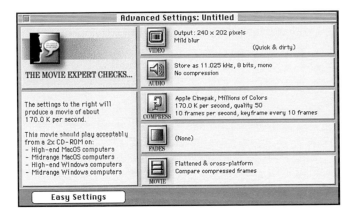

Movie Cleaner Pro has some additional capabilities such as batch processing and enhanced cropping and resizing options. It is also strongly recommended for the Power Mac platform. There is also a new product in this series specifically geared to bringing movies to the Web, called Web-Motion, which is a plug-in for Movie Cleaner Pro. This adds Web-specific descriptions to the left-hand panel you see in Figure 7.25 (which previously pertained primarily to CD-ROM playback). Movie Cleaner Pro claims to have filters to "make video look better at low data rates" and gives you accurate control over data rates as low as 1.4K/sec. In making some of the decisions, Web-Motion shows you clips and you choose the one you like best. It even generates HTML with EMBED tags for your page! Get all the details and the program itself at http://www.terran-int.com/webmot.html.

Desktop Video Software

As with audio, we will briefly discuss some software that can be used to edit and enhance video before moving onto the file formats and the actual process of getting video to the Web (the section "Delivering Video on the Web"). Here we will mention three applications:

- Premiere—The most widely used and least expensive of the three

- Avid VideoShop—A bit more powerful and more expensive

- Adobe AfterEffects—A high-end tool for adding incredible effects and layers in a video

All three are cross-platform; however, they are all for use with QuickTime, but Adobe Premiere for Windows enables you to work with AVI files.

Adobe Premiere

```
http://www.adobe.com/prodindex/premiere/
```

This is the program we use the most often for working with video. We find its interface intuitive and friendly (see Figure 7.26). The Construction window is where the project is put together; each horizontal row is a track (information stored separately that will eventually be played simultaneously). You can see and adjust how the tracks relate to each other, including video tracks, video super-impose ("S"), transition ("T"), and audio tracks (up to 99 video and 99 audio tracks). You can drag-and-drop clips along and among these tracks. You choose transitions from the animated Transitions window that displays a sample of each transition. The Controller enables you to play the movie-in-progress (displayed in the Preview window), displays key data, and enables you to mark frames during previewing. The Project window is where you organize the elements, and the Info window displays crucial information in one concise panel: duration of movie, frame size, and so on. Note that it does not display data rate, which would be nice! Premiere for Windows can save movies as either QuickTime or AVI files.

305

Strata VideoShop

http://www.strata3d.com/products/VideoShop/VideoShop.html

This program can perform all the tasks that Premiere does, but its interface is quite different (see Figure 7.27). The Sequence replaces the Construction window but also enables you to add tracks and to drag-and-drop to rearrange clips. The Canvas enables you to control the preview playback directly from the window instead of from a separate controller. You can actually view source tapes and select clips from them before you bring them into the application. The major improvement over Premiere is that VideoShop enables you to capture video directly into the application from a camera or VCR connected to the computer. It gives quite a bit of control over the digitizing process (more than the utilities that come with most capture boards). Another feature not present in Premiere is the desktop window (in the top middle of the figure, called "elroy in 17 sec"). This is like a mini-desktop displaying icons for the various components you are working with.

figure 7.26

The Construction, Transitions, Controller, Project, Preview and Info Windows in Adobe Premiere.

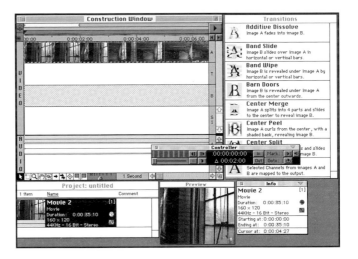

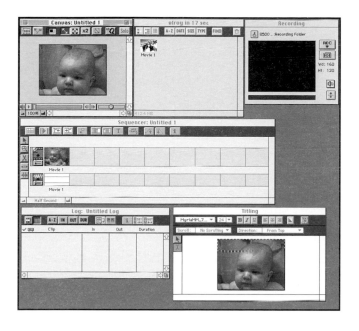

figure 7.27

The Canvas,
Desktop, Recording,
Sequencer, Log and
Titling Windows in
VideoShop.

Adobe AfterEffects

http://www.adobe.com/prodindex/aftereffects/

This program is an additional tool for adding effects and combining movies, not an alternative to the editing software packages discussed above. Adobe calls the process you perform with the application *modeling*, not editing. AfterEffects has quite a price tag, but once you've worked with it you don't want to give up the power it gives you to add depth and a layered feeling to your video. Its biggest strength is merging graphics with video footage for more of a "multimedia" feeling. The interface is not unlike some animation programs in that it uses a timeline, called the Time Layout (see the lower portion of Figure 7.28). You can also see the Project window, which is not unlike a Macintosh Finder window, the Composition window, and the audio palette with sliders. Below them you see a toolbar (with a nice compact set of eight tools), and an info bar that displays information about (are you ready for this?) the *pixel* you have your cursor over! My favorite option is "hide shy layers."

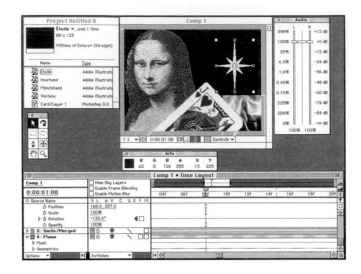

figure 7.28

The Project, Composition, Audio, Tool, Info, and Time Layout Windows in Adobe AfterEffects.

File Formats

Originally each compression system, especially each hardware-based compression system, created a different file format. Now three major file formats—or more properly, file format standards relevant to the Web—are QuickTime, AVI, and MPEG, and they are each associated with a platform.

If you are working on the Macintosh platform, QuickTime is really your best option as a developer (it comes with the system). If you are on Windows, you are pushed toward AVI (which comes with the system), but QuickTime is available to you. Unix supported only MPEG for a while, so it was the format of choice on that system. Those that are seeking the best-quality, most-compressed video will strive for MPEG, but there are hardware requirements for both creating and *viewing* MPEG files. Just as your platform influences your choice of format, your choice of format you use will influence (if not determine) how you can to bring your video to the Web. This is discussed in detail in the next section. As with any battle for standards, the one that gains the most popularity will win; the jury is still out. Our vote is for QuickTime as the most cross-platform-friendly.

> **NOTE**
>
> The site at http://www.microsoft.com/ie/challenge/compari-son/multimedia.htm has a clip of Jay Leno at the Windows 95 Launch available in all three formats. The QuickTime (MOV) file size is 797K, the AVI file size is 503K, and the MPEG file size is 121K. Of course, we do not know what codec was used with the MOV file!

The QuickTime Standard

QuickTime is free; you can get it from `http://www.quicktime.apple.com`.

You can get a lot of information about QuickTime at the QuickTime FAQ site: `http://www.quicktimefaq.org`.

QuickTime is a system extension originally created for the Macintosh system, now available for the Wintel platform, which makes it possible to view video (and/or animation and music) on your computer. The file format associated with QuickTime is referred to as a QuickTime (or QT or MOV) file and it uses the suffix .mov. QuickTime also has a control bar (see Figure 7.29) built into every QuickTime movie (although you can choose not to display it).

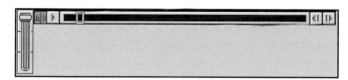

figure 7.29

The QuickTime control bar.

NOTE

QuickTime is not an application that plays or edits movies! To play a movie you must either be within a properly configured Web browser or use a small application such as MoviePlayer (Macintosh) or MediaPlayer (Windows). QuickTime is not an application at all, but a system software extension that provides a standard: for example, the standard video compression slider that editing and compression utilities use.

Although we refer to the file format as "QuickTime," it is really a standard that enables the movie to be relatively independent of the way it was digitized and the compression used by the digitizing card (the card has to conform to the QuickTime standard). This is a big improvement over the many different formats generated by the various proprietary cards and compression software (AVI and MPEG are competing standards). QuickTime is the easiest format to port across platforms without much special preparation of the files: the Macintosh will play QuickTime created on the Wintel platform. From a Mac you must "flatten" a movie to bring it to the Wintel platform—a simple option in the saving process of most software that adjusts the file for cross-platform use.

The AVI Standard

This Microsoft software (file extension .avi) comes with the Windows operating system as an element within the Videos for Windows product package. AVI stands for Audio Video Interleave, which refers to the fact that the audio and video data are stored consecutively in the format's file. In other words, segmented audio data follows segmented video data, imperceptibly to the audience. This format cannot be played directly on a Macintosh without being converted to QT (see sidebar earlier), so it is out of the question for Macintosh-based developers.

MPEG

MPEG stands for Moving Pictures Experts Group, where the compression scheme originated. As can be seen from the note at the beginning of the "File Formats" section and Table 7.1, this is by far the most efficient compression available. It also is the highest-quality video of the three. The problem is that MPEG is still largely dependent upon having MPEG playback hardware. There are many, many cards for the PC, and Apple now offers one for the Mac. While it might be a reasonable investment to get a card for the kind of compression MPEG offers, the trick is to get the movie to play on the client's CPU. The developers are working hard to get a software playback solution for MPEG.

Two players specifically for the Web enable you to play MPEG files without the specialized hardware decoders or proprietary video servers. In addition to playing files over the Web, you can use Netscape to play the file *locally from your hard disk* (so you as a developer can view an MPEG video without the playback hardware). It seems that it took the pressure of the Web to bring the software solution! Please read on in the plug-in section below.

> **NOTE**
>
> MPEG, with regard to use on CD-ROMs or the Web, is technically called MPEG-1. MPEG-2 is broadcast-quality video.

AVI and MPEG to QuickTime Conversion

To convert AVI to QT on a Macintosh, use Microsoft's Video for Windows Converter from `ftp://ftp.microsoft.com/developr/drg/Multimedia/VfW11-Mac/`.

To convert AVI to QT on Wintel, use Intel's SmartVid converter (for Windows or DOS) from `ftp://ftp.intel.com/pub/IAL/multimedia/smartv.exe` *or* `http://www.intel.com/pub/IAL/multimedia/smartvid.htm`, *or The San Francisco Canyon Company's TRMOOV.EXE from* `http://www.sfcanton.com/`.

QuickTime for Windows supports MPEG compression (it's simply another codec), but you must have MPEG playback hardware.

On a Mac, you can use a freeware utility called Sparkle (`ftp://mirror.aol.com/pub/info-mac/gst/mov/`*), which enables you to play the movie, or if you have MPEG playback hardware you can follow a complex series of steps outlined at the QuickTime FAQ site (*`http://www.quicktimefaq.org`*).*

Delivering Video on the Web

There are basically two directions you can go to deliver video on the Web: you can use the Netscape EMBED tag and expect viewers to have plug-ins, or you can use Microsoft Internet Explorer's Dynamic Source attribute for the image tag and expect visitors to have the ActiveMovie Control that comes with Explorer 3.0. At the moment, the safer bet is with Netscape's system, simply because Explorer has reluctantly agreed to support the EMBED tag and plug-ins (see `http://www.microsoft.com/ie/support/docs/tech30/nsplugin.htm`). It remains to be seen whether Netscape accepts the IMG DYNSRC tag.

The EMBED Tag and Plug-Ins

The basic HTML for embedding video is:

```
<EMBED SRC="video.xxx">
```

Further parameters depend upon the plug-in used and are inserted before the closing bracket, such as this LOOP parameter:

```
<EMBED SRC="video.xxx" LOOP=TRUE>
```

You do not have to do any special HTML to call upon the correct plug-in; the file suffix (extension) will do that. Be sure the suffix is lowercase; depending on your Web server platform, it could make a difference. The viewer *must* have the correct plug-in to view the movie.

If pages using the EMBED command for any of the following examples are browsed with Explorer 3.0, Microsoft asserts that the browser will play the files using ActiveX.

The QuickTime Plug-In

This plug-in now comes built into Netscape 3.0. This is the number one reason that QuickTime is the preferred plug-in. It will play QuickTime movies on both Windows and Macintosh triggered by the .mov suffix. The parameters you can specify are as follows; all are optional except WIDTH and HEIGHT. "Default" tells you what is set if the parameter is not specified:

- WIDTH = [number of pixels wide for video frame; mandatory]

- HEIGHT = [number of pixels tall for video frame; mandatory]

311

- AUTOPLAY=TRUE/FALSE [begins play automatically/or not (default)]

- CONTROLLER=TRUE/FALSE [displays control bar(default)/ or not]

- LOOP=TRUE/FALSE/PALINDROME [loops continuously/no loop/ plays forward, back, forward, back continuously]

- PLAYEVERYFRAME=TRUE/FALSE [do not set to true if you have any audio with your movie; movie may play more slowly if true/ allow to skip frames to keep smooth playback (default)]

- HREF=URL [makes movie a link to URL]

- PLUGINSPACE=URL [gives the URL for acquiring plug-in]

TIP

You can also instruct your visitors that they can start and stop the QuickTime playback by clicking on the movie (if the controller is absent). For the Macintosh it is double-click to start and click to stop; for Windows it is click to start and click to stop (an on/off toggle).

When the page is browsed with Netscape, the movie will begin to play after 90% of the file is loaded.

NOTE

There is a rival plug-in for QuickTime by Intelligence at Large called MovieStar that is available for Windows and Macintosh. This claims to begin playing the movie "as it is being down-loaded" if you prepare the movie with the application MovieStar Maker. Get more information about this and other proprietary video plug-ins at `http://home.netscape.com/comprod/prod-ucts/navigator/version_2.0/plugins/audio-video.html`. MovieStar's biggest disadvantage is that it does not come built-in with the browser, so your visitors would have to download the plug-in.

The LiveVideo Plug-In: AVI Files

LiveVideo plays files in AVI format (currently available only for Windows 95 and Windows NT). It is discussed primarily because it comes built in with Netscape. The plug-in is triggered by the .avi suffix. The parameters are:

- WIDTH=[number of pixels wide for video frame; mandatory]

- HEIGHT=[number of pixels tall for video frame; mandatory]

- AUTOSTART=TRUE/FALSE [begins play automatically/or not (default)]

- LOOP=TRUE/FALSE [loops continuously/no loop]

WARNING

Check syntax carefully (for any plug-in). If possible, copy from a text file downloaded from the Web. It is easy to get confused; for example, QuickTime uses AUTOPLAY and LiveVideo uses AUTOSTART.

The InterVU MPEG Plug-In and Players

There are actually two products enabling you to play MPEG files over the Web without requiring MPEG playback hardware (decoders). These are not built into Netscape; at this point your visitors would have to acquire them to see the video. The first plug-in is Action, by Open2U, but it is available for the Windows platform only (see `http://home.netscape.com/comprod/products/navigator/version_2.0/plugins/audio-video.html`).

IntcrVU MPEG Player is cross-platform, available for Mac and Wintel (`http://www.intervu.com/`). It has some classy features such as its own control icons for starting and pausing (one replaces the other as appropriate). As the file is downloading you see a symbol telling you whether or not the file includes sound (a speaker, or a crossed-out speaker). InterVU MPEG Player even gives you a little disk icon that you can press to save the file!

> *VivoActive Player by Vivo Software*
>
> *A rival plug-in to LiveVideo is the VivoActive Player. Its advantage is that it is available for both Mac and Windows platforms; its disadvantage is that it is not built into the browser and so your viewers would have to get the plug-in. VivoActive Player claims to be the fastest way to get video clips on a Web page, compressing AVI files 250:1. Best of all, it transmits the file using HTTP, so even folks on a Mac platform can see your AVI files (it is not the AVI file per se that is playing; the HTTP protocol is reading and serving the data). There are tools for developers on Mac and Wintel platforms (`http://home.netscape.com/comprod/products/navigator/version_2.0/plugins/audio-video.html`).*

The plug-in is triggered by the .mpg (or .mpeg) suffix. The parameters are:

- WIDTH=[number of pixels wide for video frame; mandatory; add 10 pixels to the width to show the frame around the displayed image]

- HEIGHT=[number of pixels tall for video frame; mandatory; again add 10 pixels for the frame, add 29 pixels for the frame and control bar]

- AUTOPLAY=YES/NO [begins play automatically/or not (default)]

- LOOP=[number of times you would like the video to loop]

- PLUGINSPAGE="http://www.intervu.com" [sends viewer for plug-in]

- FRAMERATE=[Number of frames per second] [If this is used it will eliminate any sound that is in the movie; the number should be between 1 and 25]

- DOUBLESIZE=YES/NO [doubles the size of the movie; you must change height and width values also; not available for 68K Mac—leaves same size (default)]

- HALFSIZE=YES/NO [halves the size of the movie; you must change height and width values also; not available for 68K Mac—leaves same size (default)]

- CONBAR=YES/NO [shows controls(default)/hides controls]

ActiveMovie for Internet Explorer

The ActiveMovie Control does not rely on separate plug-ins for each file format but rather neatly handles QuickTime, AVI, and MPEG with the same system (version 3.0 of Explorer required)! It is the video component of an integrated multimedia system, ActiveX. What a wonderful idea! The ActiveMovie Control is cross-platform for Macintosh and Windows (both for development tools and viewing). Sounds great! The catch is that it is a Microsoft Internet system; there is no support for it from Netscape (as of this writing). Can anyone really afford to shut out viewers who come with Netscape? As we saw in the discussion of the Netscape tags above, Explorer is supporting the EMBED command and triggering ActiveMovie to play the file if the plug-in is not present. Therefore you are, at the moment, in a no-lose situation in going with the Netscape system.

Things may change tomorrow, however, in terms of what browser supports what, so here's how you do it. You do *not* use the EMBED tag; you use a traditional IMG tag but with a dynamic source:

```
<IMG DYNSRC="video.avi">
```

or

```
<IMG DYNSRC="video.mov">
```

or

```
<IMG DYNSRC="video.mpg">
```

There are parameters, just as with the plug-ins, only this time you only have to learn *one* set for all three formats! Again, the parameters come after the filename and before the close of the bracket. You can apply all the usual parameters that you would to an IMG element:

- ALIGN=TOP, MIDDLE, BOTTOM
- ALIGN=LEFT, RIGHT
- ALT="text"
- BORDER=[width of border in pixels]
- HSPACE=[pixels]
- VSPACE=[pixels]
- And so on, and so on

Having the ALT text is especially sensible so you can send a message while the movie is loading or if it cannot load. It is sensible to use tags we are already very familiar with from IMG (because this *is* an IMG element). Note that you can specify both an SRC="still.gif" and DYNSRC="movie.mov"; then the movie will be seen if the browser supports it and the still image will appear if not. The unique parameters for DYNSRC are:

- CONTROLS (there is no value needed for this parameter; just insert the term and the controls will appear)
- LOOP=[number of loops/INFINITE] (default is to play once)
- START=FILEOPEN/MOUSEOVER (video will play when file is opened (default)/will play when mouse is over movie; you can actually specify *both* these parameters by entering FILEOPEN, MOUSEOVER, so that viewers can replay movie with the mouse)

315

The other aspect of the ActiveMovie/ActiveX system is that you can use the ActiveMovie add-on toolkit to create movies that stream. This involves something called the ActiveMovie Streaming Format (ASF), which enables multiple kinds of media, such as stills, audio, video and URLs, to be combined in one multimedia file.

To learn about the ActiveX multimedia approach, go to `http://www.microsoft.com/ie/support/docs/tech30/mmedia.htm`.

Case Studies

Here are the case studies at the end of the chapter rather than in a discussion of a delivery system, because the discussion of plug-ins and formats was so technical it seemed best not to interrupt your concentration with a fun case study! So here is your reward for reading all that stuff! One example is a very straight live video capture and one is our emersion movie, which has no live video whatsoever! (You can see both on the CD-ROM.)

The New bYte a tree Studio Space

As we mentioned in the section on "Installments of an Event," we have put up a Web page at our site showing video clips of our progress in designing our new studio space. This example will explain only the original (raw space) capture because we honestly are not going to get any further with it until this book is finished! By the time you are reading this, it will be beautiful (we hope).

We shot the video using a tripod in the middle of the space using a Hitachi VHS camcorder. We used a Power Macintosh 8500, which comes with a built-in video digitizing board (and also comes with VideoShop). If you are considering getting into video and need a new station, the price of this entire station is much less than a comparable station plus a video capture card.

We connected the camera to the video in jack and used Apple Video Player (which came on the system) to control the digitizing process. Figures 7.30 through 7.31 show three stills of the movie in the Video Player window. This shows you the movie and the Video Player interface, but the figures of 10 frames per second tell me that these figure were created when viewing the final movie later—remember that you always capture at the full 30 frames per second and reduce it later.

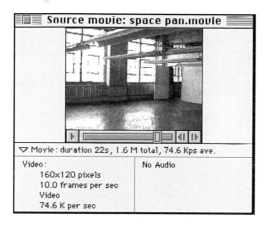

figure 7.30

The clip viewed in Apple Video Player.

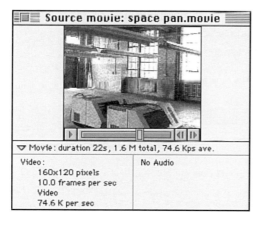

figure 7.31

Another view of the high-tech space for bYte u tiee.

Since we did not want to add any effects to the movie (it speaks for itself in a raw kind of way), we did not use any video editing or effects software and simply brought the clip into Movie Cleaner Lite. There we chose the following settings (see Figure 7.32):

- Smooth/blur: moderate (to keep the camera pan closer to smooth than if there was higher blur).

- First and Last frame high-quality (so that when the movie is stopped before or after playing it looks decent).

- The frame size of 160×120 was chosen as the smallest size at which anything would be visible.

- The "Talking heads" filter, which is intended for an interview in which the subject is simply talking and there isn't much movement, is *not* appropriate.

- Quality set to Quick & dirty (to make a smaller file for the Web).

figure 7.32

Setting up options in
Movie Cleaner Lite.

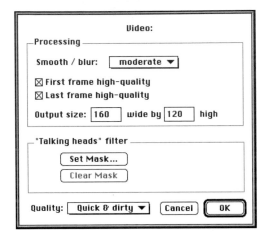

Next, in Movie Cleaner Lite the codec Video was chosen, to give good compression (we just liked the look of this better than Cinepak for this clip). This was at Medium quality, and the frame rate set to 10 frames per second (see Figure 7.33). When we clicked OK, Movie Cleaner began its processing, with a progress bar telling how long it would take (see Figure 7.34).

figure 7.33

Setting the Video
compression codec
and frames per
second in Movie
Cleaner Lite.

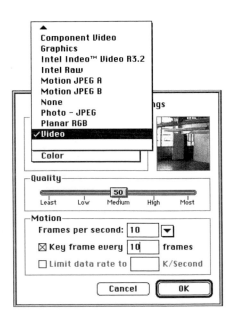

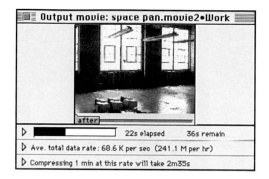

figure 7.34

*Movie Cleaner Lite
processing the
compression.*

The final file was given the suffix .mov and placed in the appropriate directory (folder, in this case called "movies") for linking to the HTML. Then in the HTML, the EMBED command was used:

```
<EMBED SRC="movies/spacepan.mov" WIDTH=160 HEIGHT=120>
```

The [e]mersion Movie

Our second case study is completely different. We wanted a mood piece showing our "out there" approach to the new era of design. You should probably view this movie on the CD-ROM before reading further so you have some idea of what we mean by that. Because we were starting from graphics and not live video, we were not constrained by the proportions set by the camera for conventional video. The frame for this "movie" is 352 pixels wide by 125 pixels tall. The type treatments were developed in Photoshop and then brought into Premiere as long horizontal PICT or vertical files (not proportional to the frame). The still images were then "panned" in Premiere (see Figure 7.35). In the example you see the file is more vertical than the frame, and the frame is literally moved across it so that it looks like the image is moving up through the frame. In the center top of the figure you see the distorted preview of one frame.

Some layers were built using type elements, each as white type on a red background, so the red could be knocked out easily and replaced by the gradated, layered image. Then the music was developed to suit the mood (we were playing music by a group called The Orb all through this process, which was inspiring). After the music was added the elements were synchronized to move with the music. Figure 7.36 shows you how there were many layers of video, four of which were in S-superimpose tracks, and it also shows the audio track.

<figure>
figure 7.35

Image Pan settings
in Adobe Premiere.

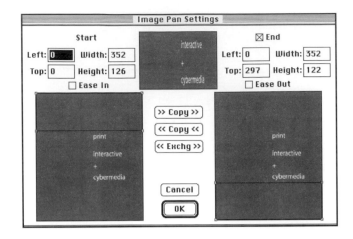
</figure>

<figure>
figure 7.36

Layers upon layers
in Adobe Premiere.

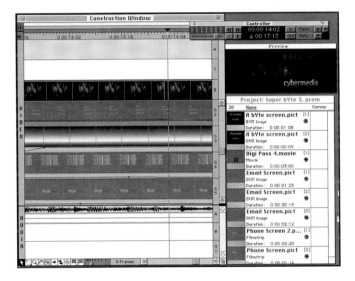
</figure>

The movie was saved as a QuickTime file (emersion.mov) and placed in
the same directory as the HTML page that will call upon it. The HTML
coding, to hide the control bar and loop continuously, went:

```
<EMBED SRC="emersion.mov" WIDTH=352 HEIGHT=125
CONTROLLER=FALSE LOOP=TRUE>
```

 *by Stella Gassaway*

Interactivity: A Richer Experience

Everyone talks as though interactivity is a new discovery. Not to designers.

Designers consider interactivity in the work they do from architectural design

to way finding. We have always asked ourselves questions such as: Will the

entrance of the building be inviting? How can I lead visitors to the locations

they wish to visit? How can the object I have created respond to the needs of

those who use it?

On the Web we are learning how to apply a new brand of interactivity to the content we design. Rather than approaching this as if it is a strange new world (as we did with audio and video), remember we are already familiar with the principles; it is the capabilities that are new. Indeed, it was a greater challenge to design a fixed product that must somehow serve a varied public, without any capacity to respond to individual needs.

The new interactivity requires designing for a multidimensional hyper-linked space. We must combine aspects of the disciplines of architecture, way finding, interface, information, and document design. An understanding of the technologies available for creating interactive art and its application within a navigational system are of primary importance to those of us designing Web sites. As with all multimedia, we must carefully combine content and innovation with the limits of current technology. The framework of our construction should be invisible and the viewer should traverse it with ease.

We define interactivity on the Web as actions the viewer initiates or participates in within the content of the site. These include:

- Membership login

- Completing online forms

- Signing guestbooks

- Playing movies

- Online training

- Threaded discussions

- Participating in games or puzzles

- Immediate feedback (such as rollovers)

- Customized content/experience

- Navigating a 3D space

The successful incorporation of many elements, devices, and techniques creates a rich, interactive, intuitive site. The designer has the opportunity to illustrate and demonstrate concepts and add depth to a site with interactive art. Actively engaging viewers creates more interest and a greater likelihood of their visiting more of the site you designed more often.

In this chapter we make the case for interactivity, discuss design considerations and technical constraints, and give tips to help you decide when and how to use certain techniques. Included are examples of interactive elements we created (many of which are on the accompanying CD-ROM) as well as those created by other designers.

The Case for Interactivity

When we are still in the womb our parents, our aunts, uncles, grandparents, and friends of the family are out purchasing every stimulating and developmental toy on the planet: mobiles to hang over our cribs, music boxes, toys with dials and buttons, rattles, and other sound-making devices—anything and everything we can play with to stimulate our brain. But stimulation is not the only point of these gizmos. One day we discover we can *control* the sounds; we can make the music play, we can change what we see. And boy is it fun! As babies we are the center of the universe. So why, as adults, should this change? When visitors come to a Web site, they again are the center of the universe.

The evidence is clear that people learn better by doing. Concepts gained from reading text or viewing videos can be reinforced with interactive exercises. The use of interactive CD-ROMs for training and reinforcement of traditional training is growing considerably and has been proven effective. Large lectures are less effective than small workshops where there is more interaction with the instructor (and other students) and the set format can be varied to meet the needs of the particular group or individual.

The first key concept is that we are active rather than passive; when demands are made on us, our brains are more fully engaged. Every teacher knows a student can't sleep in the back of the classroom if his or her participation is demanded on a regular basis. The second key concept is that actions have results; the environment changes in response to our input. The response is what makes the action satisfying and can give us a sense of effectiveness.

This active engagement of the person browsing is in large part responsible for the immense popularity of the Web. The Web opened interactive opportunities to a large audience beyond that reachable by human educators, entertainers, or sales representatives.

Hyperlinks on the Web were our first introduction to interactivity within a graphical interface on the Net. With a click we could be sent to locations near and far. Technology has come a long way, and still the simple idea of a mouse click leading you to new experiences is the heart of the Web. This basic interactive environment is the seed for the growth of the interactive experiences that come with new and ever-evolving technologies.

It is meaningless to discuss "introducing" interactivity to a Web site because by its nature the Web is an interactive experience. The viewer must interact with the user interface of the browser to access and navigate through screens or pages. Experienced Web surfers demand control over their environment and look forward to interaction at the sites they visit.

The basic interactive nature of the Web is illustrated concisely at Brian Mcgrath's site. Figure 8.1 shows the flexible boundaries within the browser. The interface is driven by the familiar element we all take for granted: the scrollbar. We naturally scroll to see the complete "page"; only then can we read the entire message and gain access to the links that enable exploration of the site. The text Mcgrath uses has a direct relationship with the interactivity he prompts from the viewer (see Figure 8.2). This site challenges designers to expand their minds and skills to take full advantage of this new medium rather than imitate the work we have done in other environments.

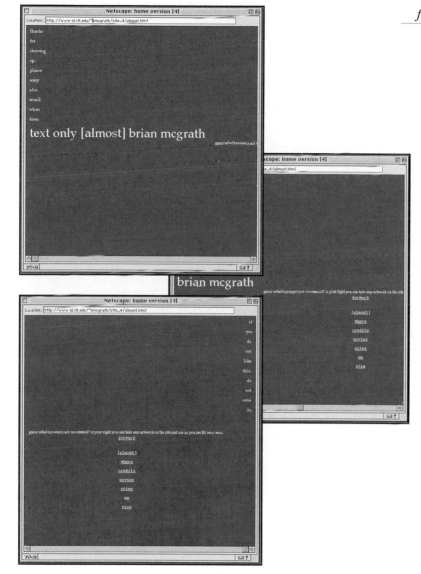

figure 8.1

An example of basic
Web interactivity at
`http://www.id.`
`iit.edu-bmcgrath/`
`site_4/`
`almost.html`.

figure 8.2

*The copy at the
Brian Mcgrath site
reinforces the points
made by the
interface.*

Design Issues

Designing for someone who is the center of the universe is actually easier
and more exciting than it may sound. As the technology gets better, the
design options grow. We spoke in the previous chapters about the
different elements a designer can use to add interactivity to enhance a
Web site: animation, audio, and video. Now we can combine these
elements to enrich a site where the visitor is a *participant*.

With the capacity to respond to actions by visitors comes the corollary: we
cannot control what actions the visitors take. Designers are flexible and
design for multiple possibilities and interactions. We don't have ultimate
control anymore; we must learn from the way visitors at our site navigate
through and participate in it. We must truly measure the effectiveness of
our design and respond to the viewer, always looking to take full advantage of the medium and not constrict it with limited expectations. We
have a more exciting and challenging environment to design within, so
let's do it.

When designing interactivity into your Web site, think about designing a print project or a way-finding system based on the interaction of a single person. Work from your frame of reference. This can make the task of designing interactive experiences less daunting. Even though the medium has changed, the methods we use to design haven't. Creating an intimate, personal, easy-to-navigate system rich in interactivity is your goal. Again, this means thoughtful design, not meaningless bells and whistles.

Consider the goals for the site. What kinds of interactivity will enrich the experience? What kinds of interactivity are appropriate? Who are the visitors to the site and what kinds of interactivity will they relate to?

After we have answered those questions we must also take into consideration the following points (covered in upcoming sections):

- Viewer/visitor control

- Interactive behavior consistency

- The context in which the interactivity will be used

- The metaphor(s) we will use

Control

As mentioned earlier, experienced Web surfers demand control over how they view the site they are visiting. But control isn't just for the experienced; it is for every visitor. We discussed the satisfying nature of an event occurring as a result of our action. This event only gives a sense of control if it is an expected event. There is a place for surprise and adventure, but visitors should have a context from which to navigate. They should:

- Know where they are in relation to their travels

- Be able to control how they get from place to place

- Be able to start and stop actions such as video or sound

There are simple ways to control some of these elements that are already well established. Macromedia Director 5.0 comes with a standard control bar that you may include in your Shockwave audio elements (see Figure 8.3). It enables you to play, stop, and control the volume of your audio. You can also create your own interface devices (see Figure 8.4). The design challenge is to create something that works as well as established interface controls. You may want to create your own interface to limit the amount of control the viewer has over the interactive element. You can see that the interface we created has less control than the built-in control bar, with no volume control available.

figure 8.3

The Shockwave audio player.

figure 8.4

This is a screen capture of some limited controls we created.

It is a struggle to create a graphical interface easily understood and accessible on multiple platforms. When we were working with the beta versions of the Shockwave for FreeHand plug-ins, we downloaded the developers' versions and instructions. Along with the plug-ins, instructions, and so on, came a GIF file. This was an unwieldy image with loads of anti-aliased text explaining how to control viewing the vector graphics (see Figure 8.5). We certainly didn't want to use this on any pages we were designing, so we set about creating our own instructions. Our directions for operation gave the viewer a test image that could be used as a demo of the incredible zooming power of the plug-in (see Figure 8.6). It worked well but it isn't perfect.

figure 8.5

This is the GIF file with directions explaining the interface of the original Shockwave for FreeHand.

figure 8.6

Our navigational directions for the same information.

In the most recent version of the plug-in, you have the option of including a navigational toolbar at the top or bottom of the image (see Figure 8.7). This bar helps create a graphical interface that is the same for Macintosh and Wintel platforms. It is a successful solution but it does take away some of the design possibilities by defining the size of your graphic. The designer, however, can still choose to explain how to use the keyboard and mouse and leave out the control bar solution.

figure 8.7

The new toolbar. You can try it out on the CD-ROM.

Designers must learn to build prototypes and test them to determine the effectiveness of the design. This is what the testing phase is about. If you have ever been in a beta testing program, you really learn what a product, such as a plug-in, can look like in its beginnings and how the careful testing and input from the testers creates a better answer. The key to giving the viewer a sense of control is to employ an easily learned interface.

Consistency

Actions and reactions within a site should be consistent; elements should have a similar feel and behavior. If, for example, you use video clips at a site, allow the viewer the same control over all the clips. Don't change back and forth from self-running to activated clips. Let the visitor know by your consistency that the clips can be turned on and off. Similarly use the same activation clues for navigational devices and other action-driven devices.

In a musical, particular songs or pieces of music created are associated with particular characters or groups of characters. These themes and variations on them are recognized throughout the play. A variation of the piece of music for a particular character may announce her appearance on stage. This thematic presence is predictable and recognizable. As designers we must create ways to inform visitors in a general way about an element or object that has particular characteristics and will most likely have a particular behavior.

The Netscape Features Demo Site

Take a look at the demo for Netscape 3.0 to see a Web example (see Figure 8.8). Here in the main menu, the visitor's action, in this case moving the mouse over a menu item, activates a rollover highlight of the area chosen. At the same time the icon above the menu reflects the choice. Ease of use = a piece of cake, Layout & Design = graphic tools. At the bottom of the bar, near the security key, is a text description reinforcing the result of the selection. The illustrations at the top of the bar are then carried to the next page with new menu choices pertaining to the subject (see Figure 8.9). In the section on Interative Navigation some ways of creating rollover highlights are discussed.

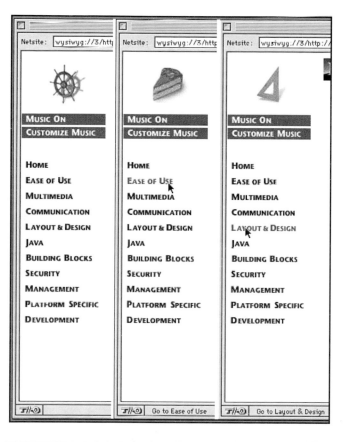

figure 8.8

A series of actions at the Netscape site show consistency of interaction (`http://home.netscape.com/comprod/products/navigator/version_3.0/`).

331

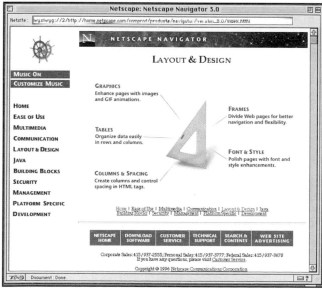

figure 8.9

The layout and design page using consistent images.

Consistency helps create a trust in the system, which enhances the effectiveness of the navigation and interactivity and creates a successful site.

Context and Metaphor

Adding interactivity and interactive elements to a site requires a great deal of consideration about the context of the activity. Does the interactivity make a concept clearer? Where is the appropriate location to add an interactive element?

Type designer Brian Sooy was seeking a method to convey the concept of a multiple master font within an article on the subject. We will discuss his solution later in the chapter, but here you see the interactive element in the context of the article describing the font's creation (see Figure 8.10). The slider and what it is trying to illustrate is explained in more detail in the section on "Conveying a Concept" later in this chapter.

figure 8.10

The slider for multiple master Veritas in context of an article (http://www.qwertyarts.com/books/qaveritas.html).

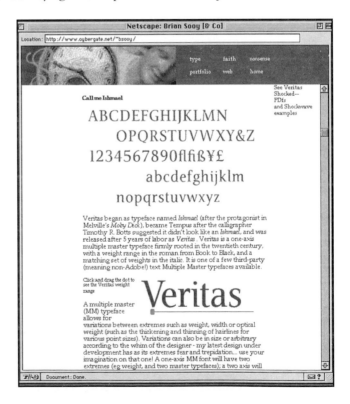

Familiar metaphors are often used to help a visitor relate to objects, information, and navigational devices at a site. The continuation of these metaphors in creating interactive objects is helpful to the viewer for continuity and spatial reference.

Most of the metaphors we see in multimedia and on the Web relate to analog systems with which we are familiar. Many of the navigational devices we see are dials, buttons, switches, and sliders (see Figure 8.11). We create interfaces to which our viewer can relate. The Net is called the information superhighway, although it is really nothing like a highway in its structure or its function. America Online calls the area where visitors have online conversations Chat Rooms when no rooms exist.

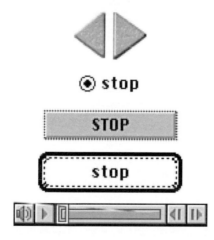

figure 8.11

Here are some of those switches, buttons, and sliders. We are familiar with these and have some idea of what will happen if we activate them.

Dial It

The Dial It site (`http://Web20.mindlink.net/ph/TV/tv_2.html`) uses a familiar metaphor: television and analog dials and tubes. The first page of the site is a large image of a television dial (see Figure 8.12). You can't actually turn to a channel, but it does give you floating numerals from which you can choose a channel. We chose channel 9. When the new page loaded, it reinforced the metaphor using a torn sheet of paper that looks like it came from a television guide in the newspaper (see Figure 8.13). The navigational devices you have to choose from are the dial, which will take you back to the "home" page, and a television.

figure 8.12

Here's the home
page for Dial It.

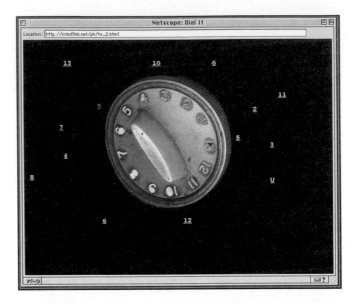

figure 8.13

We chose channel 9
at Dial It, and this is
what we got.

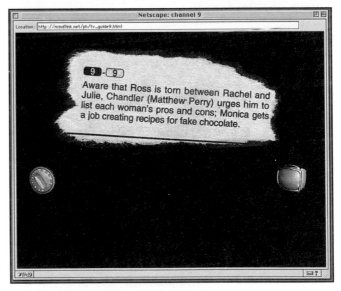

Let's click the television. The next page consists of a question, an interactive text box, a television, and a transmit button. Everything on the page carries the use of the metaphor through. Even the "submit" button for the message the visitor can enter says "transmit" (see Figure 8.14).

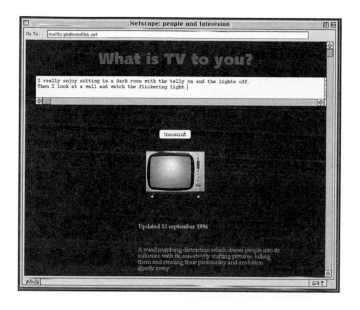

figure 8.14

We chose the TV icon at Dial It, and this is what we got.

The Variety of Interactivity on the Web

As we have mentioned, a site's goals and audience determine the relevance of any element. Content that includes text, images, animation, audio, video, and interactive elements drives a Web site.

What are the goals of the site? There may be multiple goals:

- Distribution of timely information and education

- Marketing and lead generation

- Retail business, sales, and ordering

- Public Relations, entertainment, and making visitors feel a part of things

Investigate your client's competition. Do they have sites? What interactive techniques do they use? What shortcomings do their sites have that you want to avoid? What good ideas do they use that you can build on?

Who is your audience? What browsers will they be using? What kind of access speed will they have? What interactive tools will you have at your disposal based on their viewing tools? Will you require them to download plug-ins or will you work with the built-in features of the browser? These are the questions you must ask before you even begin to design interactive elements for incorporation at the site you are designing.

What? You aren't designing the site? You've been asked to enhance an already designed and active site? The questions you must ask are the same, but the statistics gathered from the site should help you to choose methods and tools to use.

In this section we will get just a taste of the wide variety of purposes for which interactivity is used on the Web, including:

- Providing information interactively

- Customizing a visitor's experience

- Interactive navigation

- Virtually visiting

- Entertainment

Providing Information Interactively

All educators know that engaging a learner interactively is half the battle won. This is not limited to educational sites, per se; often in the normal course of business it is essential to get information across in order to create interest in a product or a service. You have to explain why you are different, and that may be a complex explanation. Try selling multiple master fonts. Flash and dash isn't going to get you very far.

Conveying a Concept

We like multiple master fonts in our studio; we love working with type. We don't cringe at the thought of designing a project using *only* type. In fact, because we design the interiors of books, we are quite familiar with type-dominated projects. We have been lucky enough to meet some wonderful type designers. One of them, Brian Sooy in Elyria, Ohio, is one of the few type designers outside of Adobe to design multiple master fonts.

We were redesigning `http://www.fontsonline.com` and asked Brian if he had any suggestions for how we could convey the concept of multiple master fonts online. We suggested using Shockwave, QuickTime, or an animated GIF because we were going to use these formats throughout the site. After a few email messages back and forth discussing the concept of the "morphing" of the font, he suggested a Shockwave graphic with a slider the viewer could control (see Figure 8.15). It was essential to have the viewer control the axis manipulation to understand the possibilities in manipulating the typeface. As the slider is pulled from left to right, the font changes through a number of weights created by axis manipulation (see Figure 8.16). The images we show here are from Brian Sooy's site.

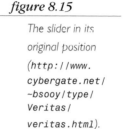

figure 8.15

The slider in its original position

(`http://www. cybergate.net/ ~bsooy/type/ Veritas/ veritas.html`).

figure 8.16

The slider showing a variation in axis weight.

337

NOTE

"A multiple master typeface allows for variations between extremes such as weight, width, or optical weight such as the thickening and thinning of hairlines for various point sizes."
-Brian Sooy

Another excellent example of informing the public about type can be found at `http://www.razorfish.com/bluedot/typo/anatomy/` (see Figure 8.17). Using Shockwave, the visitor can drag one character outline on top of another so that the subtle differences between the two are readily apparent (see Figures 8.18 and 8.19).

figure 8.17

The introductory page of the Razorfish typography site.

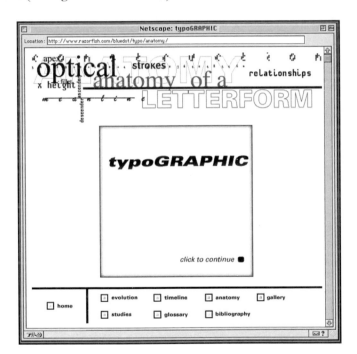

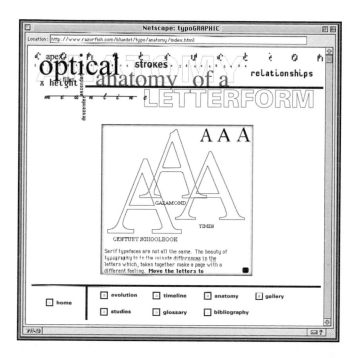

figure 8.18

Here you see the
outlines of three
different serif fonts.

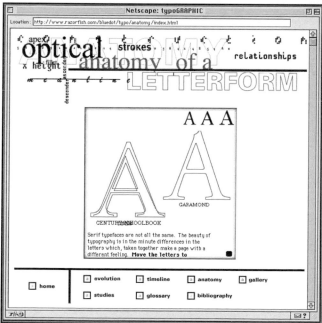

figure 8.19

You can drag a
letter onto another
to compare their
shapes.

It's All in the Data

We've all seen database interfaces that leave us cold and gasping for the information we urgently need. One small electronics manufacturer has taken the simple idea of a database of attributes of microwaves and camcorders into an experience truly designed to fit the consumer's needs. What do you want to do when you shop for electronics? You want to *compare* the products. At the Samsung Product Browser (`http://www.sosimple.com`), this is very easy to do.

First things first: this is a fun interface, and well-designed, too. Simple scrolling and pop-up menus give you criteria with which you will search. We decided to start with microwaves. We're looking for a new one for the studio, so why not check them out (see Figure 8.20)? Let's take a look at them all so we have an idea of what is available. Click here, scroll there, okay, click Search. Well, we get another screen that asks about watts and defrost and a few other things. We answer those questions in the same manner.

figure 8.20

Microwaves: who would have thought they could be so macho?

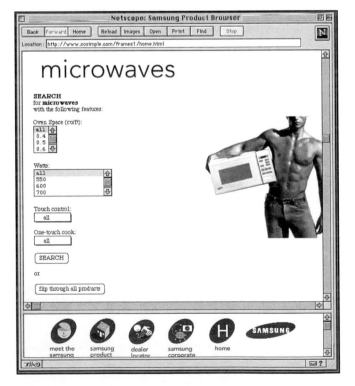

We then find two models we like, put x's in the boxes, and click compare. We've got a side-by-side comparison, feature by feature. Very cool (see Figure 8.21). Now we take a look at camcorders (see Figure 8.22). We select citeria in the same way we did with the microwaves. This time there is only one item meeting our criteria and the interface shows us all its features (see Figure 8.23). When we take a look at all the features, we can sce we have the option by the arrow-embellished page icons to move forward and back through this visual catalog.

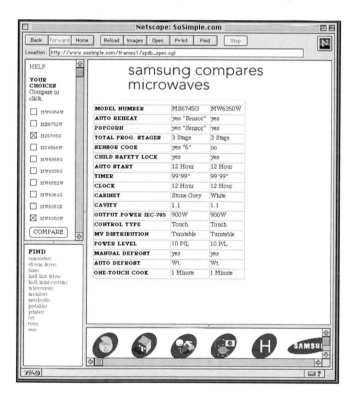

figure 8.21

Comparing two microwaves.

figure 8.22

Okay, so I guess camcorders aren't macho.

figure 8.23

The bulleted list of features.

Frames are used judiciously here. They are used where they are helpful—like when you want to select one or more models for comparison or to access another product in "find."

The use of images for the products was interesting, too. The man holding a microwave under one arm—to indicate that it is of manageable weight and size? And the woman holds the camcorder with one hand—small, light, easy to handle, even for a woman. Stereotypes or measuring devices? The information has been presented in a clear, easy-to-access interface that is a pleasant surprise.

Customizing a Visitor's Experience

One of the greatest advantages of designing for the Web is customizing a visitor's experience. Designing areas that can be manipulated by the reader or visitor requires a working knowledge of the site's content and additional Web resources that relate to the site. Customizing the experience can be a totally invisible experience for viewers, or the customization can be driven by viewers.

The following two examples show considerable viewing preference manipulation. Both sites have engineers to handle creating the code required to create these options. Be wary of overwhelming visitors to your sites with preference options.

They are good examples to illustrate the possibilities, yet a bit too much to go through, in my opinion. Be careful how far you push the viewers' tolerances. We suggest testing on a number of folks to get a feel for their tolerance levels. Pick folks that are newbies as well as seasoned surfers.

Netscape's PowerStart

At the Netscape site, a visitor-driven option is available to design a personal "PowerStart" page at `http://personal.netscape.com/custom/` (see Figures 8.24 through 8.28). This demo page is designed to show the level of customization available within the Netscape environment.

figure 8.24

*Netscape's
PowerStart opener
leaves the frames to
the left and bottom
empty until you
enter the
customization menu.*

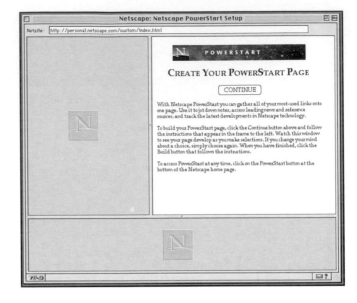

figure 8.25

*The instructions and
preview show up
side-by-side in the
frames interface.*

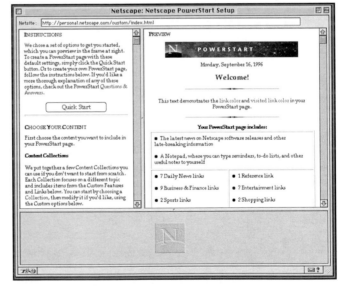

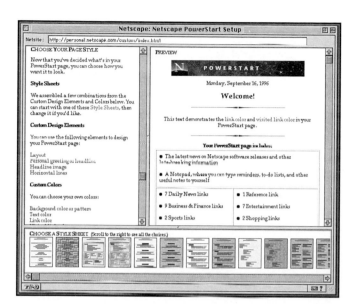

figure 8.26

Select from the style sheets and design elements.

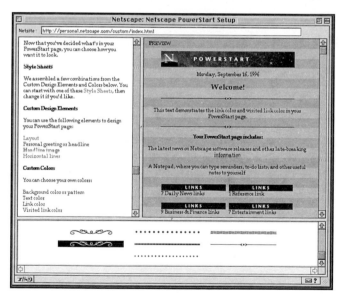

figure 8.27

Apply the choices and the frame on the right updates to show the selection in context.

figure 8.28

After following all the steps, the preferences chosen are applied and the page is available.

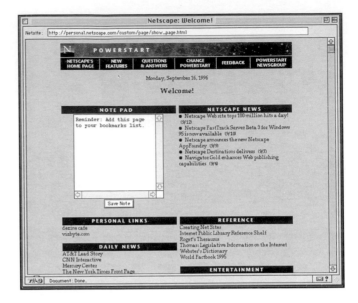

The PowerStart page provides a number of choices in creating a page that is your starting point (if you designate it as your home page within the browser preferences) when you launch your browser. It takes a bit of time to set up these preferences, everything from background color and graphics to sets of news links and a notepad. Customize by selecting content and design elements from the menus made available.

So, now the browser keeps track of your preferences through a "cookie" it has received from the server. As a result of that cookie information, a script creates a page from a database based on the preferences you selected. The next time you go to your PowerStart page, the browser remembers all of these choices you made by consulting the cookie. We discuss cookies in the "Cookies" section later in this chapter.

The designer of this interface had a lot of work to do combining information design, interactive design, page design, and communication with the engineer who implemented the interface to build the custom HTML page.

HotWired

Another example of this kind of customization with a less daunting interface and pretty clean page design is the customization of the member interface at HotWired (`http://vip.hotwired.com/login/subservices.html`). A registered member can set preferences for visiting the site. When these preferences are set, the member logs in and HotWired remembers what the preferences are, making new content that fits the set preferences available. This customization makes it possible to have new information, and information that may be nested, available at more accessible levels. This is sometimes referred to as "surfacing" information. The visitor doesn't have to navigate down many levels to get past previously experienced or irrelevant content.

At HotWired there are four categories for "personalization." Similar categories could be used in designing almost any site. It is not necessary to use all the possibilities. The viewer at HotWired also has the ability to set some preferences and leave the defaults for others. There is also the possibility of changing the preferences at any time the viewer wants. The levels of choice and customizing are considerable.

- **Member Information:** One of the cool features here is the option to make your email address and URL active links when posting to Threads (a threaded discussion list). This enables other participants in the discussion to click to send you email or visit your Web site (see Figure 8.29).

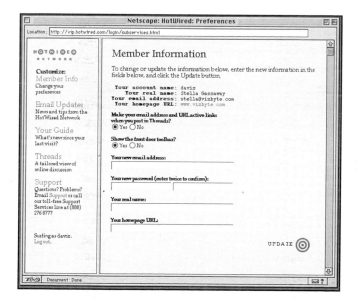

figure 8.29

Enter the HotWired Member Information customization menu.

347

- **Email updates**: I don't always surf the Net. I want to check out stuff when it changes and I don't want to waste time. I like getting notices (when I request them) from sites I find interesting. The folks at HotWired have an update email list as part of their customizing option. Simple radio buttons let you answer yes (mail me) or no (don't bother me). Pretty cool stuff (see Figure 8.30).

figure 8.30

Email updates selections.

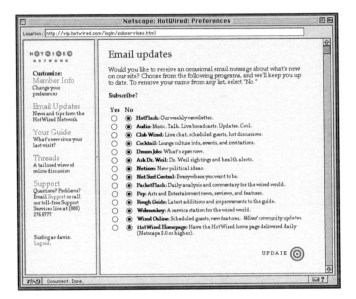

- **Program Guide**: HotWired enables you to create a guide that appears each time you visit the site. The purpose is to indicate items new since the last time you visited. They are displayed and marked "new." This is helpful for at-a-glance reference, and is important at a site with changing content and considerable depth (see Figure 8.31).

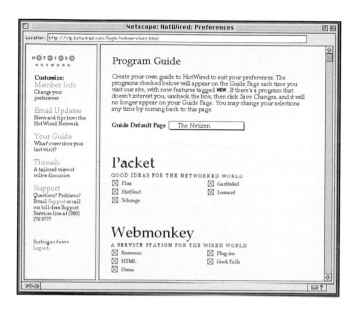

figure 8.31

Program Guide.

- **Threads**: The Threads discussion groups are available for much of the content at HotWired. To save you a little time, you can choose how to view the discussions (see Figure 8.32).

figure 8.32

Tailor your view of Threads.

After you register as a member and set your preferences for the view you want to see, try logging in. A simple page appears where you enter your member name and password. Click the log in button and you are welcomed (see Figure 8.33). You can select an option to have HotWired save your name and password with a cookie (see the discussion of cookies later in this chapter).

figure 8.33

Logged in at HotWired.

The interactivity of becoming a member to HotWired gives the visitor a sense of control. Preferences have been set and now a special view, a view requested by the viewer, is furnished by the server.

Yahoo!

Another example of a simple and transparent use of server smarts can be found a `http://www.yahoo.com`, where, when you search in a particular category, you are served up an ad that pertains to the search (see Figure 8.34). This provides advertisers with a targeted market for their ad. An ad will show up when a category is chosen and when search results are returned.

This is a great way to guarantee an advertiser an audience; careful planning that isn't too obvious and is always considered helpful. It's a lot like asking you if you would like fries with your burger.

figure 8.34

An advertisement pertaining to the search criteria is served up at Yahoo!.

Interactive Navigation

One source of the instant gratification that is increasing in popularity is rollover navigational elements. The rollover is a very simple and rewarding experience: you put your cursor over something and presto! it changes in some way. That could be anything from a simple color change or a brightening to a complete transformation. Because this is the Web, there is a natural connection between rollovers and navigational icons for two reasons. First, the fact that something changes alerts the visitor to the fact that this is an active graphic and implies that something even more will happen if it is actually clicked! Second, every designer is faced with the challenge of offering many navigational choices and giving information about those choices without cluttering the page. A rollover can be used to display additional information when activated that neatly disappears when the cursor is removed.

Packet

An excellent example of the value of roll overs is at `http://www.packet.com` (see Figure 8.35). Here at the bottom of the page in a frame unto itself is the navigation bar. This bar is run by a Java applet. It could just as well have been done in Shockwave. If you don't know, Java rollovers have been big in Director for quite some time and are making their way onto the Web in a big way. Of course with Shockwave you have to worry about having the plug-in.

figure 8.35

The first page of
Packet.

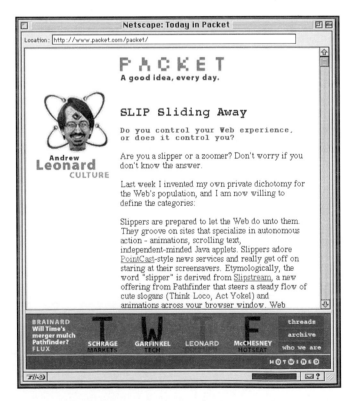

Here in a rather compressed space a designer could fit in the titles of the lead articles on each day of the week. When the arrow travels over the day of the week and columnist's name, activating a hot spot, a new image appears giving the article title. Pretty simple, you say. Sure it is; most good ideas seem that way when you stumble upon them.

Rollovers also highlight the threads, archive, and who we are sections (see Figure 8.36).

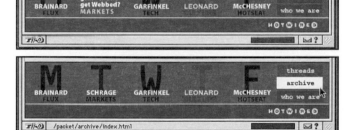

figure 8.36

Here you can see a couple of the other active rollovers in the navigational bar.

Chrysler

Every once in a while you should just click some of those ads you see at search sites. A click away can be some surprising and clever things. And here's one I found at an unlikely spot: http://www.chrysler.com.

On the first page of this new site is a Shockwave animation. Then we get to the surprise: another short animation in the type as you see in the first screen capture (see Figure 8.37); the logos show up and there you are, ready to choose a Chrsyler brand vehicle. When you move your mouse over the brand identifier, an animation is triggered. Each animation relates to the personality attributed to that vehicle (see Figure 8.38). I just had to look at what the Jeep would do. When you roll over the Jeep identifier, a Jeep appears, the engine makes a roaring sound, and it four-wheels off. You get a rollover animation and a sound cue in one interactive moment.

353

figure 8.37

This is the "new"
chryslercorp.com
site.

figure 8.38

Four wheelin' on the
Web.

This is pretty cool stuff, and even though with quite a bit of programming you could probably have Java do this, I wouldn't suggest it. This is where Shockwave is a good choice. With audio compression the file doesn't get big, either.

Guinness

Someone mentioned I should check out the Guinness site (`http://www.guinness.ie`). He mentioned something about a Widget. Well, you can find out about the Widget and a whole lot more about the brewery when you head on over to this Shockwave-driven site. Figure 8.39 is a capture of a bubbling animation. The bubbles have symbols and a simple rollover gives you a hint about where you are going to go if you click. A very dandy interface; check it out. We talk later about another interactive spot at the site.

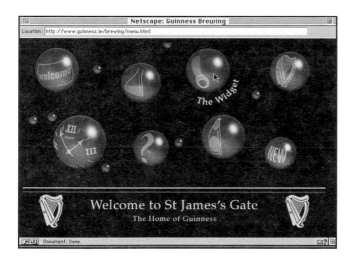

figure 8.39

Check out the Widget.

Macromedia

The renovations at the Macromedia site (`http://www.macromedia.com`) are welcome improvements over its old image-heavy navigation. The new design uses white backgrounds on the pages, one of those "workarounds" for the unsightly white box with its logo that greets you before the file has loaded. Choose any background, any background at all as long as its white. Yes, I do want Macromedia to fix this so that we can really create interactive environments without having to put up ugly signs saying "loading" or "one moment please." I'm an ungrateful designer. I want it perfect now. Okay, the design rant is now over.

Back to more interesting things like the very cool, fun, and amusing navigational device at the entry page to the site (see Figure 8.40). When the imagemap loads, it comes in gracefully from a ghosted image to vibrant primary and secondary colors. Numerous navigational choices are immediately apparent, but when the visitor places the cursor over the objects on the screen, sounds surprise you, animations are triggered, and other options appear (see Figure 8.41). Each of the objects on the screen has a sound, animation, and hot spot to a location at the site. You'll probably play around a whole lot before you even choose to go anywhere. The first time the guy that looks like a government agent from the '60s appeared, everyone in the studio laughed (see Figure 8.42).

figure 8.40

The Macromedia interactive navigational map.

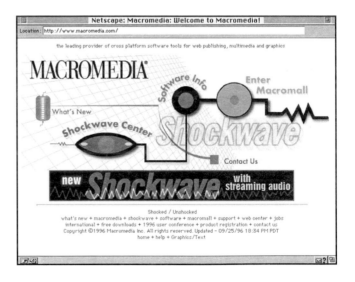

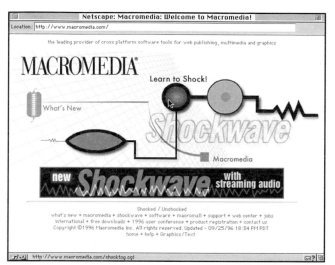

figure 8.41

Other options
appear on rollovers..

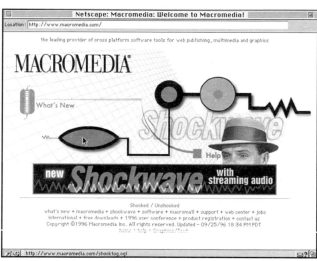

figure 8.42

Some of the
animation is
extremely silly.

This element is the integration of numerous goals in one element:

- Art created in FreeHand (probably)

- Animation and interactivity in Director

- Shockwave integration

- Compression

- Navigational imagemap

The really fun thing about the interactive imagemap is the animation that runs continually, shooting little shockwaves through the schematic drawing in the map. This is a really fine piece of interactive navigation. Visitors come back to the site often but won't be bored by this demonstration of interactivity brought to us by the folks that want us to buy their tools to do this stuff. Macromedia has created a sample and set a standard at the same time. This is an excellent tool for marketing and visitor experience. Don't you wish you had done it?

Virtually Visiting

Creating a virtual space for visitors is one of the ways to bring an environment to the visitor instead of the visitor to the environment. Many corporations create video tapes and send them with or without a sales person to distant customers. The tapes have been created as a plant or office tour to give a feel for the people and environment. A virtual storefront is more than an online catalog. It's a space that can be navigated and explored; it is more like the in-store experience.

With the Web and the new interactive tools available to us, it is possible to create an atmosphere online with video, sound clips, music, and text controlled by the visitor. Now the visit isn't a linear video tape; it's an interactive visit, not unlike a personal tour at a facility.

As we discussed in the video and audio chapters, the independent music industry has been at the leading edge of technology, bringing both recorded and live performances to the Web. These virtual clubs are an exciting part of virtual places on the Web. They are not 3D simulations; they are actual places with live content available on the Web.

Creating a site for *virtual visiting* requires total integration of multiple technologies and a seamless, intuitive interface. The designer has to be tenacious to create an environment retaining the viewer and suspending reality during the visit.

Club Congress

At bYte a tree we're really interested in QuickTime VR, so we decided to check out the Apple QuickTime Web Challenge Video/QuickTimeVR Winner: Club Congress at `http://phoenixnewtimes.com/ads/congo/`. It's always exciting when you visit a site and say, "Wow, I wish I did that." I don't know about you, but for me uttering those words is the highest praise I can give.

When first arriving at Club Congress, a sound-only movie loads and plays as you enter the club (see Figure 8.43). Click the club logo and enter the main screen to "The World's Darkest Nightclub." Here you can select where in the club you want to go (see Figure 8.44). We came for the VR, so let's check it out.

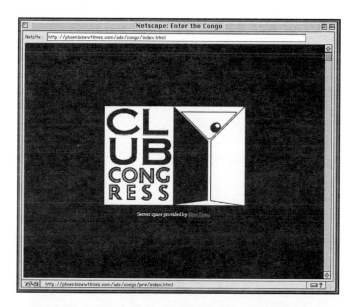

figure 8.43

The entrance to Club Congress.

figure 8.44

Visitors use the icon menu bar to the right to choose their destinations at Club Congress.

In the first room entitled "Kiss" (see Figure 8.45), we enter "The World's Darkest Nightclub." QuickTimeVR enables a 360-degree panoramic view, zooming in and out, and clicking hotspots. With keyboard controls a visitor can walk into one room, look around to see if there's anyone he knows, and if not proceed to another room in the club using the navigational buttons in the viewing frame. In this case we went forward into the room called "Dance" (see Figure 8.46).

figure 8.45

One of the VR rooms at Club Congress. You can zoom up close to the regulars.

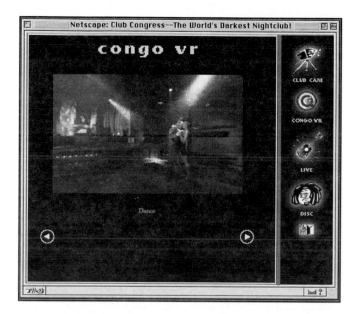

figure 8.46

The dance floor at Club Congress.

You can move around quite a bit within each room; the club atmosphere gives you plenty to investigate. The atmosphere at Club Congress is thick and as you wander through the different rooms you become totally caught up in the experience. You want to know who the people are by the bar, and just what are those folks doing in the other room? What about the dancers? Did they meet each other tonight? The only thing we found missing is a continuous sound track. A simple MIDI piece would have worked well without much additional download time.

361

The skillful design and technological knowledge to build this virtual club experience doesn't end with QuickTime VR. You can also check out the live Club Cam that updates ever 15 seconds (see Figure 8.47). Click the "LIVE" icon and check out the concert schedule brought to you live through the net. (We discuss this is the video chapter.) The folks at Club Congress have done everything it takes to build a successful, easy-to-navigate, interactively rich environment on the Web. When you enter Club Congress you are virtually there.

figure 8.47

Live look from the
Club Cam.

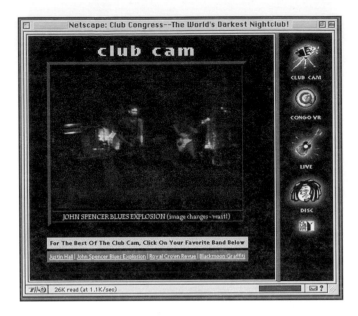

Toyota

All right, we've gone to the Chrysler site; what do those folks at Toyota (`http://www.toyota.com`) have happening? It's always a good thing to check out your competition. Well, one of the most fun, interactive parts of the Toyota site is a great marketing tool. You can cyber-drive up to the Toyota Model Lineup for the year (see Figure 8.48). When you select a vehicle to look at, you have quite a number of choices. You can look at large photos such as the ones in print catalogs, take a look at spec charts, take a "walk around" using QuickTime VR, and use the PhotoBubble Viewer to sit in the car and get a full 360-degree view of the interior.

It's exactly like the Web site says: "Virtually everything but that new car smell"—and I bet you they're working on that.

We chose to take a look at the RAV4. The PhotoBubble viewer (a downloadable viewer link is available at the Toyota site) is pretty cool and the resolution was still good even when we zoomed in on the dashboard (see Figure 8.49). The mouse will let you zoom and spin all around the interior; it feels pretty real.

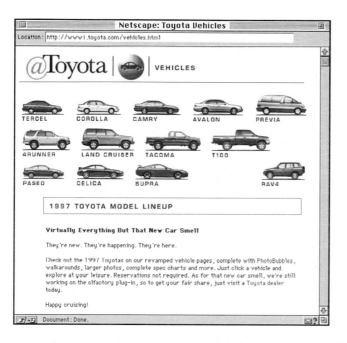

figure 8.48

You can choose a vehicle to experience in the PhotoBubble Viewer.

figure 8.49

Shots from inside the RAV4.

Have you bought a new car lately? Still feeling the trauma from trying to figure out what you wanted and making a deal for the car or truck you bought over a decade ago? Well, here you can check out the options and features, practically sit in the vehicle, and find out where the nearest dealers are. You can make your decision to buy a Toyota model and options, and all before hitting the road to visit the dealer. When you don't have to go to the dealer it will be perfect.

Toyota has made it possible for a potential buyer to check out its offerings without any pressure. There are lots of ways to get information, view the vehicles, check their specifications, and find dealers. That's a value to the potential buyer. The experience is interactive and the potential buyer has control. This is a very different feeling from what traveling to several dealers would be like. Now if only you could kick the tires.

Blue Wolf Net

For a different kind of virtual experience, visit Blue Wolf Net (`http://www.bluewolfnet.com/`), especially its Browseteria (see Figure 8.50). This is a 3D VRML world that reveals some of the power of VRML—and the power of experiencing an immersive, truly 3D experience. It still crashes my Mac, but hopefully VRML will become more stable soon!

figure 8.50

The VRML world of
Browseteria.

Entertainment

Now the chance to talk about just plain fun stuff. Well, of course it has another motive, but the fun is still there. Entertainment is a great way to get folks to visit a site. They don't have to be interested in what you offer to pass the word about some terrific game that can be played live. Those who are interested in the content at your site will be glad to experience something amusing. Corporations love to have the public feel all warm and fuzzy in association with the company name.

Games on the Web

I'm not much for playing simple games on the Net, but I found two that because of their context really made me chuckle. The first is Crash and Burn, which can be found at the creative and technologically hip Razorfish site at `http://www.razorfish.com/bluedot/drive/drive.html`.

If you've never been to the Razorfish site, go there and be inspired! Here you can find some of the most elegant solutions to design problems. Crash and Burn is just such a solution. It is a simple game fashioned after original 4-bit games created for arcade or television play. It pays homage to the days when the definition of interactive games and the technology used to create them were much simpler.

As you can see by the screen captures, it's a simple game (see Figure 8.51). The player tries to drive the car down the road without crashing into other cars or obstacles that may be in the roadway. The player is given three lives, and for me they were very short ones. No coins are needed for another game and play can continue as long as the player wishes. It's simple and silly and you'll chuckle while you play it. And see, it works, because I'm telling you to visit the site.

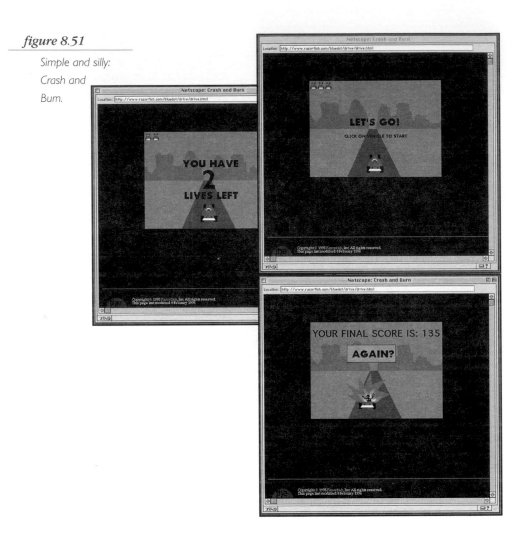

figure 8.51

Simple and silly:
Crash and
Burn.

The second example is at a place you would expect silly games. Point your browser to `http://www.cornpops.com` (see Figure 8.52).

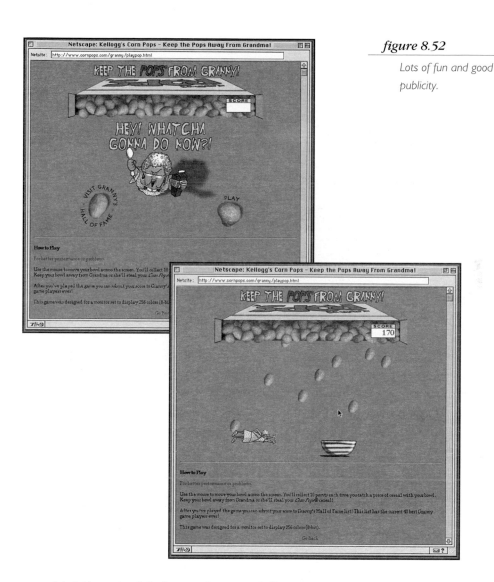

figure 8.52

Lots of fun and good
publicity.

Lighthearted Information and Propaganda

While corporate sites are more likely to attract visitors with humor and
entertainment than dry information, their efforts to be lighthearted leave
many sites simply vapid and cutesy. An inspiring exception is the daz-
zlingly clever and amusing `http://www.guinness.ie` from Ireland (see
Figure 8.53). Each part of the site we visited was Shockwave-driven except
for the opening screen. We discussed the rollover highlights in the section
on interactive navigation earlier, but now we're off to visit the brewery.

You can visit Ireland, fun I'm sure, or stop in at the local pub. The visit to the brewery has a catch; you have to try out being brewmaster.

figure 8.53

Choose your path.

You make selections and follow directions to add the ingredients and chill and ferment to make the perfect pint of Guinness (see Figures 8.54 through 8.56). We didn't know too much about the task but adventured to try entering different data just to see the results. The brewery calculator told us we were pathetic at the job. We did, however, answer the extra point question correctly indicating how many kegs we would have to brew to meet the needs of Guinness drinkers in the whole of Ireland.

figure 8.54

Mixing the brew.

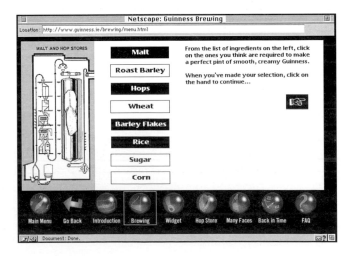

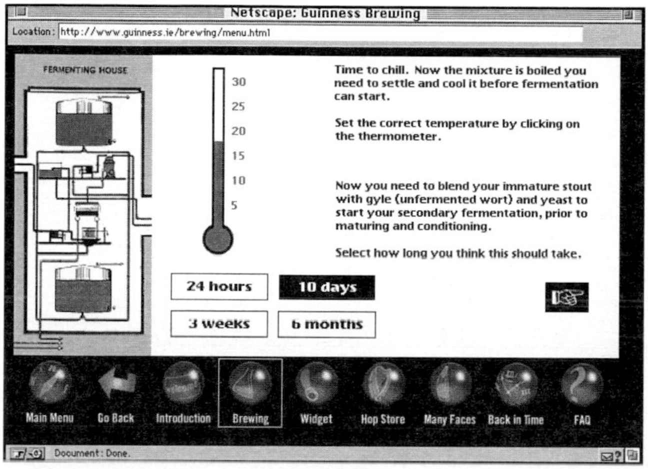

figure 8.55

Just the right temperature for the right number of days and...

figure 8.56

...you find out how well you did.

This is a fun, interactive experience and you can actually learn some basics about brewing the brown stuff. It's probably even more of a challenge to those who drink the stuff or have given homebrewing a shot.

The interface for the visit was organized and obvious (perhaps in case you had too many pints). It was fun and I can think of at least a dozen friends that would enjoy it for different reasons. I'm sure the site has done everything the designers had planned for it. It engages the visitors, informs them about brewing, tests their knowledge about the ingredients of the beverage, and instigates them to have their friends stop by and check it out.

The use of Shockwave may not have been the original intention. The presentation seems as if it was made for another prurpose and then later shocked and put on the Web. It works well, looks great, and was a good use of Director. The whole experience was actually absent of most of the hassles of waiting for other forms of interactivity to load or process on the Internet.

Chats and Discussions

It seems like chats are all the rage on the Web these days. To be honest, we spend most of our time trying to talk clients *out* of doing chats. Why? Because chats invariably turn into social get-togethers that accomplish nothing (for either the chatter or the company hosting the chat) and because the technology for implementing chats is too complex and, simply put, ugly.

But of course that doesn't mean it's going to be this way forever. So here's a very quick overview of the varieties of chats available.

Live Chats

In this variety of chat, everyone gets on the same Internet "phone line" and talks at the same time. This can certainly build a sense of place and community at a site, and it can also build a sense of a crowd of people all yelling simultaneously.

The basic live chat is text-only, just like IRC (Internet Relay Chat). This is appearing on more and more sites recently. You arrive at a Web page that uses CGI or Java to create several areas of the screen (some sites use frames): one in which everyone's messages display, one for you to use to type messages, and often another area for navigation, ads, or logos. Check out the chat areas at `http://www.theglobe.com/chat/` for an example.

Other chat areas are more graphical, enabling the chatters to choose icons that will represent them in the chat area. The Palace (`http://www.thepalace.com/`), from GNN, is a popular example of this graphical chat. The Palace works via its own server and client software that you have to download first. After you connect to a site using the Palace server, you move your icon/character around several realistic-looking rooms, chatting via text with other strange-looking characters as you go (see Figure 8.57).

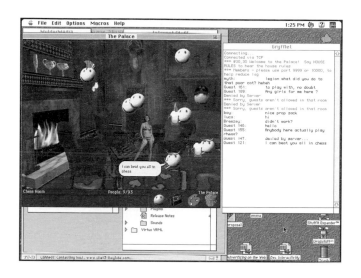

figure 8.57

Chatting in The Palace.

A third kind of live chat takes this graphical approach to the extreme by placing you (as an avatar, or 3D character) into a virtual 3D space (much like the Blue Wolf Net site mentioned earlier). You can literally walk around rooms and "bump" into other people, talking with them via text or (in some cases) voice. Eventually we'll see these 3D spaces done entirely in VRML, but for now most of them are proprietary systems that require a server and special software to view. You can check out a few of these systems at `http://www.chaco.com/`, `http://ww3.blacksun.com/`, and `http://www.onlive.com/`.

Discussion Groups

Another way to create a "conversation place" on your site is to avoid the "live" chat entirely and instead use a discussion group concept. In this scenario, visitors leave messages posted long-term for others to see, and they can also respond to the postings of others (much like you find in a Usenet newsgroup).

The advantage here is that these kinds of discussions are usually filled more with content you care about than with social chatting. You can browse through the various topics discussed and read only what interests you. And unlike live chats, these discussion areas are going on all the time, so you don't have to coordinate schedules and time zones to arrange a specific time to meet online.

On dezine café, we created tanGo (`http://www.dol.com/tango/`), a discussion area consisting of several topic areas: one for talking about the site, one for rants, one for product reviews, and so on. (see Figure 8.58). It's a great way for people to interact with each other and with the site, and it keeps them coming back.

figure 8.58

On tanGo, visitors can talk back about the site they're browsing.

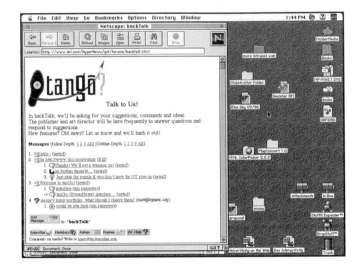

For tanGo, we used HyperNews, a free discussion CGI program available at `http://union.ncsa.uiuc.edu/HyperNews/get/hypernews.html`. It's relatively easy to set up on a server, and it even supports threading, which means that messages on the same topic appear grouped together for easy skimming and reading. Definitely check it out.

Options for Introducing Interactivity

There are almost as many technical options for bringing interactivity to the Web as there were for animation, including Shockwave for Director, Java, JavaScript, cookies, VRML, QuickTime VR, and more.

Shockwave for Director

To create a rich interactive presentation, this is the tool most accessible to the developer. We already discussed bringing Director presentations to the Web using Shockwave in Chapter 5, but we will recap the pros and cons briefly. We hear that Netscape 4.0 will include the Shockwave plug-ins as a part of the browser. This means users won't have to get a separate plug-in to view Shockwave movies, which makes Shockwave an even more attractive option for bringing interactivity to a site.

Pros include the following:

- True visitor-initiated interactivity

- Excellent compression (using Afterburner for Director)

- New audio SWA sound compression and streaming audio

- Relatively easy HTML coding using the EMBED tag

- Bandwidth-friendly if you are not carried away

- You can control palette of HTML page from director movie if desired

- If not afraid of Lingo, you can build in URL links

- Cross-platform support

Cons include the following:

- Plug-in needed (Netscape 4.0 will change this)

- Entire presentation must load before it will play

- Ugly white box shows up no matter what color background, so Macromedia's ugly embossed logo shows up as solution while movie loads

- Expensive application (Director) required for creation

- Relatively steep learning curve

- Poor documentation

- Support for QuickTime within the presentation is under development

- Requires server configuration

Shockwave for Director works as a plug-in for Netscape 2.0 and 3.0 that users have to download. Fortunately, for version 4.0, Shockwave capability will be built into Netscape, so no separate download will be required. Internet Explorer 3.0 supports Shockwave natively through an ActiveX Control.

373

Embedding Shockwave movies into HTML is fairly easy. The basic EMBED tag looks like this:

```
<EMBED SRC="rollover.dcr" WIDTH=100 HEIGHT=125>
```

The WIDTH and HEIGHT tags are mandatory to specify the size of the image in pixels. The Shockwave movie may not play if these sizes are not specified.

There are also optional attributes you can add to the EMBED tag for Shockwave movies:

- `PALETTE=foreground` gives you control over which color palette the browser uses when it plays the movie. "foreground" means the browser will load the Director movie's palette and use it as the palette for the entire page. (Internet Explorer 3.0 does not support this attribute.)

- `PALETTE=background` prevents the palette of the Director movie from loading, and instead the browser uses the system palette. This is the default setting under the EMBED tag.

- `BGCOLOR="ffffff"` (Shockwave for Director 5 only) lets you specify in hexadecimal the solid color to display behind the movie.

You can also specify alternative information in case a browser doesn't support Shockwave. Simply use the NOEMBED tag like this:

```
<NOEMBED><IMG SRC="button.gif"></NOEMBED>
```

In this case, the browser will show the standard button GIF if it can't display the Shockwave movie.

For details on other EMBED attributes and workarounds, see `http://www.macromedia.com/shockwave/director5/browser.html`.

Tools

Essential tools for working with Shockwave for Director include:

- Macromedia Director (information at `http://www.macromedia.com/software/director/`)

- Afterburner for Director (free download at `http://www.macromedia.com/shockwave/devtools.html`)

> **NOTE**
>
> Other tools we recommend are good books on Director and/or Shockwave. A couple you might consider are *Inside Director 5* (New Riders), *Macromedia Shockwave for Director* (Hayden Books), and *Shockwave Power Solutions* (New Riders).

bYte a tree: An Introduction

One of the coolest things about the Shockwave technology is being able to bring projects created for other environments to the Web with very little additional effort.

One example is an interactive presentation we created to introduce our multimedia division to our established clients. We created this simple introduction to fit compressed on a disk; you can experience it on the CD-ROM (see Figures 8.60 through 8.62). This presentation had to fit on a disk for mailing and be a self-running application with viewer interactivity. It had simple goals:

- Announce that STELLARViSIONs had a new multimedia division

- Give the recipients an idea of what we could do for them

- Use images and type identified with STELLARViSIONs and combine it with the new division image

- Reflect our studio personality

- Tell them to call us

375

figure 8.60

The intro to the piece; if you don't take action you get the "ahem."

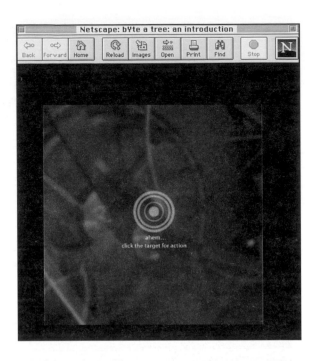

figure 8.61

One of the vizbytians, Gerry, is introduced.

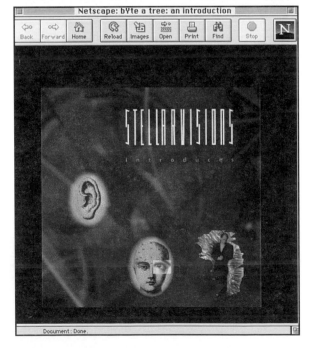

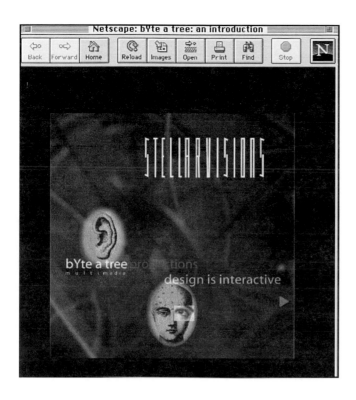

figure 8.62

*The primary
interactive screen.*

We wanted to Shock this Director piece and put it on the Web in our portfolio section. Here on the Net we didn't have to worry about cross-platform difficulties of delivery. With this new option for an online portfolio, we could now invite our clients and potential clients to investigate our work without sending any media. This is just the first of a number of pieces that will be available at our Web site.

Oh, did I say it went smoothly? One glitch. The original QuickTime movies that had been linked files in the presentation now were adapted and recreated as Director animations so that we would be sure the sound would be in sync. You can link other assets to Director Shockwave presentations, but you can't be sure that the QuickTime movies will be fully loaded when the viewer begins to interact with the piece.

Java

Java is an object, platform-independent programming language from Sun Microsystems. This is the most powerful way to bring interactivity to a site and control what the user experiences. The programmer can use ready-made objects and classes that can bring multimedia effects into pages. The object has all the information necessary to make a functional effect, but you can change certain variables (color, size, message displayed, and so on).

Java actually controls the Web browser and was specifically developed for the Internet. Unlike CGI, the Java applets are executed by the client's computer and therefore the speed of connection is not as critical.

A tiny self-running application, called an applet, is sent to the client's computer when called on by the browser. When the browser sees the APPLET tag, it downloads the applet from the server and executes it. This application is designed to operate only within the browser, therefore it cannot run amok on the client's hard disk.

To call on an applet, insert a line in the HTML that gives the applet name and the amount of pixel space desired for the element:

```
<APPLET CODE="appletname.class" Width="x" Height="y">
```

Pros include the following:

- Powerful, flexible language creates many possibilities for interactivity

- Cross-platform support

- Some tools exist which are making Java programming easier for non-programmers

- Very secure, so it won't mess with users' systems

- Supports many multimedia elements, including sound and (eventually) video

- Hundreds of public domain applets freely available

- Backwards-compatibility friendly (unlike plug-ins)

Cons include the following:

- A very steep learning curve to learn the language

- Not fully stable, still being developed

- Doesn't function identically across platforms

- Often slower than Shockwave for Director or other interactivity options

Java is still a young language. As time passes, we're bound to see people doing more and more things with Java as awareness increases and the language evolves.

There are three ways to incorporate Java into your Web page:

- Learn the programming language from the ground up.

- Hire someone else to program in Java for you.

- Customize ready-made Java applets that you find and download from other sites.

Teach Yourself

Java is a full-blown programming language. For the most part it requires a background in basic C++ programming and a mind like a steel trap. This translates into a very steep learning curve. But if you're up for the challenge, go for it. As for myself: no way.

But if you want to dive in, I recommend doing so via these books: Wintel people, go get *Teach Yourself Java in 21 Days* (Sams.net); Mac users, seek out *Teach Yourself Java for Macintosh in 21 Days* (Hayden Books). Have fun!

Hire Someone

Let's face it. You've got enough to do already. Leave programming to the experts. As you get deeper and deeper into bringing multimedia and interactivity to the Web, you'll have more and more need for a good programmer who can whip out CGI programs and Java applets for your every whim. Why not start developing that relationship today?

For example, HotWired (`http://www.hotwired.com/`) is one site that you'd expect to use interactivity all over the place. And in fact, the folks there have begun experimenting with interactive interfaces, especially on the channels Webmonkey (`http://www.webmonkey.com/`) and Packet (`http://www.packet.com/`). As it turns out, one of the techie geeks there created a custom-made Java applet that HotWired's non-programming designers could use to easily create and customize Java applets. The designers were thus freed up to create the navigational interfaces you see for Webmonkey and Packet (see Figure 8.63). For details on this story, see `http://www.webmonkey.com/demo/96/37/index4a.html`.

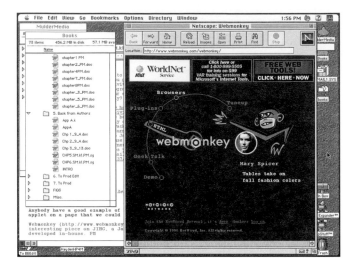

figure 8.63

The custom-made Java applet that helps you navigate around Webmonkey.

Customize Ready-Made Applets

A great short-term solution for making Java come to life on your site is to copy-and-paste someone else's Java (with their permission, of course!).

Many sites offer ever-expanding collections of ready-made Java applets ready for downloading and complete with instructions for customizing them for your specific needs. This can be a great first option to explore because chances are the interactive effect you have in mind may already be in existence. Why reinvent the wheel? The best Java site to explore is Gamelan (`http://www.gamelan.com/`) (see Figure 8.64), and especially this page at the site: `http://www.gamelan.com/pages/Gamelan.sites.collections.html`.

figure 8.64

Gamelan: EarthWeb's Java directory.

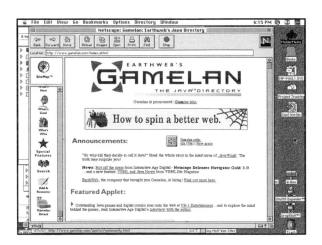

There are more and more applets available that can be adapted for use in a specific situation by setting the appropriate parameter tags PARAM in the HTML, which give information to the applet. The applet, for example, might describe a circle with a "color." The following line of HTML...

```
<PARAM name="color" value="green">
```

...tells the applet to make the circle green. Some applets require certain parameters to be set, and other parameters may be optional. The author of the applet needs to provide a list of parameter names and permitted values, specifying which are required and which will default if not specified.

The Hayden Books Web site (`http://www.hayden.com/`) uses this method. The folks there wanted buttons that lit up when your mouse rolled over them, and when they came across the GrowButton Java applet, already compiled and ready to use at the Apple Flavored Java site (`http://www.mbmdesigns.com/macjava/`), they knew they had a solution. Hayden got permission to use it, downloaded the applet, and changed the HTML to name the buttons they made in Photoshop: one GIF for the normal button, one for the "lit up" button, and a third for the "clicked on" button. The power of Java without the programming (see Figure 8.65)!

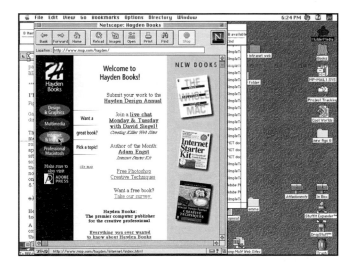

figure 8.65

The Java-enabled buttons in action at Hayden Books.

In the midst of this new technological fever, designers want to remain designers, not programmers. If we have a knowledge of our tools, ask software developers to give us what we need, and demand reliable tools, we'll have all we need. All the great features that come in software updates are suggested by designers such as us. Be involved in the development of tools such as AppletAce mentioned below. These graphical interfaces for customizing available applets will become a big part of the future. Ready-made objects for the Web will grow and the devices to customize and write them are already hitting the scene. It may be a while or maybe never that we see a tool for Java that will make the programming invisible. One thing is for certain: programming that is simple enough to be packaged will be for us, and the more difficult stuff will be left to professionals as it should be.

Another alternative to keep in mind is that there are new tools and applications coming out all the time that make creating or customizing Java applets easy for the non-programmer. A few examples include:

- *Macromedia's PowerApplets/AppletAce* (`http://www.macromedia.com/software/powerapplets/`). PowerApplets are ready-made applets you can download for free, and AppletAce is the stand-alone application you can use to customize PowerApplets. The PowerApplets are fairly basic right now, but it's a nice, easy-to-use package (see Figure 8.66).

figure 8.66

Customizing a PowerApplet in AppletAce.

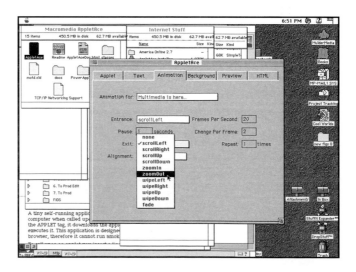

- *Jamba* (`http://www.aimtech.com/prodjahome.html`). An authoring tool enabling you to create rich, interactive Java applets without programming.

- *Sanga Pages* (`http://www.sangacorp.com/`). This new product offers the same advantages, although it also requires a server.

And that's just a taste of what's out there. Java is here to stay.

JavaScript

Unlike an applet, which resides on the server and is downloaded to the client, JavaScript is ASCII text within an HTML document that controls the browser functions. A typical example would be a command to open a new window in the browser (see Figure 8.67). This kind of scripting is not as complex as Java programming itself, but it still requires rigorous discipline to learn and use effectively. What's nice is that you don't need any special software; you can create JavaScripts with the same text editor you use for writing HTML.

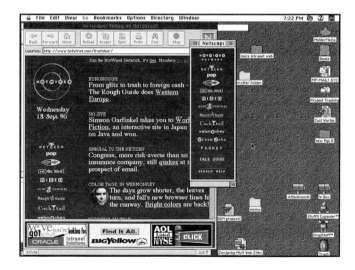

figure 8.67

The navigation window that pops up (via JavaScript) when you enter HotWired (*http://www.hotwired.com/frontdoor/*).

Just to give you a feel for it, here's the JavaScript code in the HTML document that creates the HotWired pop-up window:

```
<script language="javascript">
var remoteWin = null;
this.name = "home";
var myBrowser = navigator.appVersion;
function startToolbar() {
```

```
    if (myBrowser.indexOf("X11") == 7) {
      remoteWin =
window.open("","Toolbar",'toolbar=0,location=0,directories=0,status=0,
menubar=0,scrollbars=0,resizable=0,width=131,height=370');
    } else {
      remoteWin =
window.open("","Toolbar",'toolbar=0,location=0,directories=0,status=0,
menubar=0,scrollbars=0,resizable=0,width=110,height=335');
    }
    if (remoteWin != null) {
      remoteWin.rootWin = self;
      remoteWin.location = "http://www.hotwired.com/frontdoor/
toolbar/toolbar.html";
    }
}
function fetch(url) {
  rootWin.location = url;
}
</script>
```

Other things you can do with JavaScript include:

- Scrolling text

- Changing background colors

- Detecting plug-ins in visitors' browsers

- Making alert boxes appear

- Capturing keyboard input

- Coordinating content in various frames

- Creating an in-line clock or calculator

- Validating forms immediately

- Detecting and customizing for browsers

- Making rollover imagemaps (Netscape 3.0)

As with Java, you can learn JavaScript from scratch or you can copy and paste cool JavaScripts from around the Web and customize them to fit your needs. The nice thing about copying JavaScripts is that the script is fully contained in the HTML file, so all you have to do to see and copy it is select Document Source from Netscape's View menu.

Two great sites to begin your JavaScripting adventures are The JavaScript Index (`http://www.c2.org/~andreww/javascript/`) and Cut-N-Paste JavaScript (`http://www.infohiway.com/javascript/indexf.htm`).

If you want to learn JavaScript, go to the bookstore and find *Teach Yourself JavaScript in 21 Days* (Sams.net) or *JavaScript for Macintosh* (Hayden Books). If you don't have the time to learn JavaScript, but want to utilize the functionality, check out *Plug-n-Play JavaScript* (New Riders).

CGI

When it comes to CGI (Custom Gateway Interface) programs, frankly, you're better off getting some assistance from professional programmers. These applications, written from scratch usually in C++ or Perl, run off a server (unlike Java applets, if you remember, which are downloaded to a PC and run on the PC). CGIs are complicated, and you need access to the server to get them running and configured properly.

Basically, if no other technology does what you want it to do, not even a Java applet, you resort to creating a custom CGI script. The variety of possibilities here is endless, from the simplest animation via CGI (that's what server-push animation is) to the most complex database-driven engine serving customized Web pages to users depending on their preferences.

A lot of CGI is behind-the-scenes, so you seldom see it. Chances are, if you're sending information from a Web page, a CGI is handling it. If a Web site is creating Web pages on-the-fly for you, a CGI is probably behind that, too.

385

Cookies

If you explore the depths of your Netscape or Internet Explorer preferences files, you'll find a little file called something such as MagicCookie or cookies. If you open this file in Word or a text editor, you'll see multiple lines of text, each with a URL (or part of a URL), and some mostly incomprehensible data after each. Each of these lines represents a cookie.

A cookie is a piece of information some Web site servers give to you when you visit their site. Your Mac or PC stores the cookie in this cookies file. Then, when you visit the same site at some later date, your browser recognizes that one of the cookies it has was originally sent by this particular server. Your browser sends the cookie back to the server, which in turn is now able to recognize you. The server remembers whatever piece of information it gave to you the last time you visited and takes action accordingly. This "action" can be almost anything depending on how much information is in the cookie and what the server does with that information.

Time for a concrete example. When you first visit the M&M's site (`http://www.m-ms.com/`), you see a nice splash screen with a rather large animated GIF (see Figure 8.68). But within the HTML document the server sent, it also sent the following line:

```
<META HTTP-EQUIV="Set-Cookie" Content="mm-pages-seen=0:0;
expires=09-Nov-99 GMT">
```

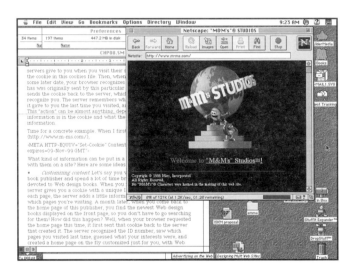

figure 8.68

The initial M&M's splash screen.

A cookie has been set! If you open my cookies file, you can see it listed there, on the last line (see Figure 8.69).

When you reload the page or come back to it later, the server sees by the cookie that you've already viewed one splash screen (page "0:0"), so now it serves up a new splash screen; this time a very entertaining Shockwave movie (see Figure 8.70). Sure enough, this HTML page sets the cookie to "mm-pages-seen=1:1." Each time you visit the page, the cookie tells the server which splash screen you've seen already, so it can serve a new one. It's a simple example of cookies used effectively to customize content.

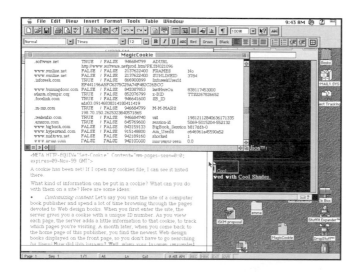

figure 8.69

The cookies file, just changed by the M&M's site.

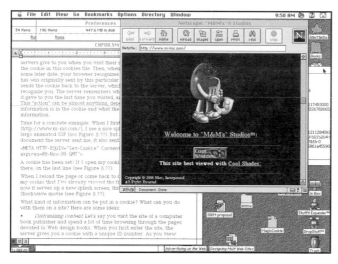

figure 8.70

The new splash screen page, customized by a cookie.

What You Can Do with a Cookie

So, what kind of information can be put in a cookie? What can you do with them on a site? Here are some ideas:

- **Customizing content**. Let's say you visit the site of a computer book publisher and spend a lot of time browsing through the pages devoted to Web design books. When you enter the site, the server gives you a cookie with a unique ID number. As you view each page, the server adds a little information to that cookie to track which pages you're visiting. A month later, when you come back to the home page of this publisher, you find the newest Web design books displayed on the front page so that you don't have to go searching for them. How did this happen? Well, when your browser requested the home page this time, it first sent the cookie back to the server that created it. The server (with the help of a back-end database) recognized the ID number, saw which pages you visited last time, guessed what your interests were, and created a home page on-the-fly customized just for you with Web design books front and center. A working example of this kind of use of cookies is the Netscape PowerStart personalized Web page service we looked at earlier in this chapter.

- **Tracking**. In much the same way, you can use cookies to track where visitors go on a site. Servers assign unique ID numbers to visitors, and then Webmasters can watch where traffic tends to flow on their sites. Webmasters can learn if they need to change navigation or featured content to direct traffic where they want it.

- **Online shopping**. You might also use cookies and ID numbers to make online shopping easy. A cookie might serve as a "shopping cart," keeping track of your purchases as you browse down various "aisles" in a virtual store and pick up items as you go. When you check out at the end of your shopping trip, the server looks at your cookie to see the list of items you want to purchase. Amazon.com (`http://www. amazon.com/`), for example, gives you an ID number cookie when you enter, which if you notice also appears in the URLs of the subsequent pages you visit. Amazon uses this number to track where you go and what you put in your shopping basket.

- **Verifying membership**. Some sites such as HotWired use cookies to make site registration easier. You register with a username, password, and other information on the site once, and the server stores just the username and password in a cookie it gives to your browser (it stores the other info, such as your email address and real name, in its own database). Then, when you visit the site in the future, the server uses the cookie to recognize who you are and let you into the site automatically, so you don't have to log in manually every time.

Okay, what *can't* be put in a cookie? The server can't figure out your name, email address, contents of your hard drive, or other personal info (unless you type it in and tell the server yourself). This is good news if you have fears about Big Brother knowing everything about you. But privacy is still a concern with cookies because even though a server might never know your name, it can usually figure out where you're visiting from (mcp.com tells the server you come from Macmillan's server, for example,), and it could easily track exactly where you've been on its Web site. That's potentially a little scary, and something to keep in mind if you want to use cookies on your site.

How to Bake a Cookie

As you can see, the M&M's example earlier uses HTML to set up the cookie (though keep in mind that at this point only Netscape, Internet Explorer, and Mosaic support cookies). But on the server side, a CGI program of some sort is needed to deal with that cookie so that when the browser sends the cookie, the server will know what to do with the information. This CGI is always necessary because most sites using cookies create Web pages on the fly based on the contents of the cookie. Yes, it's a task for a programmer.

Many sites are now using JavaScript for setting cookies. JavaScript is quite flexible for taking input from a visitor and immediately setting up a cookie. (You'll also come across Perl CGI scripts for doing this.)

Here are some places to get started to learn the fine art of cookie baking:

- Andy's Netscape HTTP Cookie Notes: `http://www.illuminatus.com/cookie.fcgi`

- JavaScript Tip of the Week: Using a Browser's Cookie: `http://www.gis.net/~carter/therest/960701/`

- Matt's Script Archive: HTTP Cookie Library: `http://www.worldwidemart.com/scripts/cookielib.shtml`

VRML

VRML (Virtual Reality Modeling Language) is usually pronounced "V R M L," but its friends pronounce it "vermel." VRML is the new hot thing on the Web. It was the hot subject at the SIGGRAPH conference this year, and the new VRML 2.0 is the topic of conversation at interactive conferences.

VRML, extension .wrl, is easily compared to HTML, as they both are ASCII text formats that can be copied and pasted. Basically, it's a code language like HTML, only instead of Web pages it enables 3D virtual worlds you can move through. VRML and HTML are similar in that they both describe where an image file is located in relationship to a text block, as well as how they're arranged on the page. But the .wrl file enables the designer to describe where an object is located in three dimensions, as well as other elements such as text, lighting, and sound. You know all those virtual reality games and movies you're seeing? That's what VRML is trying to do: immerse you in an entirely different world you can move around in and interact with.

In HTML, the designer pulls in a composition of text, images, and different media formats. In VRML, you can pull in other .wrl files from other URLs and explain where you want to have the object located. Both use text-based descriptions, although VRML is more intensive due to the way its descriptions include lists of coordinates making up the individual points in the polygons defining the object. VRML has a mystique about it that makes people think it is very complicated, and in fact, if you want to write VRML code from scratch, it's very difficult. The trick is to use authoring environments that output VRML code for you (we'll get to that briefly).

NOTE

Mark Pesce has been a leader in the VRML movement since it began. His vision has shaped much of VRML. You can check out the early vision at `http://vrml.wired.com/concepts/visions.html`.

So, what's VRML being used for? Not much—at least for now. The potential for VRML and 3D, interactive worlds on the Internet, is amazing, but the reality is still very clunky and bandwidth-heavy.

Here's what VRML might enable in the future: Instead of going to a Web site of a specific brand of automobile and viewing pictures of the cars and reading about the braking times and leather seats, you enter a 3D space in which the car (looking fairly realistic) appears in three dimensions. You can move around it, fly over it, and open the door and sit in the driver's seat. You can go for a test drive down a virtual street and see how the car responds and how well it brakes. You can (eventually, perhaps) feel the texture of the leather seats. And, chances are, you can be forced to deal with a virtual salesman who comes up to you and tries to make a deal...

Much of this is years down the road yet, but a lot of VRML experiments today are moving in exciting directions. And the software needed to view VRML files is becoming more and more stable. The Live3D plug-in is Netscape's official VRML browser and supports many of VRML's features. VRML 2.0, the most recent specification of the language, is bringing exciting new features to 3D worlds, such as background sound that varies in volume depending on your distance from it, objects with behaviors (such as a dog that barks only when you approach it), and more. Cool stuff.

Want to learn more? I don't blame you. Here are a few sites to check out:

- The VRML Repository: `http://www.sdsc.edu/vrml/`

- VRML Update Newsletter: `http://cedar.cic.net/~rtilmann/mm/vrmlup.htm`

- IAT VRML Forum: `http://www.iat.unc.edu/technology/vrml/`

If you want books, here a couple of good ones: *Laura Lemay's Web Workshop: VRML 2.0 and 3D Graphics* (Sams.net), *Creating Your Own VRML Web Pages* (Que), and *Special Edition Using VRML* (Que).

Want to try your hand at creating a VRML world? There are plenty of authoring tools coming out all the time that make this relatively easy. Here are a few of the options:

- Caligari Pioneer (`http://www.caligari.com/`). A powerful authoring tool and browser for creating realistic 3D worlds. Wintel only.

- Virtual Home Space Builder (`http://www.paragraph.com/vhsb/`). Very easy to use, but perhaps not as powerful. Wintel only.

- Virtus 3-D Website Builder (`http://www.virtus.com/3dwb.html`). True WYSIWYG for VRML. A great tool for getting started. Wintel and Mac!

- WebSpace Author (`http://Webspace.sgi.com/WebSpaceAuthor/`). Sophisticated stuff: imports 3D models, creates links, and enables great flexibility. SGI machines only.

391

QuickTime VR

This software from Apple enables you to immerse yourself in a scene created from a series of still images (photographs or illustrations). The viewer can change the point of view and perspective remains intact, which gives the impression that you are looking around the scene. You can go closer to areas (depending on the resolution of the original image). An excellent example of this has already been discussed earlier in this chapter (`http://phonixnewtimes.com/ads/congo/`). Another use of QuickTime VR is, rather than turning your head in an environment, you can turn an object and view it from all sides. At an Italian site selling NICE watches (`http://www.benice.it/english/vr/`), you can see all sides of the various watch models (see Figures 8.71 through 8.73).

figure 8.71

This is the "baby" watch showing the VR controls.

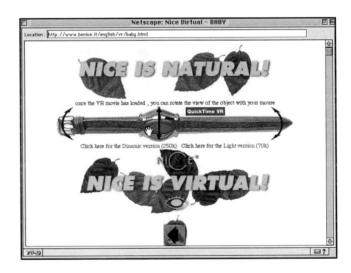

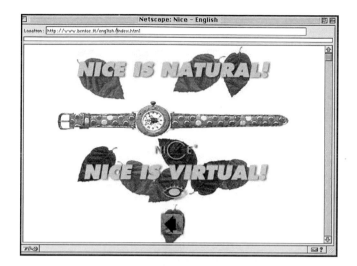

figure 8.72

The watch is turned to face the viewer.

figure 8.73

The watch is turned in profile.

To create a QuickTime VR experience, you must set up a camera (preferable with a wide-angle lens) on a tripod. If this is a digital camera, you will not have the painful step of scanning all your still images. To create an atmosphere for the viewer to enter, pan left to right and up and down, shooting stills with overlap. To create an object that can be spun in space, the object is turned in between shots (or the camera must move around the object). Alternately, you can render a series of overlapping drawings.

Using a utility called Stitcher, which is a part of the suite of tools that comes with The QuickTime Authoring Tools Suite, the images are linked together seamlessly. Check out more of the details at `http://qtvr.quicktime.apple.com/`.

This is a moderately priced method of bringing powerful virtual reality to the Web.

QuickTime

Under normal circumstances, the interactivity built into QuickTime is quite limited, consisting of starting and stopping the playing of a movie. However, this simple feature can introduce a great deal of interactivity if there are multiple QuickTime movies on a page. Please refer to Chapter 7 for a full discussion of QuickTime technology; we will limit ourselves here to discussing a couple of unique applications.

A Puzzling Brew at the dezine café

We are constantly looking for new features to add to the dezine café. The visitors to this site include those interested in design, a professional audience very critical of the site's content and design. They are also a savvy audience looking for creative uses of new technology.

The QuickTime plug-in for the Netscape browser had been announced and was available for distribution on the Net, and we wanted to incorporate this new technology at the dezine café. We periodically introduce contests or games to keep our visitors amused and offer an example of the new possibilities on the Web.

The bad boyz at bYte a tree had an idea to make a steaming cup puzzle using the new QuickTime plug-in. The steaming cup is the emoticon logo for the dezine café. The puzzle is similar to hand-held puzzles that are a single image broken down to numerous square tiles. Instead of dragging the tiles, you must stop each at the correct tile (see Figure 8.74).

There were only two QuickTime movies created: one was a series of tiles
(the Photoshop illustration broken down) and the other was the sound.

The exact same .mov file was embedded in the HTML 16 times, to save
download time and memory. Each placement of the movie was positioned
into a grid on the page. We used the LOOP value for the EMBED command to change how some instances of the movie played. To make it
more challenging, three of the movies were embedded as palindrome, so
they did not loop through the images in the same way as the other tiles.

The amount of memory we saved using the same movie also gave us some
room to move on the audio front, and we added a ticking sound (as a
separate movie) to make the experience more game-like, as if time were
running out. If the sound were part of the repeated movie, there would be
multiple layers of sound playing simultaneously and out of synch!

The timing of the movies was critical. We had to make the puzzle slow
enough for a player to solve but not too easy. Our original test showed
that the movies were way too fast, and the experience was frustrating
rather than fun. The timing was adjusted and several folks asked to test
the puzzle were able to solve it in about five minutes (see Figure 8.75).
This was an acceptable amount of time to be engaged in the puzzle.

395

figure 8.75

*This is the
completed puzzle.*

When a visitor-player completed the puzzle, he or she could print it out as proof and enter an ongoing drawing to win a dezine café T-shirt.

bYte a tree: The Atmospheric Sound Generator

The sound bYtes project described in detail in Chapter 6 is another example of multiple QuickTime movies, where the visitor is engaged interactively. Here (`http://www.vizbyte.com/sound/soundbytes.html`) visitors create their own atmospheric sound by combining the various QuickTime (sound-only) movies that are displayed.

The goals here weren't deep. This part of the site is a place for adventure, visual interest, and exploration:

- Use original sound

- Create an interesting interface, one that would be a bit cryptic.

- Use QuickTime for compression and viewer control

- Keep download time less than three minutes at 28.8

We created this sound generator for the Apple QuickTime Web challenge and were excited to hear that the QuickTime plug-in would be bundled with Netscape Navigator. This would mean we could use QuickTime more, since more people would have it.

NOTE

UPDATE: Now, Shockwave would be the way to create this page. Its new audio compression would save lots of loading time. We'll probably rebuild it soon to save some bandwidth.

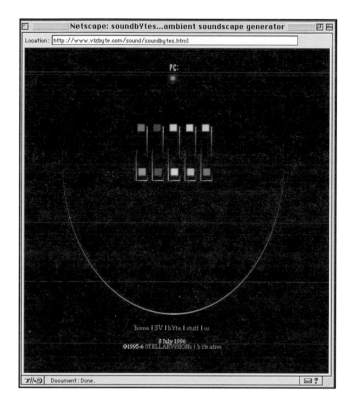

figure 8.76

The soundbYtes sound generator.

Shockwave for FreeHand

The Cup Hunt at designOnline can be experienced on the CD-ROM or live online at `http://www.dol.com/shock.html`. This is a series of eight FreeHand illustrations, and to get to the next illustration you must locate the tiny hidden coffee cup emoticon. Each illustration brings out aspects of the host site; dezine cafe.

In the first illustration, the cup is centrally located in the "o" of doL, encouraging the viewer to enter into the central "depth" of an illustration, and it is relatively easy to find, to give encouragement (see Figure 8.77). When you click the cup, a URL attached to the element in FreeHand (using the URL Xtra) takes you to the next illustration in the sequence.

figure 8.77

The designOnline
illustration for the
Cup Hunt with the
emoticon hidden in
the center.

The dezine café illustration has URLs attached to words, such as "conversation," as well as to the cup (hidden in the center of the bun, of course). As the sequence progresses, the cup gets slightly more difficult to find—at least the same "hide it in the center" technique is not used! See how you do when you try it (see Figure 8.78). Our goal, which from observation seems to have been effective, is to draw visitors in with the search for the cup and then dazzle them with the other elements and humor of the illustration that convey the essence of the dezine café.

figure 8.78

Another FreeHand
illustration online in
the Cup Hunt, this
one for the café.

appendix A

Online Resources

Here we've collected links to some of the most useful sites we've found for designing Web multimedia. They're organized, like the book, into the following sections: general design, graphics, animation, audio, video, and interactivity. Have fun exploring!

General Design and Development Sites

David Siegel's *Creating Killer Web Sites* pages:
`http://www.killersites.com/`

designOnline™ and the dezine café™:
`http://www.dol.com/`

Designer's Guide to the Internet:
`http://www.zender.com/designers-guide-net/`

Web Page Design for Designers (discusses technical limitations, color palettes, and navigation; has links to software and HTML references):
`http://ds.dial.pipex.com/pixelp/wpdesign/wpdintro.htm`

BrowserWatch (for keeping an eye on the latest plug-ins and browser rumors):
`http://browserwatch.iworld.com/`

Information on copyright infringement:
`http://www.copyright.org/`

Yale Center for Advanced Instructional Media (a handbook on site design):
`http://info.med.yale.edu/caim/C_HOME.HTML`

The MIT Media Lab (if you want to get excited about the future):
`http://www.media.mit.edu/`

Works of the Visual Language Lab at MIT:
`http://design-paradigms.www.media.mit.edu/projects/design-paradigms/`

zoecom site:
`http://www.zoecom.com/`

SIGGRAPH, Special Interest Group on Computer Graphics (lots of resources):
`http://www.siggraph.org/`

STELLARViSIONs & bYte site:
`http://www.vizbYte.com/`

The Virtual Library of WWW Development:
`http://www.stars.com/Vlib/`

MediaNews:
`http://www.medianews.com/`

Microsoft ActiveX Gallery:
`http://www.microsoft.com/activex/gallery/`

WebHints: Web Design:
`http://www.rocksoft.com/webhints/design.html`

Animation House site:
`http://www.animationhouse.com/`

Adobe's home page:
`http://www.adobe.com/`

Macromedia's home page:
`http://www.macromedia.com/`

Graphics Sites

BoxTop Software (home of the PhotoGIF and ProJPEG Photoshop plug-ins):
http://www.aris.com/boxtop/

Lynda Weinman's page on the browser-safe color palette:
http://www.lynda.com/hex.html

GIF Construction Set:
http://member.aol.com/royalef/toolbox.htm

JPEG FAQ:
http://www.cis.ohio-state.edu/hypertext/faq/usenet/jpeg-faq/top.html

IMA (Interactive Multimedia Association):
http://www.ima.org/

Tools and tidbits for developing sites (at the IMA):
http://www.ima.org/tools/

Debabelizer:
http://www.equilibrium.com/

Optimizing Web Graphics. (create faster-loading, better-looking graphics for the Web; includes the 216-color nondithering palette):
http://www.webreference.com/dev/graphics/

Adobe's GIF vs. JPEG page:
http://www.adobe.com/studio/tipstechniques/GIFJPGchart/main.html

Bandwidth Conservation Society:
http://www.infohiway.com/faster/

ColorMaker Resources (Web color reference):
http://www.missouri.edu/~c588349/colormaker-resources.html

Animation Sites

Royal Frazier's GIF animation site:
http://member.aol.com/royalef/gifanim.htm

Enviromedia:
http://www.enviromedia.com/

FutureWave Software:
http://www.futurewave.com/

Apple Computer's QuickTime site:
`http://www.QuickTime.apple.com/`

GifBuilder:
`http://iawww.epfl.ch/Staff/Yves.Piguet/clip2gif-home/`
`GifBuilder.html`

Apple's QuickDraw 3D:
`http://quickdraw3d.apple.com/`

Totally Hip Software:
`http://www.totallyhip.com/`

Audio Sites

RealAudio:
`http://www.realaudio.com/`

Production Elements Library:
`http://www.networkmusic.com/prod.htm`

IUMA, The Underground Music Archive:
`http://www.iuma.com/`

Cowboy Junkies site:
`http://www.geffen.com/cowboyjunkies/`

New York Online (hear the jazz riff):
`http://www.nyo.com/samsung/docs/toc.html`

Sony:
`http://www.sony.com/`

Geffen:
`http://www.geffen.com/`

EMI:
`http://www.EMI.com/`

Word, the online journal/magazine:
`http://www.word.com/`

CNN interactive news network:
`http://www.cnn.com/`

National Public Radio site:
`http://www.npr.org/`

Video Sites

QuickTime information:
`http://www.QuickTimeFAQ.org:8080/`

Terran Interactive (home of Movie Cleaner Pro, Web-Motion and Movie Cleaner Lite):
`http://www.terran-int.com/`

Apple Computer's QuickTime site:
`http://www.QuickTimc.apple.com/`

Apple's Webcasts:
`http://live.apple.com/`

Data sheet on QuickTime:
`http://www.tietovayla.fi/CLARIS/apple/asindex.dir/productinfo/datasheets/as/quicktime.html`

VDOnet:
`http://www.vdo.net/`

How to make better movies (tips from MacUser):
`http://www.zdnet.com/macuser/mu_0995/feature/sidebar1.html`

Mission Impossible site:
`http://www.missionimpossible.com/`

The archive section at the Mission Impossible site:
`http://www.missionimpossible.com/g/index-frm.shtml`

Because I Am (an independent documentary film site):
`http://www.becauseiam.com/`

CNN interactive news network:
`http://www.cnn.com/`

MSNBC news network:
`http://www.msnbc.com/`

c|net:
`http://www.cnet.com/`

ABC news network:
`http://www.abc.com/`

CNN video streaming site:
`http://allpolitics.com/`

Nice Cork Watch site:
`http://www.benice.it/english/`

Clinton Gore re-election site:
`http://www.cg96.org/main/d/video/`

STELLARViSIONs & bYte a tree studio:
`http://www.vizbyte.com/newspace.html`

Merce Cunningham Dance Foundation:
`http://www.merce.org/`

Merce Cunningham's living sketchbook:
`http://www.hotwired.com/kino/95/29/feature/`

Sparkle (a Mac freeware program that plays MPEGs, PICTs, and QuickTime movies):
`http://www.quick.net/ftp/MAC/`

New Vivo video player:
`http://www.vivo.com/vivoactive/player_form.html`

Interactivity Sites

Firefly (the personalized music and movie service):
`http://www.ffly.com`

Interactivity Matrix:
`http://www.uarco.com/doctech/matrix.htm`

Club Congress, the darkest night club on the net:
`http://phoenixnewtimes.com/ads/congo/`

Brian Mcgrath (student interactive site):
`http://www.id.iit.edu/~bmcgrath/site_4/almost.html`

Razorfish: Blue Dot typography:
`http://www.razorfish.com/bluedot/typo/anatomy`

Shock-Bauble Showcase:
`http://207.69.132.225/abtboble.htm`

JavaScript Authoring Guide (from Netscape):
`http://home.netscape.com/eng/mozilla/3.0/handbook/javascript/`

Brian Sooy Type (also check out the animations and buy some great type):
`http://www.cybergate.net/~bsooy/type/`

veritas:
`http://www.cybergate.net/~bsooy/type/Veritas/veritas.html`

eclectic two:
`http://www.cybergate.net/~bsooy/type/eclectics/ectwo.html`

Mark Pesce's VRML vision:
`http://vrml.wired.com/concepts/visions.html`

VRML repositories:
`http://www.sdsc.edu/vrml/`
`http://www.vrml.org/`
`http://cedar.cic.net/~rtilmann/mm/vrmlup.htm`
`http://www.sdsc.edu/SDSC/Partners/vrml/repos_software.html`

Kinetix's VRML browsers:
`http://www.ktx.com/`

Java (Sun's Java page):
`http://java.sun.com/`

World's WorldShaper 3D:
`http://www.worlds.net/`

Express VR:
`http://www.cis.upenn.edu/~brada/VRML/ExpressVR.html`

Macromedia (Director, FreeHand, Authorware, Fontographer, Extreme 3D, and SoundEdit):
`http://www.macromedia.com/`

Gamelan (Java directory):
`http://www.gamelan.com/`

Shockwave:
`http://www.macromedia.com/shockwave/`

mFactory (mTropolis a better Director? check it out yourself):
`http://www.mfactory.com/`

405

What Every Multimedia Designer Should Know About MIME Types

MIME stands for Multipurpose Internet Mail Extensions. It was created to

enable multimedia files within electronic mail. The standard was first

published in 1982 in the Internet document entitled RFC-822. Later stan-

dards were determined in RFC 1521 and RFC 1522. They can be found at

`http://www.oac.uci.edu/indiv/ehood/MIME/MIME.html`.

MIME Make Up and Function

It is important for the multimedia Web designer to know that the MIME type, in conjunction with the browser settings, determines which plug-in or helper application is activated for each file. In other words, the MIME file tells the recipient of the electronic message how to interpret the content.

A MIME type's basic function is to identify the rules for decoding the otherwise unstructured ASCII (plain old, boring text) body of the electronic message. Each MIME type defines whether the digital information is in the form of text, image, audio, video, application, multipart, or message. An eighth type for VRML was under standardization process at the time this appendix was written. Read more on that under the listing of MIME Types Defined. Each of these types is then further defined with a subtype and an optional list of parameters as seen in the Action field in Figure 1.14. Types and subtypes are written with a forward slash between them as in quicktime/mov. An extension is then added to trigger the application to implement the file with the MIME type indicated.

RFC-822

RFCs (Request For Comment) have come to be defined as the standards documents of the Internet Engineering Task Force (IETF). If you would like to read or skim over any of the many RFCs from as early as 1969 to the present day, they can be accessed a couple of ways. The most direct way to see the one referred to in this discussion of MIME, RFC-822, is through `ftp://ftp.cslab.vt.edu/pub/rfc/` `rfc822.txt`. *There are RFCs on numerous Internet standards topics and a good search engine will provide links when you type in RFC + the subject in question. Generally speaking, RFCs are weighty and technical(dull), although those found dated April 1 of any year are usually (geek) fun reading.*

About MIME Types

Text format is automatically set at default and is the same as RFC-822 content. Its subtypes enable revisable formats of text. Each of the multimedia types have applicable subtypes, such as video/mpeg or image/gif. Application types are MIME designs for the use of message-enabled applications and the exchange of such data, as in application/postscript. They enable the exchange of proprietary word processor and spreadsheet data. The standard definitions of the types are listed later in this chapter, as well as a table of each MIME type. Many sub-types and extensions *often* used as standards have not been determined for extensions. To stay current with all the latest sub-types refer to information `ftp://` `ftp.isi.edu./in-notes/iana/assignments/media-types.`

MIME Types Defined

Text—Used to represent textual information in a number of character sets and formatted text description languages in a standardized manner.

Multipart—Used to combine several body parts, possibly of differing types of data, into a single message.

Application—Used to transmit application data or binary data, and hence, among other uses, to implement an electronic mail file transfer service.

Message—For encapsulating another mail message.

Image—For transmitting still image (picture) data.

Audio—For transmitting audio or voice data.

Video—For transmitting video or moving image data, possibly with audio as part of the composite video data format.

X-world or Model—At the time of this writing, x-world, a MIME type for virtual reality data, was on the threshold of becoming a standardized MIME type. VRML 2.0 was on the verge of becoming official, and x-world had begun the RFC process, although Netscape had enabled it in Navigator. At the time, it was proposed that the MIME type name be changed to Model from X-world.

What's in a Name

It's easiest to understand MIME by viewing Navigator's helper applications configurations using a PC (see Figure B.1). The Mac's view of them is not as detailed (see Figure B.2). With Navigator running, select General Preferences from the Options menu. The Helper folder lists File type, Action, and Extensions.

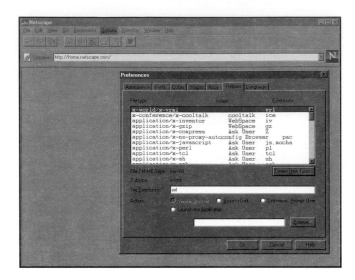

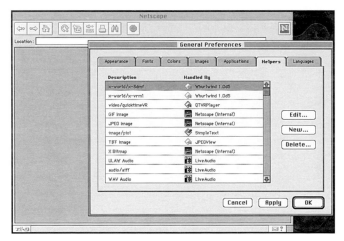

Scrolling through the list, you can clearly see:

- The File type field, which lists the MIME type and its subtype (for example: application/jpeg).

- The Action field, which tells you if the file is handled through the browser or asks you to name the extension (for example: freehand.exe), or says you will be required to specify what the browser is to do with it (Ask User). In most cases the browser will save the file to the hard disk.

- The Extensions field, which names all the extensions that will be recognized by various operating systems (for example: jpeg, jpg, jpe).

In Conclusion

The circumstances for configuring a MIME are becoming fewer because most plug-ins do it automatically or the browser is set up for the MIME. It's not an unheard-of situation, however, for Web designers, especially those who use multimedia, to need to configure a MIME file.

Not all browsers can handle some of the file types internally. Most will then send a file to an external application if it's been properly associated. That's why it's important to be aware of the different MIME types when designing a multimedia site. The server and the browser that the plug-ins are running on have to be configured to run the plug-ins for the correct MIME types. Mac users particularly need to be reminded of the importance of including the extension letters when naming a file because extensions aren't standard for the Macintosh.

MIME Table

The following table lists all MIME types, many subtypes, and several common extensions. Extensions have yet to be standardized.

411

TABLE B.1

MIME Types, Subtypes, and Extensions

Type	Subtypes	Common Extensions
text	enriched	
	HTML	html, htm
	plain	txt
	tab-separated-values	
	richtext	
application	activemessage	
	andrew-inset	
	applefilr	
	atomicmail	
	cybercash	
	director	dir
	dca-rft	

continues

TABLE B.1, CONTINUED
MIME Types, Subtypes, and Extensions

TYPE	SUBTYPES	COMMON EXTENSIONS
	dec-dc	
	eshop	
	mac-binhex40	
	macwriteii	hqx
	mathematica	
	msword	
	news-message-id	doc
	news-transmission	
	octet-stream	
	oda	tar, dump, readme, uu, exe
	pdf	ods
	postscript	pdf
	remote-printing	ps, eps, ai
	riscos	
	rtf	
	slate	rtf
	wita	
	wordperfect5.1	
	x-authorware-map	aam
	x-dvi	dvi
	x-director	dir, dxr, dcr
	x-hdf	hdf
	x-powerpoint	ppt
	x-sea	sea
	x-sgml	sgm, sgml
	x-stuffit	sit
	x-tar	tar
	x-tex	tex
	zip	zip
image	gif	gif
	ief	ef
	jpeg	jpeg, jpg, jpe
	rgb	rgb
	tiff	tiff, tif
	xbm	xbm
	x-freehand	fhc
	xpm	xpm
	x-xwindowdump	xwd
	x-pict	pict

TYPE	SUBTYPES	COMMON EXTENSIONS
audio	aiff	aif, aiff
	basic	au,snd
	midi	mid,midi
	unknown	gsm
	wav	wav
	x-aiff	aif,aiff,aifc
	x-midi	mid,midi
	x-wav	wav
video	mpeg	avi
	msvideo	mpeg,mpg,mpe
	quicktime	qt,mov
	x-msvideo	avi
	x-sgi-movie	movie
multipart	alternative	
	appledouble	
	digest	
	header-set	
	mixed	
	parallel	
message	external-body	
	news	
	partial	
	rfc822	
x-world model	x-vrml	wrl
	x-vream	vrw

index

417

W

X-Z

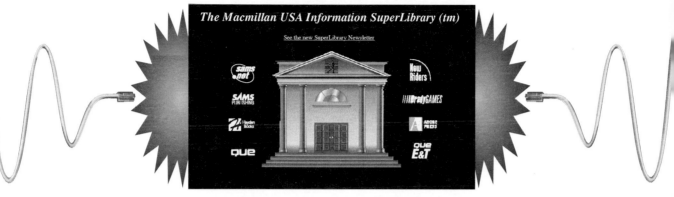

REGISTRATION CARD

Designing Multimedia Web Sites

Hayden
Books

Name _____ Title _____

Company_____Type of business _____

Address _____

City/State/ZIP _____

Have you used these types of books before? ☐ yes ☐ no

If yes, which ones? _____

_____

How many computer books do you purchase each year? ☐ 1–5 ☐ 6 or more

How did you learn about this book?_____

☐ recommended by a friend   ☐ received ad in mail
☐ recommended by store personnel ☐ read book review
☐ saw in catalog   ☐ saw on bookshelf

Where did you purchase this book? _____

Which applications do you currently use? _____

Which computer magazines do you subscribe to? _____

What trade shows do you attend? _____

Please number the top three factors which most influenced your decision for this book purchase.

☐ cover   ☐ price
☐ approach to content ☐ author's reputation
☐ logo   ☐ publisher's reputation
☐ layout/design   ☐ other _____

Would you like to be placed on our preferred mailing list? ☐ yes ☐ no e-mail address _____

☐ **I would like to see my name in print!** You may use my name and quote me in future Hayden products and promotions. My daytime phone number is: _____

Comments _____

_____

_____

Hayden Books Attn: Product Marketing ◆ 201 West 103rd Street ◆ Indianapolis, Indiana 46290 USA

Fax to **317-581-3576**   Visit our Web Page **http://WWW.MCP.com/hayden/**

Fold Here

Other DESIGN/GRAPHICS Titles

Designing Business
Provides the design/business communities with a new way of thinking about how the right design can be a strategic business advantage. It is the definitive guide to presenting a business identity through the use of traditional media vehicles and emerging technologies.

- CD-ROM (dual-platform) exhibits interactive prototypes of multimedia brochures, interactive television, and Web sites as developed by Clement Mok designs Inc., one of the most sought after interactive design agencies in the world
- Shows how effective communication is one way to out-think, out-plan, and out-perform the competition

Clement Mok
1-56830-282-7 ▪ $60.00 USA/$81.95 CDN
264 pp., 8 x 10, Covers PC and Macintosh, New - Expert
Available Now

Adobe Persuasion: Classroom in a Book
1-56830-316-5 ▪ $40.00 USA/$56.95 CDN
Available November 1996

Learning Adobe FrameMaker
1-56830-290-8 ▪ $60.00 USA/$81.95 CDN
Available Now

Adobe Illustrator for Windows: Classroom in a Book
1-56830-053-0 ▪ $44.95 USA/$59.99 CDN
Available Now

Adobe Pagemaker for Windows: Classroom in a Book
1-56830-184-7 ▪ $45.00 USA/$61.95 CDN
Available Now

Adobe Photoshop: Classroom in a Book
1-56830-317-3 ▪ $45.00 USA/$63.95 CDN
Available October 1996

Advanced Adobe PageMaker for Windows 95: Classroom in a Book
1-56830-262-2 ▪ $50.00 USA/$68.95 CDN
Available Now

Advanced Adobe Photoshop for Windows: Classroom in a Book
1-56830-116-2 ▪ $50.00 USA/$68.95 CDN
Available Now

The Amazing PhotoDeluxe Book for Windows
1-56830-286-X ▪ $30.00 USA/$40.95 CDN
Available Now

Branding with Type
1-56830-248-7 ▪ $18.00 USA/$24.95 CDN
Available Now

The Complete Guide to Trapping, Second Edition
1-56830-098-0 ▪ $30.00 USA/$40.95 CDN
Available Now

Design Essentials, Second Edition
1-56830-093-X ▪ $40.00 USA/$54.95 CDN
Available Now

Digital Type Design Guide
1-56830-190-1 ▪ $45.00 USA/$61.95 CDN
Available Now

Fractal Design Painter Creative Techniques
1-56830-283-5 ▪ $40.00 USA/$56.95 CDN
Available Now

Photoshop Type Magic
1-56830-220-7 ▪ $35.00 USA/$47.95 CDN
Available Now

Photoshop Type Magic 2
1-56830-329-7 ▪ $39.99 USA/$56.95 CDN
Available November 1996

Adobe Photoshop Complete
1-56830-323-8 ▪ $45.00 USA/$61.95 CDN
Available October 1996

Production Essentials
1-56830-124-3 ▪ $40.00 USA/$54.95 CDN
Available Now

Stop Stealing Sheep & find out how type works
0-672-48543-5 ▪ $19.95 USA/$26.99 CDN
Available Now

Visit your fine local bookstore, or for more information visit us at http//:www.mcp.com/hayden

This product includes a copy of Shockwave™ for Director®, which enables the playback of high-impact multimedia on the World Wide Web. For further information regarding Shockwave, including upgrades and available add-ons, please see the Shockwave Technology section on the Macromedia World Wide Web site (http://www.macromedia.com).

MACROMEDIA END-USER LICENSE AGREEMENT FOR SHOCKWAVE™ RUN-TIME SOFTWARE (the "Software")

PLEASE READ THIS DOCUMENT CAREFULLY BEFORE FIRST USING THE SOFTWARE. THIS DOCUMENT PROVIDES IMPORTANT INFORMATION CONCERNING THE SOFTWARE, PROVIDES YOU WITH A LICENSE TO USE THE SOFTWARE AND CONTAINS WARRANTY AND LIABILITY INFORMATION. BY FIRST USING THE SOFTWARE, YOU ARE ACCEPTING THE SOFTWARE AND AGREEING TO BECOME BOUND BY THE TERMS OF THIS AGREEMENT. IF YOU DO NOT WISH TO DO SO, DO NOT USE THE SOFTWARE.

1. Important Notice

   Shockwave software is a unique addition to Macromedia's Run-Time software library, allowing End-Users to play applications created with Macromedia's authoring software, available on the World Wide Web. The Software is an object code package that is designed to run with and will run only with an Internet browser which is licensed to contain and contains Macromedia Player software. If your browser is not one of these, the Software may not function properly.

2. License

   This Agreement allows you to:
   (a) Use the Software on a single computer.
   (b) Make one copy of the Software in machine-readable form for backup purposes.

3. Restrictions

   Unless Macromedia has authorized you to distribute the Software, you may not make or distribute copies of the Software or electronically transfer the Software from one computer to another. You may not decompile, reverse engineer, disassemble, or otherwise reduce the Software to a human-perceivable form. You may not modify, rent, resell for profit, distribute or create derivative works based upon the Software.

4. Ownership

   This license gives you limited rights to use the Software. You do not own and Macromedia retains ownership of the Software and all copies of it. All rights not specifically granted in this Agreement, including Federal and International Copyrights, are reserved by Macromedia.

5. Disclaimer of Warranties and Technical Support

   The Software is provided to you free of charge, and on an "AS IS" basis, without any technical support or warranty of any kind from Macromedia including, without limitation, a warranty of merchantability, fitness for a particular purpose and non-infringement. SOME STATES DO NOT ALLOW THE EXCLUSION OF IMPLIED WARRANTIES, SO THE ABOVE EXCLUSION MAY NOT APPLY TO YOU. YOU MAY ALSO HAVE OTHER LEGAL RIGHTS WHICH VARY FROM STATE TO STATE.

6. Limitation of Damages

   MACROMEDIA SHALL NOT BE LIABLE FOR ANY INDIRECT, SPECIAL, INCIDENTAL OR CONSE-QUENTIAL DAMAGES OR LOSS (INCLUDING DAMAGES FOR LOSS OF BUSINESS, LOSS OF PROFITS, OR THE LIKE), WHETHER BASED ON BREACH OF CONTRACT, TORT (INCLUDING NEGLIGENCE), PRODUCT LIABILITY OR OTHERWISE, EVEN IF MACROMEDIA OR ITS REPRESEN-TATIVES HAVE BEEN ADVISED OF THE POSSIBILITY OF SUCH DAMAGES. SOME STATES DO NOT ALLOW THE LIMITATION OR EXCLUSION OF LIABILITY FOR INCIDENTAL OR CONSEQUENTIAL DAMAGES, SO THIS LIMITATION OR EXCLUSION MAY NOT APPLY TO YOU. The limited warranty, exclusive remedies and limited liability set forth above are fundamental elements of the basis of the bargain between Macromedia and you. You agree that Macromedia would not be able to provide the Macromedia Software on an economic basis without such limitations.

7. Government End Users   RESTRICTED RIGHTS LEGEND

   The Software is "Restricted Computer Software." Use, duplication, or disclosure by the Government is subject to restrictions as set forth in subparagraph (c)(1)(ii) of the Rights in Technical Data and Computer Software clause at DFARS 252.227-7013. Manufacturer: Macromedia, Inc. 600 Townsend, San Francisco, CA 94103.

8. General

   This Agreement shall be governed by the internal laws of the State of California. This Agreement contains the complete agreement between the parties with respect to the subject matter hereof, and supersedes all prior or contemporaneous agreements or understandings, whether oral or written. All questions concerning this Agreement shall be directed to: Macromedia, Inc., 600 Townsend, San Francisco, CA 94103, Attention: Chief Financial Officer.

Macromedia is a registered trademark of and Shockwave is a trademark of Macromedia, Inc.

About the CD-ROM

The *Designing Multimedia Web Sites* CD-ROM is packed with Mac and Windows tools and examples for bringing animation, sound, video, and interactivity to your sites.

The Best Web Multimedia

- Example Web pages discussed in the book, so you can see the multimedia in action
- Sample animations
- Shockwave movies
- Audio clips
- QuickTime movies
- And more

Demo Versions of Major Software Applications

- For animation: Infini-D, Adobe Dimensions, Extreme 3D and Strata Vision 3d
- For audio: SoundEdit 16 and DECK II
- For video: Adobe Premiere and Adobe AfterEffects
- For interactivity: Macromedia Director

Essential Multimedia Tools

- GifBuilder
- GIF Construction Set
- FutureSplash Animator
- Emblaze Creator
- QuickTime for Windows and Macintosh
- Movie Cleaner Lite
- D-SoundPro
- SoundApp
- SoundHandle
- And much more!

NOTE

Some of the software included on the CD-ROM is provided as shareware for your evaluation. If you try this software and find it useful, you are requested to register it as discussed in its documentation.